Praise for Heather Child

A chilling fable for the social media age – fierce, compelling and utterly believable – **M.R. Carey**

The People's Republic of Love balances beautifully in that strange space between the online world and the real world, caught between desire and emptiness, offering glamorous highs and horrifying lows. A smart, scary and ingenious read – **Aliya Whiteley**

Heather Child continues to impress. One of our most promising new voices – **Gareth L Powell**

Heather Child has taken a classic locked room mystery and given it a Black Mirror-esque twist, to create a compulsively readable vision of a future that may be just a bare step from our present – **Anne Corlett**

A truly thought-provoking novel that delves into the darker side of the desire to be visible – **Jen Faulkner**

Heather Child has an uncanny ability to tap into our deepest fears of the increasing influence of social media on our lives, and turn them into all too realistic nightmares. Her books are compulsive reading – a glimpse of a future that is frighteningly possible – **HJ Reed**

The People's Republic of Love

Heather Child

SRL PUBLISHING

SRL Publishing Ltd
London

www.srlpublishing.co.uk

First published worldwide by SRL Publishing in 2026

SRL PUBLISHING
THINKING DIFFERENTLY, DELIVERING CHANGE

Copyright © Heather Child, 2026

The moral right by the author has been asserted in accordance with the Copyright, Designs, and Patents Act 1988.

ISBN: 978-1-915073-56-3

1 3 5 7 9 10 8 6 4 2

This book is sold subject to the condition that it shall not, by way of trade or otherwise, be reproduced or transmitted in any form or by any means, electronic, mechanical, photocopying or otherwise, without the prior permission of the publishers.

No part of this book shall be used in any manner for the purpose of training artificial intelligence (AI) systems or technologies.

SRL Publishing and Pen Nib logo are registered trademarks owned by SRL Publishing Ltd.

This book is a work of fiction. Names, characters, places, and incidents are either a product of the author's imagination or are used fictitiously. Any resemblance to actual people, living or dead, events or locales, is entirely coincidental.

A CIP catalogue record for this book is available from the British Library

SRL Publishing is a climate positive publisher offsetting more carbon emissions than it emits.

I often do the most silly useless things to appear to advantage before or attract the attention of those I shall never see again or whom I care nothing about.

Isambard Kingdom Brunel

Winning doesn't matter. Not any more. Charlotte would rather not play at all, but it's in the contract. In the large as well as the small print it says that you can't just leave the game, you have to lose it. You have to be a loser.

Sounds so easy.

She steps into the escape room amid excited murmurs from the other contestants, the air charred with a touch of oil, though the machinery is almost silent. In a moment spotlights will snap on, illuminating whatever horrific scenario they have created. *Escape*. You just have to escape. Ignore the puzzle, even if it's simple and easy to solve – don't solve it. Fingers cold, pressed against your temples. *You can do this.*

Water starts swirling across the linoleum floor, and at once Charlotte knows what is going on. She knows instantly, as though a cloud has passed overhead and cut off the sun. Liquid gushes in, soaking her canvas shoes, and her companions make worried and disgusted sounds, sharing this primal aversion to a rising water-level. At first it is a lukewarm ocean broth, but then there is the tang of sewage, so subtle you would hardly notice – unless you were expecting it.

Charlotte covers her mouth and nose. She squeezes her eyes shut and, involuntarily, her brain strings together images of all the people she loves, like fairy lights, lingering on her friend Tamsin's amused smile, the hug as they parted, the cool press of her rain-ruddy cheeks. *If you don't share it, it never happened.* They'd enjoyed arguing about this, a psychometric survey question for this very show. She handed Tamsin the umbrella, and that was the last time they saw each other.

Now her skirt is plastered to her legs again, and home is far away. She takes a deep, juddery breath, then a tiny step, finding it slippery underfoot. People are calling her name. The filthy liquid consumes her knees, then chills her thighs, and she holds her arms aloft and keeps moving, hollow and heart-heavy as she comes to a decision. This time, she'll have to play the game.

Part One

TUNNELFAIRY

One

Sometimes you step inside a building and sense, instinctively, that it's unsound. It might be a crack in the corner of your eye, a creak on the edge of hearing, or a right angle that looks wrong. Tamsin slows as she walks through the office. There are too many people here – surveyors she hasn't seen for months, graduate engineers who should be on the floor below. They are grinning like they know something she doesn't. In a paperless workplace, people are clutching sheets of paper, the dry rustle unfamiliar. For some reason they have used one of the photos from the recruitment shoot to mock up something resembling the front cover of *Vogue*, and have printed several copies.

'You got me,' she shrugs. 'It's a bit of a pose.'

Honestly, though, why is everyone acting like it's such a big joke? She grabs one or two of the printouts and fulfils requests for autographs, writing personalised abuse. The photo is pretty good. She is by the brick arches of London Bridge station, one bum-cheek on the wall, a strand of hair wisping from her hard-hat, laughing in the lemony sunlight that so captivated the photographer when they emerged from the tunnel.

Finally, she makes a beeline for the office she shares with her supervisor, only to close the door and find him staring at her.

'What?'

Ted has been described by older members of the team as having something of the Womble about him. When Tamsin looked up this reference, she could see what they meant. He pushes his glasses up the bridge of his nose and mustard stubble crinkles below pursed lips.

'Did you give permission?' he asks. 'I assume you did. I was just a bit surprised.'

'Permission for what?' She yanks off her body warmer and hurls it at the coat stand.

These days you can only buy printed magazines at boutique shops, so she is not expecting Ted to hand over a glossy edition of *Vogue*. On the cover is a sticker saying HR COPY DO NOT REMOVE. Something begins to spiral through her innards, a combination of excitement and dread. This can't be happening, but here is an actual magazine, and she is on the front. Written across her hip, it says *Careers edition* and something about women in science and engineering.

'The marketing department have fingers in a lot of pies,' says Ted. 'Would you like a drink of water?' No doubt the colour has drained from her face. He nods back to the open plan office. 'They're chuffed to see their little Tam, suddenly a star.'

She doesn't know what to feel. Help us recruit more female graduates, they said. Get something for the 'Visibility' section of your employee assessment – the section she falls down on year after year. Tamsin doesn't enjoy having her photo taken, but she was willing to grin and bear it for the sake of her career. Plus it was a noble cause. Despite being one of the biggest engineering firms, Ogilby Dobbs lags behind on diversity. It pays well and gives her experience on huge projects, but culturally it needs a kick up the arse.

Her middle finger trails across the cover. Maybe it's not so bad. It is not exactly an embarrassing photo, though her top looks a bit tight. The photographer has caught her in a post-laugh glow, a bit of blush in her cheeks from having carried the core drill up the incline of the tunnel, her skin dewy. They had been flirting, just a little, since she assumed the shoot was over. Did the words pass her lips, as the camera flashed unexpectedly? 'Don't use these!' She can't be sure. He must have been lucky with the images. That perfect turn of her head, and the makeup... perhaps she reached for the mascara that morning and triggered a whole day of flukes.

London's rickety old Underground is springing leaks as water levels rise in the clay, and repairing it is a job never done. At her desk, Tamsin sips the grey-hued coffee Ted has made and steals glances at the magazine. The picture makes it look as though she is on a site visit without a protective coat, her hat worn like a fashion statement.

'Do you think it matters that I look a bit... informal?' she asks her supervisor.

He shrugs, stirring his breakfast cup-a-soup.

'The usual suspects have had things to say about following PPE rules on a site visit. But you know what it's like around here, the arse doesn't know what the elbow is doing.'

Her stomach sinks into her boots.

'But I did follow the rules. We took so many pictures with me in full gear.'

'And you wonder why they didn't use those, with the jacket reaching to your knees...'

She turns away from his permanent, cynical half-smile. It's not her fault that PPE is one-size-fits-all, and that size is 'Yeti'. The only way she can work in gear is by making ruthless use of the Velcro straps and securing her rolled-up trouser legs with hair elastics. She spent an hour in the tunnels being photographed in neons and steel toe cap boots, then relaxed for two minutes at the end. It's hardly fair she has been immortalised as unprofessional.

What makes it worse is that she is the last person to cut corners. Getting here has been a long road. The drop-out rate on the Ogilby Dobbs graduate programme is two in three. Survival meant months – even years – of being ignored, baited and talked-over, or occasionally coddled, feeling a sweat-heavy jacket land on her shoulders during some impromptu outdoor lecture, or being given whispered 'tips' she already knew. Supervisors used to snort and roll their eyes at her cautious approach, and for a while she thought she'd be among the quitters, the ones who hid tears behind smeary goggles as they nodded along, falling behind. That was until she began to study the gangly coffee-fuelled men who ran the place. She learned to stand her ground, to cultivate a steely gaze. Now she can blag with the best of them. She takes zero shit and has a laugh when they go out for drinks. Her feet are far enough under the table that it has felt safe to relax now and then, to let her guard down. Was that a mistake?

'Let people say what they want,' Ted goes on, 'you've just got Ogilby about a million quid's worth of publicity, so they've got nothing to complain about. Have you seen the rumpus online?'

He leans across her desk and brings up the company's Social page, headed, of course, with her picture, the sight of which is already beginning to curdle her stomach. Why are there so many comments? It takes a minute of reading to realise that, perhaps inevitably, someone has accused Ogilby Dobbs of using a model for this shoot instead of a real engineer. Tamsin's mouth drops open as she reads:

So Ogilby Dobbs is making amends for their past sexism by trying to recruit more women... using a hired model who looks like a construction worker's WET DREAM. *Slow hand clap gif*

Then, in a move that must have given the HR department enormous satisfaction, there is a chirpy little retort from Ogilby:

Tamsin Wilde, @TunnelFairy, is a geotechnical engineer working to keep your London Underground running safely and smoothly.

What a curveball, to include her handle. They must have thought they were doing her a favour. She switches to the LOVE social network, to her profile, and tumbles down a waterfall of new comments. The numbers are unreal. Since it is semi-automated, anyone who shows more than a passing interest is added as a follower, and people are looking her up to establish if she is a model or an actor, or just AI-generated. A cold vibration runs through her bones as she reads the remarks. Inevitably, people describe her as 'cute' – always a bugbear since school – but it gets worse:

OMFG! She can have a go with MY helmet
If she really does work at Ogilby ... WHAT A WASTE.

A hard-won qualification, followed by five years of tunnel engineering experience, and the world just wants her to get her top off.

Shutting it down, she turns instead to the three-dimensional hologram model of a tube station projected above her desk. There is a service hatch that needs looking at, but her mind is going to other portals, doors she opened years ago. Doors that can never be closed. There is, of course, a reason she avoids posting selfies on her LOVE feed. It is safer that way. Occasionally a certain group of people find her photos. They make gleeful remarks. Sometimes they paste her face onto their websites, like a deer's head nailed to the wall. *This is how Tammy May Wilde looks now.* Imagine the excitement this new windfall will generate.

A grunt draws her attention to Ted, who has melted his sandwich packet to the kettle and is scraping ineffectually at the molten plastic. She tries to focus on her scribbled calculations, the strata beneath her station, but part of her is still scrolling through that torrent of joyous outrage against Ogilby Dobbs: people digging up old scandals, questionable views expressed by the CEO, sexual harassment allegations, and that story about waste oil dumped in a river, settled out of court. Amid so much sleaze and spin, the company would surely think nothing of dressing up a model as an engineer… and so she is caught in the middle, the internet on one side, her employer on the other. Ogilby have trumpeted the positive quote she gave about working there, slapping @TunnelFairy on everything. Now countless strangers are following her. *Following* her – has no one noticed how creepy that sounds?

She pushes the coffee away, wishing she had a pint of ale instead, that she was sitting with Charlotte at their favourite sooty-fronted pub. Her friend would tease out the lighter side of this situation. 'You lucky git,' she'd say. With all these fans falling into her lap, Tamsin would be the envy of anyone working in the arts. You don't get signed or auditioned or published without a decent following, and you don't get the followers until someone cuts you a break. It took Charlotte years to escape this chicken-and-egg situation. When she finally won a dating show and was famous, one of the first things she did was to recruit other influencers as mentors for young artists, doing what little she could to pay it forward.

Right now Charlotte is back in the fray herself, cut off from the outside world while filming a reality television show. It is easy to forget this, to start typing a message only to remember she cannot be reached. As Tamsin turns back to her tunnels and escalators and ventilation systems, she is ashamed to remember that she promised to keep up with the episodes. It is difficult to find time, now the end of this project is so near, the final calculations that will ensure her station structure stands firm amid the treacherous London mud, which often catches you out with a few metres of quicksand. She needs to focus, but the cover of Ted's magazine reflects a lot of light, like a small rectangular puddle in which she can see her watery, distorted face. A ripple of fear crosses her heart. *Please don't let this be like last time.*

Two

Charlotte arrives in a motorboat of the kind they usually rent to tourists in the People's Republic of Love, with sun shade and solar fairy lights. Each contestant is supposed to emerge sexily from the ocean, but the good-hearted skipper takes her almost to shore, the water only thigh-high. She dips herself to get her bikini wet and then strides out of the surf between the two camera drones, flicking seawater from her fingertips, covering her mouth dramatically as she sees the villa up ahead.

Bundles of vines are draped across the swanky steel-glass construction. According to the show's concept statement, it is a *mysterious beach house, long since abandoned by its tech tycoon owner.* As well as all the usual pools, bars, and other luxury features, it is supposed to have an escape room, run on artificial intelligence which, left alone too long, has gone rogue…

Not for the first time, she wonders whether this description is intentionally vague, to ensure her stomach is filled with butterflies as she walks up the beach towards what will be her home for the next few weeks, so long as she avoids getting evicted.

The air is salty, and her agent's glottal voice popcorns into her memory: 'It projects,' she hiccupped, 'the algorithm projects a 300 per cent uptick in followers, just for going on the show. And if you make it through…' Her agent is called Orla, a woman of fifty-five with a dicky digestive system. Although she has let her client slip several letters down the celebrity alphabet, Charlotte doesn't have the heart to fire her. 'On the plus side,' Orla added, when the offer came in, 'It's not a dating show. The set up is… have you ever done an escape room?'

'Who hasn't?'

They are hard to avoid. Escape rooms are big business, with whole department stores being repurposed to offer live action experiences – treasure hunts, team challenges and life-size boardgames. Every October, when Tamsin's birthday rolls around, an escape room will almost certainly be on the cards.

'Great. It'll be you and some other celebrities in a sort of desert island scenario,' Orla went on. 'Directors will see what you can do. You can show off your… emotional intelligence.'

This had a slight aroma of bullshit, since producers would only be interested in the numbers: how many followers, and how often has she trended? How much advertising revenue will she bring to the venture? Like everything in the Republic, it's about the money.

Charlotte remembers flicking the topmost needle of her agent's desk cactus as she was told about the rules, the contract – always scarily permissive in terms of what the producers could do – and the prize, the ten thousand Luvcoin that would propel her bank account out of the red. This was what made the show impossible to turn down. A few more months and she would find herself without sponsorships, utterly broke and forced to limp back to the UK, maybe having to live at home again. Even now, under the scorching tropical sun, the thought makes her shiver. For two years she has resided in the funfair paradise of the People's Republic of Love, a cluster of private Caribbean islands that recently declared itself a brand new country. It's a two-hour hop from Miami, full of influencers and entrepreneurs all raising a middle finger to that dirty, dated word – *politics* – and making their own rules. Every morning she sees their yachts dotted along the horizon like a row of perfect teeth. The grass is always cut and watered, the gardens full of waxy banana leaves, the cocktails frothy flowers on thin glass stems. No, she thinks, as she climbs the steps to the terrace, brushing powdery sand from her feet. This is worth it. She has nailed a reality show before, and she can do it again. Her game plan, as ever, is simply to be herself.

Palms poke through carefully sawn holes in the decking, the cookie-cutter leaves of plastic vines already a little bleached. A thin, fresh odour of laundry detergent falters in the heat, and the brimming infinity pool burbles. When she goes over to the alfresco bar, she finds the owners supposedly left in such a hurry that they failed to unplug an entire fridge of champagne.

It cheers her to pop the cork and start filling a slender glass. Overhead, palms interlock their green fingertips, rustling companionably as birds flit and sing. Pieces of fibrous coconut husk have gathered around the base of the steps, and the air is warm, laced with nectar. It is heavenly. Then, like a key-change in this perfection, a buzzing sound makes her turn, eyes blinking away the heat that precedes tears. It is surely a bee, a big, tropical one, sent to her at the beginning of this experience for good luck. It would mean so much to see one right now. But it is just the next motorboat bobbing its way towards the beach.

She finds more flutes and arranges them on a tray, feeling the advantage of being the first to arrive. Her drink looks so tempting: floral, dry and ice-cold. Out of habit she blinks twice, but of course she is not wearing her smart contact lenses so no photo is taken. There are no devices allowed, no phones, smartspecs, or wearables. She couldn't even bring her smart bikini that senses UV rays, turning stripy when she is in danger of sunburn. A light sweat comes over her, and she has to inhale slowly and remind herself there are cameras everywhere. Nothing is being lost. She takes a sip of her drink and feels comforted. Here, she will be seen, every moment of every day. A sultry, woody haze rises from the decking as the sun inches lower, as though the villa is embracing her.

Will her friends and family be watching? It is so hard, here, to picture people going about their day in Liverpool and London. A heart-shaped, impish face comes to mind, and a comforting clockwork gait. Tamsin is that rare thing, a friend from the before-times, still dusted with the playfulness of their years at junior drama club. She reminds Charlotte of who she used to be, though since then they have trodden wildly different paths. No matter how much Tamsin hates the showiness of these shows – being the kind of person who will even shy away from a nice selfie – she'll be watching.

No need for a suitcase, they told her. Everything would be provided by the show's sponsors. She has found her bedroom which, rather strangely, opens directly onto the living room. Or maybe it is the lounge itself that is odd, the kooky sofas and chunky coffee tables attached to the walls with an empty space in the middle. The metal floor sounds hollow underfoot, reminiscent of a shipping container. Perhaps it has to be basic so the cleaning bots can cope.

All the other contestants have arrived and their chatter echoes across the terrace, startlingly loud after those first minutes when she was alone. Charlotte checks her appearance in a mirror positioned a fraction too low on the wall, pleased her hair is still a smooth, coal-dust cascade despite the humidity. She has exchanged smiles and introductions, warmed by a promising trickle of anticipation. Maybe Orla has got it right this time.

Back in the living area, the top surface of the coffee tables has vanished, revealing plates of tacos and nachos and a feast of finger food. So that explains their shape – the room is half lounge, half vending-machine. Overwhelming quantities of aftershave and body spray combine as everyone moves indoors. She meets a Somali-Norwegian make-up guru, a TV chef who has gone slightly off the boil, a vlogger who looks about twelve, and a drag queen known for lip-syncing all the US president's speeches. It is not as though she expected major celebrities, but the lack of solid names puts a damper on things. There is a woman made famous by a single viral video – not hugely flattering – of her attempt to gulp down a pint of molten marshmallows, nearly choking to death. 'It started out like a milkshake, I swear,' she proclaims. Finally Charlotte meets a man whose skinny vest can barely contain his armfuls of muscle, whose voice sounds like it has echoed around a cavern before emerging.

'Asher,' he introduces himself, crushing her hand and leaving it a little powdery.

'Bodybuilder? A wild guess, obviously…'

His posture changes, a nerve plucked. 'Award-winning,' he sighs, 'but it's acting I wanna do. What about you?'

'Same. Can't you tell?' Charlotte laughs, flexing her muscles. 'Actually, I think I've had enough of acting… the nice thing about presenting is that you can be yourself.'

She discovered this while filming *Spill It – The Inside Scoop on Your Groceries*, which was two seasons of the most fun she has ever had, stamping around small-town America in branded leathers, learning to ride a Harley.

Asher smiles, dips a nacho and looks around.

'Have you found where you'll be sleeping yet?'

She nods towards the nearest door. 'This is me. Yeah, they must think I'm the party animal or something. You?'

'I'm sharing with that guy,' he points at the chef, not looking too thrilled. 'We're next to the games room.'

The beach house is a sprawling place. A metal staircase leads up to a mini-gym, pool table, and ping-pong, plus a couple of bedrooms and another bar.

'Any idea where the escape room is?' She was imagining an industrial-looking door, ominously locked, but nowhere seems out-of-bounds. Asher shakes his head.

'No, but we'll find out soon enough,' he grins. There is a gravity to him that she finds calming, and his reasons for being here make sense. Most of the others, with the possible exception of Mak – a friendly kids' TV host, who is also the only other Brit – are already making her squirm, but she can get along with anyone temporarily. As her eyes roam over the tanned skin, the perfect lipstick and peeping tattoos, she pictures a sort of red glow concealed deep in every contestant's chest, their desperation-meter, everyone hiding it under a facade of cool. To be here, what inhibitions have they overcome? What stories are they telling themselves?

Asher is right to be wary about the escape room. Neither of them are under any illusions about how these shows work. Entertainment must be generated, and that means rubbing people up the wrong way until sparks fly. Audiences have been promised a house that swallows people who fail to solve its riddles. Whatever that looks like, she will have to deal with it.

The moment comes sooner than expected. Before they have finished their meal, sofas and tables begin to suck themselves back into the walls, shutters sliding into place over all the exits. Their nervous giggles create a tinny echo. Then the floor splits, and the two sections alongside the crack begin to sink, followed by the next two strips, grinding on hidden gears, the floor transforming into two matching sets of stairs, forcing everyone to stumble downward. Charlotte loses her balance and clutches Asher's warm, thick arm as they make the last knee-high leap into a basement they had no idea was there. Then, like a garage door closing, the stairs lift back up to become the ceiling. Slow, theatrical lighting reveals a mustard-yellow room decorated with hieroglyphs. It is stuffed with jars, treasure, and three cocoon-like sarcophagi, the whole thing a mixture of props and holograms, the air dry as paper. Here we go, Charlotte thinks, as a booming voice reads out the riddle. She must have done an Egyptian-themed escape room before. How hard can it be to navigate a few mummy jokes?

The clock is ticking and they need to find the first clue, so she tries to concentrate, but her heart is going crazy. There is something in the air, some wisp of a scent perhaps, that is reaching inside her, urgently familiar, sweet but not exactly pleasant, and impossible to identify while her senses are overwhelmed with all this activity, the scuffling feet and eager voices. Someone says her name, and she snaps out of it. Focus, she tells herself. If you lose the game, you lose everything.

GOGGLERS (LOVECAST 2270) 'WE WATCH SHIT'

DOC: [READING] Twelve celebrities prepare to find a way *Outta My Room*.
DICK: *Outta My Room*?
DOC: It's an escape room thing.
DICK: Sounds like an angry teenager.
PACEY [ON SCREEN]: It looked like a milkshake, when they were melted. For reals!
DOC: They've really scraped the barrel with this lot.
DICK: I liked *Naked Down a Mine*. Or what was that one in a brothel? *Man Vs Sex*.
DOC: *Naked Down a Mine*? Shut your face was that a show.
DICK: Much better than this shit. One of the trackers went on the blink and they nearly lost someone under Pennsylvania. A girl fell into an underground lake and they just did her stitches and put her straight back down the hole, then it went septic…
CHARLOTTE [ON SCREEN]: Yeah, they must think I'm the party animal or something.
DICK: What's that, Liverpool? Feel like I know her.
DOC: Scouse, yeah. Don't you remember Charlotte Hardey? She won *Six on the Beach* season three. With Rollo. I thought she was alright.
DICK: Oh here we go… down, down into the basement!

Three

London feels achy, like it wants to stop the traffic and stretch. Tamsin opens the door of an auto-haircut emporium. When she was young, there were tatty magazines in hairdressers. Now she is grateful not to be sitting around flicking through them, to be standing instead in this queue of people staring at their devices. No one seems to be noticing her, thank goodness, not like the first salon she tried. If this *Vogue* business doesn't die down, she'll have to seriously consider deleting her LOVE account. The man beside her glances up, but then continues to scroll through US election news. Luckily, only a few people besides herself are wearing smartspecs, the spider-thin devices that sit above eyebrows and annotate the world with useful information – including facial recognition.

Tamsin squeezes a button on the corner of her specs to fire up her smartface virtual assistant.

'Hey Red,' she says quietly, 'can you show me *Outta My Room*?'

'Sure thing.'

The opening credits are projected just ahead of her eyes, showing a glassy turquoise sea and a palm-fringed beach. She sighs. A couple of weeks in the sun would really hit the spot. Charlotte doesn't swim, but Tamsin would be straight into that warm-bath ocean, floating on her back and losing herself in the endless sky. At least on a film set there would be no access to the outside world, no temptation to look at her LOVE account. Someone has set up a poll, showing most people still don't believe she is an engineer. They have started puppeting her in their arguments about women's innate aptitude – or lack of – for science and engineering. What a dinosaur of a discussion. How can it still be taking place in this day and age?

On *Outta My Room*, the opening salvo gathers pace, drums combining with the pop and sizzle of technology gone wrong, unsuspecting celebrities fetching up at a mysterious beach house, not knowing that the inbuilt escape room has been left alone with its algorithms for too long… or so says the announcer.

Tamsin leans in, seeing they have made the escape room into a cartoonish Egyptian tomb. It reminds her of that Liverpool museum with the big Egyptian collection that she visited several times as a child, keeping Charlotte company when she was dragged along by Kathleen – her dad's new wife. Apparently Kathleen was much kinder to Charlotte when there were two of them, though it was awful being in the museum office with that woman; her perfume used to fill the air with a sickly, cough-syrup sweetness.

The contestants whisper nervously together, not a stray hair between them, while the narrator explains that it is a team game, only one 'winner' key to be found. Three clues later, Tamsin has worked out the solution, and wants to yell: *Don't you people know how escape rooms work? There's obviously a secret compartment behind the bird symbol.* Her friend moves sluggishly and Tamsin knocks her knuckles together, 'Come on, no time to daydream.' This show is the career-boost Charlotte has been after for ages, and she needs to give it her A-game. Pity there is no way to message her with some encouragement, reassure her that people are already chatting about *Outta My Room* on the Tube, on websites and podcasts; they are one-click-buying the outfits Charlotte is wearing. The show is definitely making people look her up and remember who she is. Tamsin closes her eyes to beam puzzle-solving vibes across the Atlantic. Think like an engineer, Charl. Think of problems as your bread and butter.

At last it is done, and the narrator wraps up the show with some choice sarcasm and terrible mummy puns. Tamsin inhales the scent of conditioner, steps closer to the greasy sound of scissors slicing. *Think like an engineer.* From her bag she retrieves the book she is currently reading – an arty little biography of Isambard Kingdom Brunel. After the bitchiness of *Outta My Room*, the cool articulacy of Brunel's letters and diary is calming, his voice ringing out clearly across the centuries.

Sometimes she feels like a kindred spirit of this

Victorian giant of engineering, who was even – like her – slightly sensitive about his height, compensating with an eight-inch stovepipe hat. As a lonely student in Bristol, something kept drawing her to his landmarks: the SS Great Britain, suspension bridge and docks. In their shapely shadows her brain must have invented the sense of a presence, to share her solitude. Sometimes she would talk to him, imagine what he'd think of the modern world. Now, whenever she has to hang out in some site manager's armpit-fugged man-cave, or deal with Ogilby politics, Tamsin finds herself drifting backwards in time until she can almost taste the smoke, dodge the sparks as rivets are hammered flat on ships' hulls, railways, and bridges. Brunel was always breaking records: the biggest ship, the longest tunnel, everything the first of its kind, as though a devil was sitting on his shoulder whispering, 'Go big or go home.' It is the ambition that inspires her, though Ted loves winding her up about her fondness for what he calls 'Fairytale engineering'. He will point out that Brunel's SS Great Eastern, built for four thousand passengers, was longer than Downing Street and too gigantic to enter most harbours. 'Bankrupting everyone involved,' Ted will say, licking his lips. 'Ahead of its time,' she will retort.

At last a booth becomes available, so Tamsin puts the book away and sits down for her haircut. 'Take it back eight weeks' she tells the screen, which searches for online images of the floppy, boyish cut she had back then. If only it was so easy to go back in time, to return to that photoshoot, keep her PPE on and avoid all this fuss. The bowl lowers over her head, its inbuilt scissors beginning to wander around her scalp like metallic insects, snipping away. There is the odd twinge as they catch a hair, a hazard of the budget option, though the results are usually fine. If she watches adverts, her cut will be cheaper still, but she swipes them away, opting for another episode of *Outta My Room*. Her smartface knows what to do, and fast-forwards any bits that don't involve Charlotte. Now it's the next day, now the day after. How much has she missed? Her friend seems to be getting on well with most of the housemates, working her usual magic. They even give her a hand in the escape rooms now and then. But the more Tamsin watches, the more she fears it won't be enough. 'What you need is me,' she murmurs, 'and I'm not there.'

As she leaves the haircut booth, she notices two more messages from Luka, who got back in touch that morning, completely out of the blue.

Sorry I've been so rubbish, he writes. *I've been LIVING in the studio this year.*

Luka mainly does voiceovers. He's one of the theatre types Charlotte got to know when she moved to London; they were sleeping together for a few months before becoming friends. Later, the three of them started hanging out at a drinking hole on the Soho fringe, spending too much but having a fabulous time.

No problem, she replies. He has been particularly lax at responding to messages since Charlotte moved abroad, but perhaps he needed to take a step back from things.

Did you say a hairdresser at Embankment? he messages. *Why don't you pop into the Pike and Pitcher afterwards? It'll be dead, and too dark for facial recognition.*

Is he still going to that threadbare little bar? She is about to decline, but with the online shitstorm still raging it would be good to talk to someone, and Luka's blunt cynicism might just take the edge off.

Neatly shorn, she cuts through to Covent Garden and goes down the steps into a pub that, as a fresh-faced student, always felt like a thrilling, dimly-lit underworld. It is years since she smelled these velour drapes, these wine-soaked barrels stacked in a triangle and lit by red LEDs on curly candlesticks. People peek from the alcoves as she passes, everyone waiting for the cast of some West End show to traipse in, as they often used to after curtain call. She orders a pint of Yippee IPA.

'Spammy Tammy!' The voice is brassy and flamboyant, and close to her ear. She flinches, and turns to find Luka arranging his frame around the adjacent bar stool. He grins, adding: 'You're all over everyone's feeds. Well, mine anyway.'

'That name needs binning.' She gives a theatrical shudder, and they exchange the usual shoulder-hug. He has the vestige of an air-kissing habit, doing a sort of tongue-click close to her left ear and then her right. His breath smells of aniseed.

'How are you and your fifty thousand followers?' He is teasing her, yet his brow twists with intrigue.

'Seventy-five.' She gives him a wry smile. It was with some disbelief that she came across a clickbait headline earlier today, declaring that @TunnelFairy was – scandalously – the first ever AI-generated model to appear on the cover of *Vogue*. Some people think Ogilby Dobbs created her entire online profile, which would explain the relative scarcity of selfies. More followers have flooded in, wanting to see if they can spot a fake. 'Not jealous, are you?'

'Au, contraire. I wouldn't trade my loyal audience for anything. That's years of loving curation, mon ami.'

Luka's favourite kind of follower is someone who has sought him out after listening to an audiobook he has narrated, impressed by how well he does all the voices. He can make words resonate like steps across a hollow stage, or pour out smooth sentences, rich as gravy, as he is doing now, making him sound more mellow than he really is.

'Have you seen Charl's new show?'

He blows a raspberry. 'Come on – the people on these programmes are so unwatchable. Ten minutes and I'm spiralling towards an existential crisis.'

Tamsin takes a gulp of her pint. 'You're fooling no one.' As if he would let all that footage of Charlotte in a bikini go to waste. 'Joking aside...' She hesitates, unsure how to express what has been nagging her as she binge-watched the show. 'The escape rooms... it's like they've been designed to get on her nerves. You need to watch it, tell me I'm not seeing things.'

A bark of laughter. 'Is that all? You can rest assured they are one hundred percent designed to get on her nerves.' He swirls his red wine, releasing a scent of stewed fruit. 'I've known some of the guys who build these shows, and there's usually an AI involved, chewing up a lifetime of data and spitting out something that'll get a rise out of them, the poor buggers.'

Tamsin realises too late she has strayed into dangerous territory.

'Charl has it easy,' he continues. 'No squishing spiders or sucking worms or letting people watch you wank under the sheets.' He thrusts a bit and the stool rocks, 'and it's all worthwhile to move a few rungs up the celebrity ladder.'

The show is popular, mainstream entertainment, three words Luka despises. This slightly puritanical streak, when it comes to his craft, is probably the main thing that stalled his relationship with Charlotte. For him the stage is hallowed ground, theatre the crucible in which a new world order will be forged, with Brecht, Strindberg, Kane, Beckett and the rest stoking the furnace. It is not a mere waymarker on the path to celebrity. All very well – Tamsin can concede – but empathy for a friend comes first.

Her long silence softens him. 'She'll smash it,' he says, and turns back to his drink, pulling at his hair as though he could make it into something other than hair, a floppy hat with feathers, perhaps, for playing those non-voiceover roles he can never land.

'You don't think I should say something, on LOVE?' Tamsin presses. The idea of Charlotte's inner demons being stirred up for entertainment purposes makes her uneasy. It has never struck her as wise to post every thought online, though Charlotte has done it breezily, almost automatically, since her early teens. It might mean she is being singled out as an easy target. 'Just to mention it's unfair.'

He peruses her unhurriedly and drains his wine.

'I wouldn't,' he says. 'She won't want you painting her as a victim. These shows are about hanging in there, taking one for the team, all that twaddle. In a few weeks it'll be over and she'll be dancing along the red carpet, happy as Larry.'

Luka is made for perching on bar stools, his feet propped solidly on the ground while Tamsin's swing.

'I'm going to go,' she says, hopping down. 'Good to see you, but I'm a famous model now… I have to go look hot someplace.'

He enjoys the joke, flashing teeth bright as footlights. As she climbs back up to street-level, she considers the irony of Luka turning up his nose at all this popular, mainstream stuff, but only getting back in touch when she is trending.

Back at home, there are three more full-length episodes to view. She has forgotten to eat and the beer's gone to her head. Or is it guilt, this lurching sensation? It feels important that she at least watches all the shows, just to support her friend.

So far, only one game has ended with someone being evicted. When all the others were hoisted from the basement after finding keys, one guy was left below, his face a mask of despair as the ceiling closed over his head, though of course he was pictured laughing in the studio moments later, being shown clips of all his best bits.

On the show, the housemates lounge around,

drumming their feet restlessly. The escape room opens at irregular intervals, and it has been two days since the last challenge. 'You had to say it,' Charlotte groans, as they all remark on this and the floor instantly begins to sink, taking them down, down into the unknown.

In the escape room, a pink wash illuminates a stage littered with props, thick curtains nudging a piano. It pleases Tamsin to see no obvious signs of anything unpleasant. Charlotte gravitates towards the instrument. She can never resist a piano, and can coax a tune out of even the most battered specimen. Back in Camden she rescued more than one from the wood recycling project behind her flat.

At last Charlotte is in her element, helping the others solve theatre-related clues. 'It's *A Dolls' House*,' she exclaims, kneeling to extract the clue from behind its tiny door. The riddles lead back to the piano, and suddenly the bodybuilder is holding a huge club hammer and someone else has a baseball bat, and they are lifting their weapons and yelling at Charlotte.

Tamsin sits up, her skin flashing hot. What the hell is going on? Her friend is pressed against the instrument and shouting back at them, and all the others are linking eyes, making a chain of fury, the beeps coming thick and fast as they swear at her. It is terrifying. One of the women marches over and tries to peel Charlotte's arm from its anchor – the wooden corner of the piano. It takes two of them to remove her, and then, with a lot of pent-up frustration, hammer and bat slam into the instrument with a loud crunch, the upper half disintegrating with surprising ease.

Tamsin draws closer to the screen, her eyes widening until they are sore. As the other contestants pick up keys, individual seats come down on wires and lift them upward, but one figure is still frozen.

'Grab a bloody key!'

Only at the last moment does Charlotte bend, almost in a trance, and reach for the shiny object that has landed nearby. It is the drag queen who ends up rifling through the debris, hardly believing all the keys have gone, and letting out a wail as the ceiling closes.

Tamsin rubs her temples, feels the prickle of freshly cropped hair. On screen, her friend retreats into a bedroom, every ounce of her usual radiance doused. Charlotte is the sort of person who brings friends soup when they have a cold, who spends hours writing words of encouragement to complete strangers. Even Luka, who rarely has anything good to say about anyone, grudgingly admits she's a lamb. Charlotte builds bridges wherever she goes, including among the terrible people on these shows. Why would anyone want to make her suffer?

Four

It was the tiniest theatre imaginable, the fringe of the fringe. A six-week run of a little-known Arthur Miller play, and money so tight that the cast took turns cleaning the toilets. Charlotte would loiter between rehearsals, making use of the piano, a Bechstein upright with a grumpy, understated personality – whose twin they have, by coincidence, plonked into this escape room. It kindles joy in her to see it, her fingers not having felt the smooth resistance of ivory for so long. Why doesn't she practice more? Before her mum started working abroad, they would have regular lessons, a bribe of honey sweets waiting behind the metronome. The piano calls to her, asking her to touch it, to find out what it can tell her, to remember aromatic sugar on her tongue. Do the others have any sense of how rare this instrument is? Superior workmanship means that a Bechstein will produce a beautiful sound no matter how many decades pass. All at once she feels protective; she hurries to solve the clues so she can lead the other contestants away from its polished lid.

Minutes later she has gone from team player to team pain-in-the-ass. The last clue flutters to the ground – *keys to keys*.

'Charlotte, get out the fucking way!'

She can't bear it – the very idea they could smash up this antique is outrageous. But Pacey's hands bruise her wrists, and then she is watching Spike insert a chisel between C and C sharp. Asher hefts the largest hammer and whacks it into the wood, the others whooping. Nobody is wearing the goggles provided and the panels come apart with ease, the piano cracking like a brown egg. Raindrop-perfect notes crunch and clash, and Charlotte feels it in the enamel of her teeth, shooting pains through her jaw. She moans, but the others don't stop, and every impact gets right into her joints, her knuckles and feet, as they chip out the chords and the strings recoil. She doesn't help, but at the last minute she gets a key, and any eyes she meets shoot her a look of contempt.

Later, she fears the jugs of limey, salty margarita on the terrace will make her throw up. It is not real violence, smashing an old instrument. No one will understand why it upsets her. If she tried to explain, they would humour her with sly smiles. *Yes, Charlotte, the piano has died… sorry you're a complete fucking lunatic.* She hurries away to her room, hoping the cameras won't follow. The sizzle in her bloodstream keeps her pacing around the bed, turning each time she reaches the mirrored wardrobe.

No one can accuse her of not staying positive, even when her legs go wobbly crossing that steel-drum floor. It's not supposed to be easy – she knows that – but she did not expect every escape room to be built of old memories, including things she can barely recall. Her agent warned her that they might use what she posted online to help construct the games, to make them personal. But where could they have got this level of detail – like the cough-syrup smell in the museum that she had almost forgotten herself? The only place this might be mentioned is in her message threads with Tamsin, going right back to childhood. If the show has mined all the data that Smarti – the biggest tech company – has on her, there is no telling what the next escape room might contain.

The other contestants are sailing through, by comparison. What is she missing here? The narrator could be saying to viewers, 'What Charlotte doesn't know is that every room has been specially designed...' Perhaps they are singling her out for some sort of experiment. How much more can she take? The duvet rescues her, for the moment, as she burrows inside, crushing a boiling rim of tears between her eyelids.

Food is what ensures most of the housemates are in the living room when its floor begins to sink. Charlotte avoids two of the next three games by skipping dinner, eating apples she gathered at lunch. She rubs a thumb over the polished skin of the granny smith, remembering when she was at a Euston cafe and some guys conjured up an apple to offer to Tamsin, who was a little drunk and blew a fuse. 'Grow the fuck up,' she bawled at the men, who found it hilarious. Afterwards, Charlotte had to apologise for laughing, but why get so sensitive about a film they did when they were just kids? If she were in Tamsin's position, getting recognised occasionally by the random, misguided people who seem to consider the film a cult classic, she would just own it, tease them right back for being fans.

All the apples are gone now, and her stomach feels like it is bunching up, complaining at the lack of a proper meal. Is that chipotle she can smell, with a crust of toasted cheese? It is impossible to resist opening her door, looking upon a feast of burritos, of tacos oozing guacamole. The atmosphere is jovial, with the housemates chattering and filling their plates. Someone new has arrived by speedboat – a rather supercilious-looking model – and all the men are crowding round her. Charlotte creeps out, takes her first bite, and it is heaven in a floury flatbread. But of course this seems to set it off. Each sofa slides back, accompanied by a faint grinding, the walls rising as her heart sinks.

She clings to Asher's shoulder as they wobble downwards. When she opens her eyes, the escape room has become a biker bar in Memphis. It smells of beer-breath and the red dust stamped in from outside. Her heart is juddering well before she starts seeing the images of cobras lurking on spirit bottles, on the doormat and on Chinese lanterns, sensing them as shivers along her skin. How can she concentrate on the clues when the room is so obviously supposed to remind her of that experience, of the inky snakes on the men's arms, the print on their jackets? A shadow makes her jump: a hologram biker passing like a ghoul. She curls onto a chair and clings to its back, closing her eyes. Luckily it is a team game, only one key for the others to find, so she can focus on blocking out the unpleasant memories. It is hard to tell how much time passes before a descending harness butts against her bare legs; she clips herself in and is extracted.

About an hour later, there is a knock on her door.

'Babe, can I come in?' The voice belongs to Pacey, the marshmallow-swallower from Tennessee. Charlotte lowers the duvet an inch. She feels filthy, half-melted into her sweaty clothes. 'You don't have to open the door if you don't wanna,' the woman continues. There are some muffled sounds that indicate others are with her. 'But we need to have a talk, okay? We gotta work together, alright, hun?' The whispering is clearly audible: 'How 'bout I just go in?' Someone else says: 'No, don't.'

The burble of voices grows as they move away. Charlotte scrunches up her eyes, rubs until sparks appear. She was afraid this would happen, that they'd notice her lack of appetite for the challenges. How could they not? She freezes every time the floor creaks, her mind involuntarily picturing roadies scurrying around below, dressing the next dreadful set. It seems like years since she was laughing with her new housemates, collecting appreciative winks for smoothing down the various tensions. A staged intervention is a bad sign. To reach this point, a lot of bitching must have gone on, and it has probably been caught on camera. The things they would say. In fact, they might as well say them to her face, since she can imagine every word.

She twists her hair until her scalp throbs. In a way, it is not important what her housemates think, though of course it bothers her, but the editors of these shows are like bloodhounds; they will sniff out the drama, waste nothing. Being on this show is the opposite of acting; it is passive, somebody else snipping you into a cardboard cut-out. The pain spreads over her skull, a migraine swirling with frown-emojis, as she pictures her followers getting the idea she is a bit of a wimp, switching themselves off, a whole city of lights going dark one by one.

Her favourite purple bra has vanished, but the drawers are full of fresh underwear with labels still attached, and all the right size, which at least shows the sponsors did their research. A loose linen dress slides over her shoulders, feeling good against her skin.

Ever since winning that first dating show, and partly because of the drama that followed, she has been known as the straight-shooting northerner who'll say what needs to be said. Her LOVE account is a sort of inverse diary: the truth of her life sent out into the world, instead of being locked away.

If her game plan is to be herself, that means trusting her current instinct to share, to seek solidarity. The others need to know there's a reason she keeps letting them down.

Ignoring the way conversations stop and heads turn her way, she asks the housemates to come outside. The waning sun is like a warm hand on the back of her neck and, once they are all perching on bar stools, she feels a buzz of positivity. This is where she poured the welcome fizz when she first arrived, when she handed a glass to each breathless, dripping individual and smiled as if she'd lived in this villa for years. She makes sure everyone has a drink, and then calmly starts to tell them about her experience in Memphis: how she borrowed the show-owned Harley at the start of the evening, and ended it thumping her fists on the door of a beer cellar, thinking she'd never again see the light of day. There was mean Kathleen's sickly perfume in the museum, and the escape rooms that forcibly reminded her of when she was penniless and desperate in Los Angeles. Time bunches, and she seems to say a lot in the few seconds before emotion blurs her vision, her voice thickening until it gums up and she covers her face.

'Anyway, that's why I end up like a bunny in headlights.'

What comes back is unexpected. She hears: 'Oh honey, you come over here and get a hug,' from Pacey the marshmallow-swallower, suddenly sweet. 'This is why we share. How're we meant to know what you was going through?'

'It makes sense?' something lifts from Charlotte's chest. 'You really believe me?'

"Course I believe you. Them rooms trigger memories all right. Hell, when I was young and poor I had a job at this little snack bar on Route 66… We were all like: dude, we're not on the menu, 'kay?' She laughs.

'I didn't like the Egypt room, either,' Mak chimes in, 'reminded me of school trips.'

Charlotte cradles her rum and coke, inhaling its caramel aroma. The terrace has acquired the soft, generous atmosphere of a support group, each person nodding and murmuring, passing out the verbal equivalent of a comforting pat.

'There've been a few creepy ones,' Asher agrees. 'Those snakes on the doormat and the lanterns? I hate snakes.' A gloom settles upon him and he won't meet anyone's eye. The pause is quickly filled by other stories of unpleasant experiences in bars, dusty theatres, tombs and bedsits. Leah, Heidi and Shelly compete with their tales of abusive men. Everyone has a setting that meant something to them. They get what she's saying.

The sugar fog clears. 'No, guys…' she hates to break up this rare moment of community. 'It really was that bar – the red skull on the wall and everything. It was identical.'

There is a pause, a certain sternness in Jake's hoarse, death-metal voice as he mutters: 'There's plenny of bars with skull decor.'

They have acknowledged that the escape rooms mean something to her, so why is it she not affording them the same courtesy? Charlotte fights the urge to smile, shrug off her paranoia and be one of the gang again. But she can't. Honesty lies just beyond this awkward moment, almost within reach. When she presses on, there is the bristle of sympathy turning spiky.

'It's more than that…' she begins to list the escape rooms again, fleshing out the memories. It is when she starts describing how she once rolled a piano on castors from the recycling yard into the bin-store of her Camden flat, hoping to save it, that she realises this is sounding outlandish. She is losing them. They are shifting backwards on their stools, swapping looks.

'Okay, sweet pea,' Pacey stands, all out of patience. 'Whatever. Just give the next one your best shot, m'kay?'

Nobody meets her eye. As the housemates begin to slink away, somehow making it look like a collective shrug, Mak sidles over, enveloping her in the unisex sandalwood perfume he developed himself. 'Hey,' he says, elbowing her gently. 'I can't be doing with you getting evicted. Promise me you'll just suck it up?'

The broken light of the infinity pool dances in his eyes. Nothing has stuck. Somehow it hurts even more to see people like Mak and Asher failing to grasp her meaning, thinking she is just making excuses. They want her to do well and don't understand why she has become so flaky. She firms up her smile, tells him she'll do her best.

Then she is alone, the bar sticky with spilled rum, a burnt sweetness in the air. The big mirror throws back an image of her looking deflated, her eyes dark holes in a mask-like face. There are editors and producers watching via the hidden camera that is undoubtedly positioned at eye level to catch people sitting here. Producers who know what they are doing.

'Every single escape room,' she finds the words pushing themselves out, 'every effing one.' Her head shakes, sways on a tired neck. 'I know it's meant to be tough. It's meant to gross us out, to see what we can take. That's the whole point – I get that.' Her mind runs through the challenges so far, the shameless plundering of her memories, of dreams and half-known fears that they must have scraped from the very bottom of the data vaults. For the first time, anger crackles in her lungs.

'It's not like I can't take a joke,' her voice goes hard as she stands, squaring up to the mirror, knowing she should stop talking. 'But… it's not funny anymore.' If only the others had listened to her, if they had backed her up she wouldn't feel this bitter, hungry hollow opening up inside, making her reckless. 'It's bullying, isn't it? I mean, I'm not being thick here, am I? This is what you're doing, and it's *not fucking cool*.' Her hand slams down flat on the bar. Faces appear in the doorway, and at first she doesn't care. Then a hot steam of shame burns up round her cheeks, stinging her eyes. She strides to the steps and clatters down, expecting to fall.

On the darkening beach, the sand has already gone cold. Her feet sink as she skirts the villa, only stopping when she can lay a hand on the rough, comforting ripple of palm-bark and catch her breath. There it is again: the *fuck-it* moment. It happens when her sense of truth begins to snag awkwardly on reality, like two continental plates catching and then breaking free. One blissful instant of release… but now aftershocks send her heart off-beat as the night closes in around her, peppery with bugs. She has kicked up a fuss, and her whole body is being nagged by the questions that follow: is it proportionate, or princessy? Now that she is getting some oxygen into her lungs, she doubts the wisdom of getting a cog on and ranting at the producers. It might make things worse. Or it might get her chucked out. Her eyes go to the bamboo fence, a subtle boundary around the set. She almost expects a door to open, some megaphone-voice telling her to mosey on out, her replacement already on a speedboat. Sudden fear flushes her face. These three years in the limelight have made her soft. This show is probably her last chance. If she can't summon the grit then she might as well go back to wearing a sandwich board on the corner of Oxford Street.

A fragrant breeze is petal-silky against her forehead. The cool of twilight is descending and insects are tuning up for the night. She takes one more deep breath, then walks back to the house.

GOGGLERS (LOVECAST 2298) 'THE MERCH'

DOC: So now we're properly watching *Outta My Room*, we obviously want the extras, so Dick has come up with...
DICK: Jerónimo's Behind-the-Scenes Vlog and Shop. Get in!
DOC: Now let's take a look at what I can buy here, if I change a few quid into Luvcoin...
DICK: What is he, crew or something?
DOC: Shitty American whisky... oh wait, empty bottles? Look at this... he's selling two empty bottles.
DICK: What the–
DOC: Oh, I get it... 'Remember Saturday,' he says, 'aka the big night of Jake-shaggery?' It's a souvenir. You can pay actual Luvcoin for that.
DICK: I'm more interested in his photos of Leah sunbathing without a stitch on. Listen to this: 'No pixel blur here!' There are samples...
DOC: 'Purple bra owned by so-hot-she's-having-a-meltdown Charlotte – bid now!' Well no wonder she's freaking out. Poor girl can't find her underwear.
DICK: That's one way to keep me watching.
DOC: He must be raiding the laundry chute. How does he hope to get away with this?

Five

One problem always hides another. You'll hit a honeycomb of old timber, the cellar of some fourteenth century boozer, and find a way round, only to end up tunnelling towards a clutch of asbestos pipes waiting like white worms in the clay.

On the plus side, Tamsin is starting to see signs that she is becoming yesterday's news. The followers are starting to fall away; all she needs is a few days of tumbleweed – if Ogilby can bear to stay out of the debate – and the algorithms will slowly revert her profile to its natural state.

She emerges from the office and walks past souvenir shops, noodle places and one of those spas where fish nibble the dead skin off clients' feet. The trouble with all this fuss online is that she has not been thinking about

Charlotte or *Outta My Room*. Has Luka seen the latest episode? She tries his number. A gaggle of teenagers walk past, eyeing her huge yellow jacket. If it were not for this site visit she'd have continued to work from home, keeping her head down.

When Luka answers, she can see from the partial view of his face that he is in the middle of rowing practice. He sounds annoyed at himself for accepting the call.

'No,' he snaps, when she asks about the show. 'I haven't watched them all yet.' The end of his reply is drowned out by the voice of a very Scottish coxswain yelling for the stern pair to set the boat.

'I'm worried about her.'

There are rapid, cut-off splashes and a glimpse of river as the boat zips along. When he replies, he is almost breathless.

'Look… Look at everything she's sacrificed to get this far. If she's had enough, she'll quit, won't she?'

'Way enough!' yells the coxswain and Luka grunts, lifting his oar. He says a hasty goodbye and ends the call.

The projection vanishes just in time for her to avoid tripping over an abandoned umbrella. Luka disapproves of Charlotte's choices – she has made her bed and has to lie in it – but he's also right. If it was beyond endurance, she'd walk out.

It's human nature to assume that other people are basically just you with another skin slung over their shoulders. Tamsin has to remember that this is not the case and if there is one thing friends do, it's respect each other's dreams. In the early days, Charlotte burned through jobs and money, getting a speaking part here, a reaction shot there. She started again a dozen times, but it did eventually lead to a break. *Six on the Beach* may not have been an acting job, but its seven million viewers translated into quite a follower boost. Charlotte really wiped the floor with the other contestants. They were all tanned and perfect, waxed to the nines, but she was the down-to-earth scouser who had a smile for everyone, even as they tried repeatedly to stab her in the back. Nor was she fazed by the barrage of twists, odd decisions and 'little surprises' from the show's producers. By season end, all the other singles had been eliminated, and she was in a ridiculously steamy relationship with her co-winner, an arrogant guy named Rollo Boone, who she dumped, live on air, soon after the show ended.

She got some stick for that, of course, but Tamsin is one of the few who understand that it wasn't done for dramatic effect. It was just a spontaneous reaction to being cornered by the interviewer, a raw burst of honesty. Luckily, Rollo's follower count went sky-high as a result, and it didn't do Charlotte any harm, either. She moved, almost overnight, to a condo in the People's Republic of Love, and got a presenting job on a light-hearted consumer watchdog show – which she loved.

So last time it all worked out. Charlotte stepped into that dazzling celebrity landscape of lights, cameras and action, all of which gave her a coiffed, carved, almost beatific brilliance. At last she was being noticed, bathed in the glow of strangers' eyes. She has always been a natural. It was obvious from their earliest days together at junior drama club.

Tamsin splashes through a puddle, her waterproof trousers doused with grit. It was just a bit of fun, something to do after school. If she had known it would get so serious… but at the time it was exhilarating to have that casting agent draw them aside after the end-of-year showcase, faces still slick with spotlight-melted makeup, and coax them into auditioning for a film, a quirky remake of *The Lion, the Witch and the Wardrobe*.

Sometimes Tamsin awakes with a jolt, clasping the side of her bed and tearing away her sheets, feeling for an instant as though she is back amid the wardrobe's tickly, oily fur coats, its old-wood smell. Charlotte would barely have to smooth down her long, chocolatey hair as she emerged. A head taller, she was perfect as the older sister, while Tamsin's puppy-dog features got her cast in the more substantial role of Lucy. She remembers swishing through drifts of flaky chemical snow in buckled shoes, pine resin sharpening the air. The assistant director positioned Tamsin too close to a fir, so it needled into the collar of her little blouse, and she caught a beery outbreath from the actor playing the faun – later to be the subject of some alarming allegations. Lucy refuses the rosy apple he rubs on his fluffy haunch, perhaps sensing what will later happen to her brother when he partakes of enchanted Turkish Delight, but the assistant director's smoke-dried voice cut her off again: 'Lucy, keep it smooth.' Her outline was being captured, crisp as a silhouette, on thousands of frames, every waver of her voice recorded. *Again. Again. Again.* She longed for Charlotte to rescue her, for a big hug and the smell of coconut shampoo, for them to go back to messing about on the creaky stage of the community hall. But she was Lucy now, and they were too far into the filming schedule for anything to be done about it.

Eternal Winter got made. At the premier, her mum wore a pink sequined dress and cried as she hugged her child-star. The excitement bubbled up, and no one mentioned that it would dry into something icky over the years. A sheepish look would appear on her mum's face each time she was forced to shut down her daughter's Social profile, because facial recognition meant that someone always found Tammy May Wilde, and something inappropriate was always said – especially a couple of years later once all that stuff about her male co-star came out. Only when Tamsin watched the film through the eyes of fellow teenagers at a house party – amid howls of laughter – did two things become clear. First, that Charlotte was unbothered about the movie being terrible, because it had already led to other things. Second, that Tamsin would always regret having allowed part of herself to be fixed in this tacky snow-globe of a film, looking as lost as she had ever been.

'More chicken on that?' says the smiley guy serving. 'How about some crisps for later? Do you have your drink?' They are always generous on-site, the food token covering as much as you can eat. She points to a can of Ade which not only claims to be zero-sugar, but also carbon neutral and 'shadow-free', whatever that means. Tamsin sits on the fold-out picnic table and rubs the hard-hat-heaviness from her scalp. She is so distracted that she keeps inadvertently breaking rules: she wore the wrong headgear and failed to report straight to the office on arrival. At this rate she'll be chucked out and will have to explain to Ted why they still don't have data on a dodgy bit of substrate behind section 21B. Nor is it a good time to be falling behind, since there are apparently still rumblings about the photo. HR have invited her to a meeting later in the week, and hopefully she will get a chance to explain.

The problem is that her mind is elsewhere. While waiting for the site manager, she streamed today's mini-episode of *Outta My Room*, and all her trains of thought thundered off the rails. There is no ignoring how terrible Charlotte looks. Normally her smile is perpetual, her top lip resting in a natural arch over large teeth. Right now, her eyes are red around the edges, her smile askew. Even her dress sense seems to have taken a hit, the flower-print shift too loose, even frumpy... and has she lost a little weight?

Amid the chatter of construction workers, the hum of traffic and drones, it is difficult to imagine that anyone's mind is being messed with on a tropical island far, far away. Right at the end of the episode, Charlotte is at the bar, gazing into the mirror, 'Every single escape room...' she mutters, then lets out a throaty yell, the camera cutting away to show the others overhearing. Tamsin cringes. This is such odd behaviour. Charlotte is not stupid; she must know her portrayal on the show is bad, that there's no way she will come out of this sparkling.

The show must be ransacking her data, the algorithm seeking locations, items, places, smells and sounds that

Charlotte mentioned negatively online, feeding them into an escape room generator. Someone should tell the producers their system is too efficient. If Tamsin is the one to do it, to say something on social media, then at least her over-inflated follower count will be of use.

Her steel toe caps tap together beneath the table as she composes her post, letting the small mountain of chicken curry cool in the river-breeze. Seeking inspiration, she gazes beyond the metal fences, finding only a concrete bridge shadowed by pollution. Unexpectedly, there is also a man gripping the barriers. A thin sound turns out to be her name, and she stands up in time to hear the almost plaintive cry of:

'Tamsin! Thank the powers, I thought you'd never hear me.'

'Luka?'

She leaves her food and goes over to the fence, not wanting to shout past the canteen van.

'What are you doing here?'

'I just came to your map-pin.'

'Is everything all right?'

'Look,' he says, blinking wildly. 'Do not, I repeat not, put anything on LOVE.'

Irritation creases her brow.

'You came all the way here to tell me that?' He has already expressed his lack of confidence in her, his belief that anything she does will mess things up for Charlotte. Why repeat himself?

'Can you come out and talk?'

'No. I'm in the middle of work.'

'Okay, how about after? Meet me at Tito's Bar, on the river. And don't post anything until we've spoken.'

'Why not?' She glances back, seeing some neon-clad workers regarding her lunch curiously. 'You know what, never mind – message me.'

'I can't,' he says. 'Just meet me later and don't post *anything*, promise?'

'Fine,' she breathes. To her relief, he turns to go, his slim frame rocked by the eddies of a passing bus. The idea of having a drink with him again so soon is not particularly welcome, but his behaviour is too unsettling to ignore. What could warrant him tracking her down by device location, like there is not a moment to lose? And why can't he message her? Even when he's really 'up' mood-wise, he is not usually like this. Shreds of his muttering reach her as he trips, rights himself and kicks a litter bin, sounding a dull clang.

'Oh, and Tamsin,' a last shout drifts across.

'What?'

'Watch the credits.'

Six

Shelly and Pacey are curled up together, regarding her through half-closed eyes. Asher swigs a beer then puts it aside, leaving big fingerprints in the condensation. As he nudges her, Charlotte cranks up a smile.

'I'm fine.'

'Sure?' His eyebrows bristle.

'Yeah.' She looks at the sofa beneath her legs; the sweat under her knees is sticking her down. Only now she is actually sitting here, for the first time in a day and a half, does she notice how creepy this room really is. The rubbery sofas look like internal organs, the coffee tables coffin-sized, the floor tinny and dangerous. Almost as though her thoughts trigger something, the bar begins to disappear into the wall and there is the whine of machinery being set in motion.

This is it: the moment she gets back in the game, faces up to the challenge. She's been readying herself for it all day. The creak, as the floor parts, is not too bad. She can do this. The others stand, stagger, chitter excitedly. A flood of ice streaks down her backbone. Oh God, the need to *run*. The decision flashes its binary code through her brain. *Do I? Don't I?* Then her body acts independently, feet clattering on metal as she throws herself towards the kitchen door. Asher meets her eye in that split second, his mouth opening – but she outruns his shout, turning sideways and diving through, not an inch to spare, before the shutters close. She lands jarringly on the floor, catching his yell in her ear like a thrown baseball, a big, round 'No!'

Above the pulsing of her blood she can hear muffled voices and scraping sounds from within the sealed living room, as the housemates are eased down to the lower level. The kitchen floor retains its odour of bleach. Stillness reigns; the others are doing the challenge without her, thinking her a coward. Asher's guttural negative rings in her ears, and what makes her feel worse is that it was kindly meant. He was in her corner, trying to stop her from running, but she let him down.

Charlotte drags herself upward, hands clammy on the worktop. There is the dusty sourness of spilled coconut milk, a lipstick-smeared tumbler she must have knocked. Hours of psychological preparation count for nothing, it seems. When the floor trembled and began to open, her lungs pressed too hard against her heart.

She stumbles outside. A banana leaf is spinning in the middle of the infinity pool. What now? If she is going to fight tooth and nail to avoid the challenges, her only achievement on this show will be to lose the respect of her followers, as she has with her housemates. It'll never be the same as *Six on the Beach*. For a long while Charlotte is motionless, watching the leaf. When it stops spinning and rocks like a boat, she straightens up and locks eyes with the mirror across the bar. It was easier yesterday, with a bit of fire in her blood. Now it's a struggle to find the words.

'I think this is it.' She bites her lip, shivers and then, hardly believing she is doing this, tells the mirror she's made up her mind to quit, right now, before she makes a fool of herself – any more than she has done already. If she is lucky they will extract her before the others have finished the escape room, so she won't have to face them again.

'Anyway, thanks for the opportunity,' she finishes, déjà vu smacking her all the way back to those clinical audition rooms, where she'd deliver her piece then merge back into the human slush-pile of hopefuls. The relief is mingled with shame, and Charlotte pinches her nose to direct the hot tears away from her cheeks, slightly nauseated by the optimistic jazz-pink of her nails. It seems crazy to be giving up something that, only hours earlier, she was terrified of losing. But it can't be helped, and maybe it's part of the process: denial before acceptance.

She has to believe there will be other opportunities, to remember what her mum wrote, after some childhood disappointment or other: *If low-hanging fruit goes bad, don't pick it. There are other branches.* What did it mean? At the time, Charlotte didn't understand. It was one of those pieces of advice that ripened slowly.

No speedboat arrived, though she watched until dark.

She spends the next morning becoming familiar with the perimeter. Young, scratchy palms sprout from their husks, pushing through the scrub and catching her flip-flops. The heavy sweetness of tropical leaf-litter brings her unwillingly to thoughts of her mum in South America, doing six-month stints with the Medecins Sans Frontieres. All day she would wait for her mum to get some reception and see her photos and videos, for the icon to change to *seen*. When the phone beeped and she got a big fat *OMG* from her mum, especially if there was some lucky shot of a bee, Charlotte could relax, knowing her day had been filled with real stuff, things that had been seen, because her mum was seeing them too.

The young palms are rubbery, fresh with sap. Deep within the scrub she finds a line of bamboo, behind which is a steel fence. Funny how the housemates have only ever discussed these barriers in terms of security. This is your natural state of mind, as a celebrity; it is always about being shielded, never shut in.

In reality TV, an hour is a long time, and a day is an age. By now she should have been picked up, dressed, powdered, lip-glossed and half-way through her post-show interview, being gently mocked by the presenter and made to grin through a compilation of clips. Maybe that's the delay, she thinks gloomily, if they are having trouble coming up with enough of her 'best bits'.

Her mind rewinds three years to the finale of *Six on the*

Beach, and the difference between then and now makes her face soften, almost to tears. The spotlights were translucent pink and mango-orange as she strode out, waving, onto the stage they had built on the sand, a live audience whooping, two fire pits at either side filling the air with floating embers and a fragrant crackle. A flash of nerves, and then she owned it: stage, audience and moment. The ecstasy, reflected equally on Rollo's face, was like nothing she'd ever experienced. They had won. Theirs would be, for a full month, the most searched-for names on the internet.

Rollo was wealthy, well-connected and already a minor celebrity, son of the playboy gym-chain owner Baxter Boone. He was a real gift to the producers, unpredictable and extreme, so although Charlotte and another guy were initially the most-voted-for couple, Rollo was the one people wanted to watch. He must have liked her enough to change his approach, to vaguely align himself with the romantic tone of the show. Only now does she realise how much she appreciated having a partner in crime. A dating show comes with its own annoyances and emotional turbulence, but at least she was never alone.

With Rollo, what began as beguilement evolved into something more. Beneath his desire to shock, Charlotte detected determination, a diamond-hard game plan. It was one performer sensing another. Instinctively, they began to create a story at the centre of the show, a relationship full of fire, because Rollo was known for being mean and Charlotte was everyone's friend. There was something almost classical about it. Could she find the good in him, and could he bring out the devil in her? It helped that she really did fancy him. Even now she can remember the supple silk of his neck, the dark hairs on his forearms, looking as though they'd catch in his watch, the baked, almost burnt smell of his chest. He had that perfect artistry of facial hair, stubble undulating around his lips and along his jawline, at once casual and minutely groomed. He was shirtless a lot – his body resisted any clothes that were there to conceal rather than adorn.

As Charlotte wanders between the palms, she almost wishes he was with her. A warm hand on her arm. A roll of the dice. A Rollo. He treated desire as a sacred thing, not hesitating to act upon it. He would put a match to her dejection, ignite it and throw it over the fence, telling the world to go fuck itself.

But no, this is dangerous thinking. She did the right thing breaking up with him when she did, though it was a bad move to do it live on television. He went properly wild afterwards, and she only ever saw him behind a veil of champagne-spray or on some DJ's pedestal. Maybe the problem – the reason she's here – is that she never propelled herself upward as he did, relentlessly and with enough momentum to become a proper star.

She walks all the way round the perimeter, collecting a mesh of red scratches on her shins. The flies rise up in angry clouds, but she has yet to see a bee on this man-made islet. She adjusts her bikini straps as she emerges into the tropical sun. Rollo had tactics she'd often admired, gained from trying to outshine his famous siblings. Her earliest visibility had come about more naturally, with the instinct of a twelve-year-old to let some of the raw grief she was holding leak out onto social media. Her mother had always made Bolivia sound like a slightly fantastical place. It was hard to accept that she wouldn't be coming back, as though a dream had swallowed her up. Not death. Not really. When Charlotte posted about it, finally, and people replied with compassion, when they peppered her profile with hearts and crying-eye faces, it made her feel something for the first time in ages. The faintest taste of that previous sweet hit, that phone-beep that said *seen*.

Since then she has been busy online. The trouble is that emojis are so small. You need a lot. Sometimes she feels like a bee herself, visiting a million flowers.

Later on, she examines the fence panels of the poolside terrace for any hidden exit. Pacey and Spike walk past, saying nothing. On one of the posts there is a black glass nub, like a fat bluebottle.

'Alright, Producer?' she says into the camera, 'I quit. Are you getting this?' Why are the producers being so childish as to ignore her? She frowns, trying to work out how this might be portrayed to the viewing public, whether they will cut these bits of footage.

'Hey,' the voice sounds like it comes from an engine rather than lungs. In Asher's sideways glance, she detects a grain of embarrassment.

'You don't have to be seen with me, you know,' she says.

'I'm just happy you're still here.'

'Yeah, lucky me,' she sighs. 'Still no response. Maybe

it's the contract… something I missed?'

He shrugs, giving her a double pat on the back that makes her wobble. 'Losing's usually the easy part.'

As he shuffles off, it hits her. Damn those producer bastards: they did put it in the contract. The grimness of it makes her buckle. It is not enough to become an outcast and admit defeat. They want her to fail a challenge.

If you want to leave, you must be a loser.

Two days pass before her stomach feels ready for it. Time's healing balm has soothed those abrasive, gut-wrenching impressions of the escape room, but this is still a big deal. As a safeguard, she has told the others to block the exits when the floor starts to sink, to hold onto her if necessary. Even the most scathing of her housemates seemed to mellow at this, agreeing to help her find courage, flexing their hands ready for a firm grip.

Just one last escape room, she tells herself, as the floor opens and every cell of her body begins to tremble. Failing shouldn't be a problem.

They are deposited in a sort of diner, with squat chairs and tables, a bar with impressive rum collection projected on the wall. The narrator's voice emerges from a speaker, a bit distorted, and she learns the challenge is an individual task, which means someone will get evicted. So far, so good.

The others begin scuttling around, looking for clues, while Charlotte grinds to a halt, mesmerised. They have included just enough detail to make her great aunt's cafe in

Grenada recognisable. There are the red plastic chairs, the swordfish complete with baseball cap mounted above the pizza oven, which has a burnt-flour odour. What are they playing at, recreating Old Sally's? She doesn't even have photos of this place.

A movement makes her look down, and then she knows. Water creeps across the floor, touches her feet, soaks through, and there are gasps from the other housemates. They make little splashes as they pick up the pace, knowing the water level will only get higher, but Charlotte cannot move. That smell, like drains, takes her right back to being shaken awake, hurried downstairs through the dawn light. She starts seeing the slippery, flashing bodies, the dead, staring eyes. Fish dying in the swirl, fish that will fetch up on doorsteps and later be swept, bloodied and muddied, into a stinking pile. November tides were bringing waves right over the flood defences, pooling in low-lying areas of town, and one of the waiters had left a door open, letting water from the alleyway into the cafe overnight. What the six-year-old Charlotte did not expect were the small fish that had been washed in too. Some were alive, most were dying, because the water was soupy with filth, like the garbage juice that drips from dustbins. Fish marooned on plastic tables gasped as she tried to get through, her skirt bunched, and all of a sudden she felt slimy things touching her bare legs. Her scream was more of a gasp, as she tried to run, but the water slowed her down. Later she would listen in confusion as they explained that her great uncle had got his leg trapped in a drain. A funeral must have taken place, though she remembers nothing of it.

Charlotte covers her eyes and nose, and tries to live inside the idea that she is not here. This is not happening. All around is a percussive splashing, abnormally loud, the others raising their voices above it, impervious to the horror. It strikes her that if she loses the game she might be trapped. If the lights go dark and the water rises until the fish are all around, she will feel their cold, broken scales against her skin. Real dead fish – silver dulled and guts trailing. All at once she is blinking herself back into the room, trying to focus; the others are opening pots and climbing about, so maybe it is a physical challenge. Mak notices her movement, and points to a couple of keys hung above the pizza oven, letting her go first, bless him. She climbs up, gets one in her hand. Then, mercifully, a wire-seat descends and two streams trail from her toes as she is lifted free, dizzy with relief.

She bows her head against the cable. It's clear what they have done here. The message is so laced with irony that it sinks to the bottom of her heart. *You can't lose.*

The floor is re-forming, but there is a sudden yell from below.

'Oh man... I can't...'

Mak has lost the other key somewhere, or perhaps another housemate took it. He is splashing in the water, now higher than the bar, his eyes almost neon with fear.

'I can't bloody swim.'

A sail of droplets obscures him, and the last she sees, as the floor closes and the water swirls, is his hair turning to seaweed, a single frond plastered across his forehead.

Seven

You forget the credits are there. Apps skip over them, taking you straight to the next episode. Even now, when she allows them to scroll, Tamsin has no idea what Luka meant when he told her to look at them. She wonders if he saw the last episode, whether he shares her concern about the nasty turn these challenges are taking: that room filling with water, dotted with little plastic fish; the grey tinge of disbelief spreading across Charlotte's face.

The bar is becoming noisier every minute as people gather, unchained from their screens, thin wine glasses refracting the light from sky and river. She moves to the periphery, leaning out and catching the scent of muddy banks below. When Marc Brunel tunnelled beneath the Thames two hundred years ago, layers of quicksand and gravel meant the only safe ground to burrow through was just below the river bed. It was madness – you could sink a diving bell amid the flowing waters and poke through to the miners with an iron rod. The third time it flooded, six people drowned, with Isambard Kingdom Brunel – Marc's nineteen-year-old son – only narrowly escaping. Tamsin can just imagine the heavy, choking torrent, all rotting weeds and filth. Hard to believe it was even attempted, that Isambard would stay down there for days with the river dripping on his head like the last seconds of his life, alongside the unfortunate miners doing the actual digging. At least that crazy enterprise turned into a genuine achievement: the first underwater tunnel in the world. Why is Charlotte still gritting her teeth and pushing on, for something far less worthwhile?

A beanpole appears, Luka in a coat with lapels up round his ears, out of breath. 'I'm getting drinks,' he says, then leaves instantly. When he sits down with two glasses of unidentified clear liquid, he mumbles something about disturbing her at work.

'Don't worry about it,' she says, nonplussed at this near-apology. Something odd is going on.

'So, why not confront the producers on social media?' he says, as though they have been conversing about it all day. 'Well, because I did, last night, and boy did I pay.'

He jingles the ice in his drink and downs a third of it, frowning as though he can't taste enough alcohol.

'What did you post?'

He does not reply, his lips stuck in a bitter twist.

'Luka?' she tries. 'Have you seen the last episode, with the–'

'Yes. Exactly. I should have listened to you and forced

myself to watch the damn thing sooner. That Caribbean bar flooding – how cold was that? I thought some of her followers would be sure to make the connection. Even if no one gets Grenada, she squirms over seafood sometimes, doesn't she?'

Surprising that Luka knows the significance of that particular cafe with the swordfish on the wall. And he has evidently been keeping a close eye on Charlotte's profile over the years.

'Anyway,' he goes on, 'I found one of the posts where she actually mentions the flooded cafe. I re-shared it, hashtagging the crap out of the show, asking why they were picking on her. I'm pretty well-versed on psychological abuse, though she probably signed all sorts of ridiculous waivers…'

'And?' She licks her lips. Her drink smells like perfume and is probably some mysterious spirit from the back of the bar.

'Someone reported me. I got a message saying I'd breached the network rules, and my account was being closed. That's it. Ten years of building a following, trying to flog my humble talent, and it's just vanished, all in the space of a few minutes.' He shakes his head, obviously still in shock. 'You keep trying to log in, using different devices, you search for your own name, you don't want to believe it… But I've been well and truly razed from the face of the LOVE network.'

Below, tourist boats chug along, furrowing the silty water, their engine vapours mingling with the scent of roasted almonds being sold on the bridge. She has shut herself off from social media in the past, but not everyone finds it so easy.

'That's shit,' she says.

'I know. Most of my work comes in via LOVE, so I'm quite possibly screwed.' He tugs at his hair, re-sculpts it, and takes a gulp of flowery booze. 'Anyway, back to Charlotte's show,' he goes on hoarsely. 'You have to look closely, and watch the part no one bothers to watch, and then you see it. Bang. Clear as fuck. Like a punch in the throat. Suddenly you understand what's happening. Did you watch the credits?'

'What am I supposed to be seeing?'

'You didn't notice?'

'All I'm seeing is that it's wearing her down, all of this. Even taking into account her need for followers, I think she's ready to walk away.'

Luka shrugs. 'It depends if she can see what's happening, if she can smell the rat.'

'What rat?'

'Didn't you see in the credits? Republi-KA Productions is the studio. Even a cursory search turns up the governor – the bloody governor of the Republic – owning most of the shares.' Passion ripens in his cheeks.

This doesn't seem like a groundbreaking revelation.

'So? It's filmed in the Republic, isn't it?'

'The governor, Tamsin.'

'I don't see the significance. You know what these playboys are like. They own a nightclub here, a production company there…'

A light drizzle begins to fall, barely wet, just enough to

sensitise her skin. Luka looks at her pityingly, like she is a child and he is steeling himself to explain.

'That means it's his show. You do know who we're talking about here?'

'Yes, of course I–' Her lips chew together, stuck on this trivia. He might as well be asking who won a certain Oscar or who is lined up to play the next James Bond, fleeting names to which she never pays attention. The governor of the Republic changes annually.

'For Charlotte, I mean, you know who that is?'

Then, suddenly, the conversation floods back. There was laughter in Charlotte's voice when she rang to share this piece of news. No need to worry about poor Rollo – in this October's 'election' he'd been named Number One Influencer resident in the Republic, which meant he would achieve his dream of being Governor. 'Maybe I should have stayed with him,' she joked.

Roland 'Rollo' Boone. Tamsin can barely remember what he looks like, though she did watch most of *Six on the Beach*. What comes to mind is tattoos: neat and geometric, and hard to ignore when he had his shirt off so often. He was late-twenties, with hair on his face – less on his head – and a golden-skinned reality-television look. A bit young and preening for her liking, and not normally Charlotte's type, either.

'So, he owns the show... and you think he's using it to give her hell?'

Luka expels a puff of air.

'Trust me,' he says. 'I know his type. Doesn't forget a knock to the ego.' He picks at his tongue, as though to remove a fragment of something unpleasant. When they watched an episode of *Six on the Beach* together, he raised a glass to Charlotte's success, but looked away as she canoodled with other men, and finally with this 'greasy peddler of protein powders.'

'But it's so–'

'Childish? He's a toddler, Tamsin.'

'Going to all that trouble–'

'It's not trouble, not to him. The governor can make anything happen – he says the word and it's law. That's how it works in their celebrity playground. Last week he made everyone in the service industry start wearing a grass skirt, just for kicks. This show is nothing. He's been waiting to punish Charl for years, and it must have been so easy, our girl so hungry for a gig.' With finger and thumb, Luka pinches an imaginary crumb of cheese from the air. 'Set, baited, sprung. And he's getting away with it, the bastard.'

A boat goes by, sounding its deafening horn. Some of the tourists have selfie sticks that resemble fishing rods attached to their heads – tiny cameras on the ends. The Houses of Parliament look down on them with a gothic frown. All at once Tamsin feels desolate. Perhaps Rollo really could undertake a vindictive project like this, gift-wrapped as a reality show, and no one would notice or care.

'I wish there was something we could do,' she says, 'tell people what's going on. Go to the police.'

He almost loses his balance with the force of his incredulous, over-pitched laugh. 'You engineers. So bloody practical.' This spurt of sarcasm settles him back into a slump, kicking his heels restlessly against the stool. 'I agree we need to do something. That's why I didn't want you squandering your shitload of followers. Something tells me they're the only ace we hold – not that I can think of a use for them just yet, given how quickly my sad little protest was quashed,' he shakes his head. 'My whole LOVE profile erased. The thought of starting all over again makes me want to weep.'

She gives him a one-arm hug. Her mind is dusting off headlines about Rollo, his celebrity relationships, talk-show appearances, outrageous partying and odd stunts all indicating a disdain for normal codes of behaviour. No wonder the escape rooms go too far.

'It's just a shame,' Luka sighs. 'There's no way Rollo's going to let her win. She'll walk away when it gets too much, but if she knew what was going on, she could do it sooner and save herself some stress.'

Clouds are gathering overhead. Charlotte is one of the few people Tamsin carries inside her mind, a kind voice that is always there even if the Atlantic is between them. She thinks of the flooding tunnel beneath the Thames, the water-filled escape room, and the flow of tears she saw, directed away from Charlotte's face as she pinched her nose, that tic no one else would notice. Logic is on Luka's side, of course, so it is hard to explain the taut wedge of concern lodged beneath her stomach. Is there something else, something they are not seeing?

She climbs down from her stool. 'Yeah,' she says, peeling off her coat so air flutters refreshingly through her clothes. 'I guess she won't put up with it much longer.'

GOGGLERS (LOVECAST 2103) 'IN YOUR FACE'

DOC: So I'm going to play the clip, and Dick will probably interrupt because he's a dick.
DICK: Nature of the beast.
FANESSA [ON SCREEN]: So he's boyfriend material, but will you be together forever?
ROLLO [ON SCREEN]: Of course. She's my soulmate.
[AUDIENCE *AWS*]
FANESSA [ON SCREEN]: Charlotte? Don't leave him hanging.
DICK: Wait for it...
CHARLOTTE [ON SCREEN]: I... I'm sorry. Hand on heart, I just can't see it. We're too different and... You don't know the real me.
ROLLO [ON SCREEN] I think I do.
DICK: Cue major awks, and she's like, 'sorry', and he's like, 'it's been a rollercoaster, but now you're crashing it?' Listen to this...
DOC: I'm trying to.
ROLLO [ON SCREEN]: Bam! You just broke me, girl.

Eight

It takes a pitcher and a half of Tequila sunrise for them to get past that image of Mak disappearing amid the swirl of dark waters, genuine terror in his cry.

'Give us a drink,' Shelly the contortionist demands, as the chef pours too slowly. 'Say, can we Irish this up a bit?'

'Irish it up? It's a fucking cocktail.'

Charlotte, from her position hunched on a sun lounger, does not hear the usual clink of glasses. People are keeping to themselves, fidgeting and preening twice as hard, as though reaffirming that they still have control over their own bodies. There is an undercurrent of tension, perhaps even guilt, as they discuss the game.

'Poor Maki,' she hears someone murmur. Friendly and funny, he was popular among the housemates. Only Pacey is upbeat.

'What you moping for?' she chirps. 'They got to have drama. They got to make the games a bit scary. Soon as we were out, they'd be straight in there with a ring – what do they call them red and white rubber rings–'

'Lifebuoys?'

'One of them, and then he'd be towelled off, fixed up for his studio appearance. Right now he's loving it, half-way to hooched, trust me.'

They nod, knowing she is right. What other outcome can there be? Mak will be striding out under the spotlights, waving, doing his little shimmy. He'll tell them how scary it was in the escape room, spill the beans about who likes who, and try at every turn to plug his range of vegan scents and toiletries.

One by one they perk up.

'Bit of drama,' says Spike, drumming two fingers on his kneecap. 'It's what they want.'

Pacey is emphatic, goggle-eyed in her agreement. The drink flows until, uneasily at first, their spirits are restored. Charlotte slips away towards the beach. The wooden steps whine at her, and it is as though she can finally understand this language. The underbelly of the show is exposed and it is not, as she first thought, an opportunity. It's a trick.

She is struck by the Catch-22 of it, the way they are driving her to leave but simultaneously making it impossible. There is no way she could be Mak, watching the light narrow to a strip, sour-smelling water creeping up her body. She would lose her footing on the plastic table, blind herself with thrashing and float around in a soup of slimy, unseen… The shivers take over and she pushes the image away. Her housemates seem certain that Mak will be extracted quickly, but she is not so sure. If it was Charlotte in there, in the inky water, the producers might drain the room in seconds, or they might not. They could leave her in there all night. It doesn't bear thinking about.

She walks through the twilight, pausing to wring water from the hem of her dress, her sodden shoes swapped for flip-flops. To get a change of clothes would mean dashing across the living room, and she is not quite ready for that. Instead she steps gingerly into the scrub, where sap shines on broken leaves, crunchy palm fronds underfoot. It would be so blissful to walk straight off the set, but soon she is up against polished bamboo tubes that make xylophone sounds when she runs her fingernails along them. She could force them apart, but the steel barrier behind looks extremely secure.

What is beyond? From the speedboat she saw a causeway stretching across to the main island – the hotel district, from memory. A land-based escape route is by far the most attractive, if only she could reach it.

Where the undergrowth thins, she emerges onto the beach. Man-made rocks frame this cove, making it look as though a giant dropped two handfuls of sugar cubes. With the sea sighing in her ears, she picks her way over textured stone. At last she finds the point at which the metal fence meets the breakwater, which rises to head-height. The bolt startles her with its freshness, the shine of it, bored into the rock. It is cold to the touch, something that says 'prison', not 'film set'. Why is this necessary on a private island, with so little risk of marauding fans? Tears spring to her eyes, the fear fizzing back through her veins. Is she an inmate?

Her toes rest in newly wetted sand, and the line of foam seems to coax her further in. A strong swimmer could strike out past the rocks, circle the island. She swallows the dryness in her throat. It is as though they knew she might come here, might have this thought, and designed the fish-filled escape room to freshen her phobia. A few strokes and the panic would kick in, the sense of things touching her submerged legs. The liquid is warm and salty, like clear blood, and she backs away.

They want her to stay, and to push her to the limit, but why? From nowhere, she remembers reading an interview with the director of a horror franchise, one she has never been able to stomach. 'There's no point hurting a fearless lion,' he had said. 'You have to hurt Bambi.' Is that what people want to see? Has she been selected for being the most doe-eyed, her good-girl reputation suddenly an Achilles heel?

Enough. She is suddenly disgusted. Victim is not a role she is willing to play. Her mind is made up: one way or another she is getting out of here.

A wardrobe is a portal across time and space. Silk caresses her cheek and each dress has an aura of jasmine or sweet citrus, or whatever scented beads were tossed inside its protective clear-starch wrap. She has opened more of these designer dresses than expected, since the automated laundry system seems to eat a certain proportion of her garments.

When it is quiet, the occasional bang can be heard from this end of her room, or sometimes a rumble that might be a vehicle. Inside the wardrobe, she puts her ear to the flimsy back panel. The villa's building materials, like everything shipped into the Republic, are as lightweight and modern as possible. She has already examined the corridors and cupboards for signs of a maintenance hatch, some way for them to intervene when a cleaning robot beaches itself or chokes on a hairclip, but there is nothing obvious.

As she listens, the door lolls closed and, out of the blue, this brand new panic hits her, moisture springing from her skin. Come on, she breathes. Remember how you used to love hiding inside the wardrobe with Tamsin? They were fearless back then, amid the thrill-infused lighting of a sound stage, in the special 'Narnia' wardrobe built by an actual props department. It was full of vintage furs, a silky, tickly, mothball-darkness with hangers jangling. From inside you could hear things being wheeled about, the creepy laugh of Mr Faun, and the slither of green screens – soon to become an ice castle, a forbidding forest, and a room with brown 1940s furniture.

When the director lost track of her two youngest cast members, she would know to open the wardrobe and find the pair of them giggling inside, 'Are we in Narnia yet?' Are these fir trees or just fur coats? Firs or furs? Charlotte was usually let off; she got only a fraction of the grief that Tamsin had to absorb from the raspy-throated assistant director. Poor Tam – no one seemed to notice the tense bewilderment creeping in beneath some of the lines they kept making her repeat. She wasn't given much of a chance to embody her role. It is hardly surprising she would rather forget the whole thing, that she cut off her hair and hid under thick black eyeliner for a while.

Nowadays it is borderline surreal to remember they were on the same path long enough to do a film together. So many exciting things happened to Charlotte afterwards, appearances on live-streamed teen channels, her 'Bee-major' vlog, her daytime drama phase… Those scenes in Narnia are like a half-remembered dream.

She traces a smudge on the ply. Tamsin's deft hands could always undo the catch on the false back of the wardrobe. It used to stick. On one occasion Charlotte went in alone – why on earth did she do that? – and managed to trap herself completely among the furs. How strange that this memory should resurface; for years she must have blocked it out. Even now she is reluctant to remember banging her knuckles raw, feeling the burn of embarrassment when Tamsin heard the noise and let her out, laughing. It took a while to make her friend drop it.

The slice of brightness widens as the door swings open and, from nowhere, an idea arrives. Tamsin is not here, but she's watching. She's definitely watching. A new energy crackles in the garments. If cameras are capturing the wild light in her eyes then so much the better.

Watch me, Tamsin.

Nine

On public transport there is an unspoken rule that you keep your eyes to yourself, secured to a screen or book. Few passengers really see London Paddington, Isambard Kingdom Brunel's late masterpiece, this cathedral-station in wrought iron and glass. Tamsin wants to go around prodding everyone, telling them to look up.

The contractor she is meeting notices her irritability.

'You okay, pet?'

'Just project end,' she says, tucking her tablet into a satchel. No point trying to explain that she is also worried about her best friend being on a reality show under the thumb of a vengeful ex, oblivious to what is really going on. 'I'd better get back.'

It would be a stressful time in any case, this final week of checks, Ted chain-drinking cup-a-soups and everyone running around like headless chickens. The Underground exists in a delicate harmony of invisible forces, and there is no room for mistakes.

She makes her way along the platform. The loftiness of this station means it is always cool, a hint of engine oil underlying the scent of coffee and baguettes. Announcements bounce off shiny floors and vibrate among the iron curls of the ceiling.

On her train, she asks her smartface how long the season of *Outta My Room* will last.

'There is no fixed length,' says the AI. 'Similar shows run for up to twelve weeks.'

Her heart crumples. A fortnight in, and Charlotte is already starting to look ragged. How much revenge is Rollo planning to exact? It still seems surreal that the governor would go to all this trouble, but then he is rich and bored and able to indulge his whims. The more she learns about Rollo, the more it unnerves her to imagine what might be up his sleeve.

Her next train glides across the bridge, the old Battersea power station looming up like a castle with four towers. She takes out a sandwich, its foil warm to the touch. On *Outta My Room*, a gaunt, hollowed-out version of her friend totters across the terrace. Charlotte's gait is graceless. Her hair drapes down – thick, black, and uncharacteristically greasy – as she goes into her room, opens the wardrobe door and sweeps the clothes aside.

'Oh, Charl,' Tamsin sighs. 'What now?'

The jittery movements cease. Charlotte turns and tilts her head upwards, looking almost directly towards viewers.

'There are no firs, only furs,' she says. 'No fir trees.'

Her arms shoot out, as though to harpoon the hidden cameras and wind them in. 'Lucy,' she adds, quietly.

Tamsin's teeth retreat from her sandwich.

'Stop. Rewind.' The last ten seconds repeat. Charlotte speaks in a sing-song way, as though she is talking to herself, but her eyes are clear. The editors are obviously trying to make it funny, adding a burst of faintly comedic music as they transition to a shot where the others are bobbing around in the pool, talking in hushed voices about Charlotte's weird, attention-seeking behaviour.

For almost a minute, Tamsin replays the words in her mind, testing their weight, until her lungs remember to inhale some air. What would fur coats mean to anyone else? Nothing. But to her it is like sky-writing, and Charlotte would know that. The powdery, slippery fur coats in that wardrobe, almost alive as they got in the way, as the two of them struggled to find the catch that would open the back panel and reveal the way into a wintery world of prickly, resinous firs.

She watches and re-watches. She misses her stop. Why is Charlotte exhuming this old joke from the musty and unpleasant memory in which it resides? As she recalls, her friend was the one who got properly stuck in the wardrobe, on one occasion, freaking out so much that she didn't even want to be teased about it – very unusual for Charlotte. After a few more play-overs, an idea begins to glow and kindle in her mind. It seems so unlikely, and she is reluctant to give it credit, but there is no other explanation. Bizarrely, Charlotte is sending a message, and doing it at the cost of alienating her viewers. What is she saying, exactly? Tamsin's mind wants to leap in a million directions, formulate countless theories, but she forces herself to trust that first instinct, to feel what Charlotte wants her to feel. The message rings with a strong association, with only one meaning: it is about something going horribly wrong.

Time slows, the air dense and stale in her lungs. If there are no fir trees, only fur coats, it means the back panel of the wardrobe is stuck. It means Charlotte can't get out.

She pictures the set. Many a prison is located on a tiny island. There is no way her friend would be employing such desperate measures if she had not already tried everything else. And it really is desperate, to tuck her SOS inside this private joke, like a message in a bottle, and cast it adrift on the airwaves. Is this the first time she has sent a cry for help? There has been a lot of footage streamed, more than Tamsin could watch, and it makes her queasy to think she might have missed earlier distress calls, aimed at no one but herself. She shifts awkwardly on her seat, only to find she has pins and needles.

'You can't be serious.' Luka looms into the screen, pinching his anorak-hood at the chin.

'It's a crime, isn't it?' Surely this lies somewhere between kidnapping and domestic abuse, though she is not sure what happens when it takes place overseas, especially in a country like the Republic.

'Going to the police? I thought you were having a laugh.'

The weather is worsening and it is nearly dark. Maybe

there is something a bit ridiculous about taking this to the police, yet she feels a compulsion to try. It is the logical course of action. If there's one thing this situation needs, it's an injection of heavy-duty, quick-drying common sense.

'I'm just keeping you informed, Luka, not asking you to help.' She hangs up.

At home, her flatmate is out, but there is one can of Irn-Bru left in the fridge. A strange idea, to name a drink after iron and make it look like dissolved rust. Amusingly, she has heard it described as tasting of 'tangerines and girders', though really it tastes like old times, teenage years. She opens her can, swigs the top inch and re-fills with rum, as Charlotte used to do. One sip takes her back a decade, to drinking on the street in Soho, two glum figures on a wrought-iron bench. How long did they sit there, messing about and doing impressions and, on that occasion, tearing men limb from limb? They would normally be in the Pike and Pitcher, but Tamsin had just found out that the barman, her boyfriend of ten months, was messing around with someone. It was Charlotte who saw them together, late one night, and was unimpressed by his explanation that this girl was a 'submarining ex', soon to deep-dive again. If Charlotte tattled, he would ban her from the pub. So here they both were, unscrewing a flat bottle of corner-shop rum amid curious pigeons. At the time, Tamsin was too wrapped up in the betrayal to realise her friend had also taken a hit that night, potentially a blow to her career. If you want to be in theatre, everyone you need to know is in the Pike and Pitcher, from agents to z-listers, and they all need to be schmoozed. It is more than a height difference that makes Charlotte the bigger person.

So Luka won't dampen her resolve. Enough pussyfooting around with social media. If Charlotte were trapped in a basement somewhere, rather than on a luxury island, the police would be there with bells on.

She gulps down the rest of the Irn-Bru, then takes a slow breath. Nowadays they like you to start by visiting the virtual police station, but she has never done it before. In a voice both nervous and determined she asks Red to connect her.

'Are you sure?'

Certain commands require a smartface to ask this of their user, an obligatory road-bump that probably does little to deter hoaxers. She gives the apartment a quick once-over to check her flatmate is out.

'Yes.'

A blue arched doorway appears in the air, a few paces ahead of her, topped with an old-fashioned gas-lamp marked 'police'. The virtual doors open, revealing a map of the city reassuringly sprinkled with police cars, lists of arrests scrolling below. Then there are a few adverts. 'Don't drink and drone,' says the grizzled maw of Ed Sheeran, followed by a shot of a pedestrian clutching their bleeding head while the police apprehend two teenagers, their drones locked in mid-air conflict. Finally a desk appears, staffed by a supernaturally attractive blonde, the buttons of her uniform almost glowing.

'How can I help?'

'I'd like to report something,' Tamsin says. 'It's a bit hard to explain.'

'We'll do all we can,' replies the hologram, smiling brilliantly.

Tamsin hesitates, knowing this will be difficult for the AI to process. She explains about Rollo, about what he is doing to Charlotte, and the coded message. This last part proves the stumbling block.

'I'm sorry, I don't quite understand.'

Tamsin gets Red to show the clip: the hunted look on Charlotte's face as she enunciates the words. It makes her shudder to hear them again.

'I'm having trouble identifying this crime,' chirps the bot.

'Imprisonment,' Tamsin says, for the third time, her voice rising just a notch. 'Isn't that a thing?'

'Please wait,' says the hologram, in honeyed tones. 'I'm going to get my supervisor.'

Following an inordinately long wait, a man's head and shoulders materialise behind the reception desk. He is obviously squashed into a seat in some call centre and, although he wears a police uniform, seems to be slowly sinking into the bog of his own flesh, his eyes barely visible under folds of forehead.

'You want to report imprisonment?' he gets straight to it. 'But it's a girl in a TV show, right?' His voice is gravelly.

'She's being subjected to psychological torture.'

'Isn't that the point of these shows?'

'But she can't leave.'

'That's right, transcript here says she made a reference to being unable to reach Narnia.'

Tamsin squirms. With the AI there were none of these

empty, expectant pauses, but he lets her words hang in the air until they dry out and curl up. Her instinct is to retreat, to make it stop. Then she remembers the pinched look on Charlotte's face, the discord in her voice as she whispered 'No firs, Lucy.' A small, hopeless hope.

'I know it sounds like I'm reading too much into it. But the message is clear, you see, it's what we'd say when we couldn't get back into—'

'Narnia, yes I heard.'

'And what she's saying is that she's stuck there.'

'On a TV show.'

'Yes.'

'But she's playing along.'

'Yes.' Her voice falters. The officer's eyes stray to the left. Steam rises, suggesting he must have a coffee just below the webcam. The yellowy light makes it look as though he is bathed in sulphurous fumes. Tamsin takes a breath and continues: 'She has no choice.'

He stabs at his other screen.

'Ms Wilde, is it?' He tugs an ear. 'If you're concerned, I'd advise you to contact the producers. Even if this was a matter for the police, and I don't think it is, the crime is taking place in the so-called People's Republic of Love, where the only laws that apply are, if you'll pardon the expression, batshit crazy.'

'But the producers—'

'Yes I heard the bit about the ex, but perhaps you could address your concerns to someone else on the production team. That's what I'd advise.'

Tamsin feels the emptiness of the room around her.

'There's nothing else you can do?'

'Ms Wilde,' he says, one finger poised over his screen, 'I've got six calls waiting and one is rape, two aggravated assault… there might even be the odd murder. So no, there's nothing else I can do.' His first swipe obviously misses the 'end call' icon, so she catches him mutter sarcastically, 'I'm a celebrity… get me *onto this show*.'

An instant later the station has vanished, and she is back in the comforting, familiar presence of her sofa, the half-squashed can and a trailing spider plant. For one surreal moment, it is like the whole conversation played out inside her head. Heat gathers in her cheeks. This was the practical option, the sensible, grown-up course of action, and it has made her feel like a complete idiot.

Worse, she is out of ideas.

Ten

Where palms spring from white sand, Spike – the boy band drummer – and Pacey are working up a sweat on one of the hammocks, filling the air with wet, sucking sounds like a squid repositioning its tentacles. This seems like footage they'll want to keep. Charlotte sneaks in close, looks around and then starts singing, 'No firs…' like it's an old song only she knows. They look up in annoyance and she gives them a defiant grin and wanders on.

Inwardly she cringes. Her no-shit persona is her most valuable possession, and she is frittering it away. Last night she hammered on the corridor wall, yelling to some non-existent maintenance person to let her out. Now the housemates hardly bother lowering their voices when they gossip about her. When she repeats her code words – for Tamsin's ears only – they stare at her in disgust. Charlotte wishes she could explain what she is trying to do, but it would sound batty. Plus it might alert the editors, and her message would end up on the cutting room floor.

Asher is lifting a fibrous log of driftwood, crusted with salt. He squats, hoists it to his shoulders and above his head; the cameras will capture slick muscles standing out on his torso and arms. It provokes a gut-punch of an idea: what if this whole thing is semi-improvised theatre, and Charlotte is the only one thinking it's a reality show? The others might have been paid to act as contestants, Z-list celebrities. Stranger things have happened. All that talk of 'teamwork', and the ways they tried to persuade her to keep doing escape rooms, and their gasps and shrieks as the water swirled in – it could all have been a performance. Are they for real? Is there a single one of them whose name she heard anywhere at all before the show began?

Come on, she chides herself. Paranoia overload. There is an ugly snort of laughter and the two love birds from the hammock stumble past, chafing her shoulder, still adjusting their clothes. On the back of Spike's vest it says 911. Just a clothing brand, yet it gets under her skin. Call 911, the shirt declares, easy as pie. In the Republic that would, she imagines, put you through to the private security firm that does some token policing of the archipelago, the guys in charcoal suits who pick wax from their earpieces and shoo away uninvited guests from VIP parties. In the Republic there wouldn't be much for a proper police force to do. If a fight spills from a bar, whoever started it will normally use provision 54, the so-called 'dickhead defence', which lets you off if the victim was being an idiot, or if they insulted you first. In Rollo's world, this gives you every right to deck them. What keeps crime down is the sheer visibility of everything. Any citizen who fails to post on LOVE almost constantly gets a written warning. Your location is always known, your face detected a thousand times a day.

The 911 vest disappears as Spike walks up the steps and onto the decking. A gust lifts the fake lianas. It makes no sense that she feels unsafe here. Visibility is what keeps the Republic so secure, and this tiny island is like a concentrated version; here she is cocooned in ten times the scrutiny, which should equal ten times the safety. Being *seen* got her almost every job she has ever had and, long before that, it was a way of proving to herself that she existed. Right now the cameras are on, but nobody can see the full picture.

Except her old friend, God willing. Hopefully there is nothing too big going on in Tamsin's life right now, no new man to distract her. Tamsin is good at putting things together, untangling clues and solving problems. She eats Sudoku for breakfast, and flat-pack furniture gets assembled in the blink of an eye, in strange new ways. When she hears Charlotte say 'No firs,' she will tear off the thin layer of riddle like tissue paper and see the SOS in all its sinister clarity.

Her foot touches a conch shell and she picks it up, a milky ceramic microphone. As she mouths the words, she wonders if it is wise to occasionally add 'Lucy'. It makes her uneasy to be acting like those geeks Tamsin sometimes encounters, reminding her of an experience she would rather forget. Perhaps it is better to keep it simple, to avoid anyone realising who she is addressing. Furs and firs will be enough.

Vaguely, she daydreams of Tamsin coming to get her,

riding atop some heavy machinery – a crane or JCB digger – crushing the chalky coral beneath its wheels. Maybe it smashes the roof off the villa with a wrecking ball, scattering the weedy decorations. There would be a big hook, and Charlotte would simply be airlifted out. It is complete fantasy, but the images come well-oiled, gliding easily into place. Tamsin is good at making big stuff happen.

Eleven

Rollo was young when he first appeared in *The Bare Boones*. He is like a little larva of himself, skin baby-soft and adorned with just the one tattoo, dress-sense still undifferentiated – a muddle of sports shirts and low-hanging shorts. The reality show follows his dad, older brother, and younger sister, plus various partners, as they manage their gym empire and generally misbehave. There is an episode in which Rollo beats someone up after a college baseball match and they show the impressive dents left in the bleachers by his bat. The story is related by the victim's father, who comes to the Boones' mansion. Glued to the screen, Tamsin fully expects to hear Rollo deny all wrongdoing, but he doesn't. The boy deserved it – he declared – and that's what you get. She blinks in disbelief as the man, whose son avoided serious injury only by being nimble, rails at the Boones, but they just make a joke of it and move on, closing their white oak door in his face.

Tamsin shivers despite the muggy day. It is hard to imagine this sort of upbringing, where you are cushioned by money and stay juvenile and thin-skinned, never knowing true risk nor the consequences of your actions. So much for the nascent idea that she could go to the media and shame him. Rollo is never ashamed.

Leaving Paddington station behind, she walks along the pungent pea-soup canals of Little Venice. Oil rainbows zigzag around narrowboats topped with potted geraniums and rusty bicycles. Like them, she is going nowhere. This is unlike any problem she has previously had to solve. Worse, Luka heard what happened with the police and is insisting they discuss it. In typical fashion, his last message says: *I hope the filth ignored you completely.*

Thanks, Luka. Very helpful. She grumps her way to their agreed meeting point, a cafe by the water. The spindly furniture looks uncomfortable, not to mention unstable. Heads turn, and she knows her face is appearing on people's smartspecs, being recognised. That *Vogue* photo will be coming up instantly, and who knows what else. The bulges in people's pockets are suddenly apple-sized, fingers curling as though about to beckon her over for selfies, autographs, conversations – wanting a piece of her. Instinctively, she turns and goes back up the canal until she finds a pop-up bar, darkened by an overhead bridge. There are tyres and bits of junk dotted around, and the tables are those wooden drum spools that once held cable.

When Luka appears, his shabby, knee-length coat is tentlike around his black, skin-tight turtleneck and jeggings.

He looks like a mime artist fallen on hard times.

'How come you changed the location?' He takes a gulp from one of the pints she has bought and shuffles his chair closer to the grime-slicked bricks. 'Never mind. Guess what I found.' On the table he projects a view from above: a sandy island with a tuft of greenery, connected to some other landmass by a thread-like causeway. She squints.

'Wow, that's not the filming location for *Outta My Room*, is it?'

'It certainly is.' He zooms in a little, to a rectangular roof which is either pixelated or thoroughly solar-panelled. There might be people down there, but the resolution makes it too blurry to tell.

'The one they show in the opening credits doesn't have a causeway, but I guess that's because it's footage of some other island, right?'

'Precisely,' there is triumph in his voice. 'It was a nightmare to find details of the real location, but I came across a blog by some dude called Jerónimo, and suddenly the trail was hot…'

The image may be small and indistinct, but it is hugely exciting. Until now, Charlotte's film set has never felt like a real place, but here it is on the map – almost as though a pin might appear to show her whereabouts. Ripples of foam are frozen on the mottled blue sea, and there are outbuildings and paths and of course that tempting causeway, straight as a seaside pier.

'So, where is it?'

'In the People's Republic of Love, naturally,' he says, spitting out the Ps like pips. 'Just a tiny man-made dot of land.'

It almost looks possible to swim back to the main island, or at least to reach the connecting road, but Charlotte would never consider this. In the water she is like a giraffe or some other decidedly land-based mammal, all limbs and no buoyancy.

'How can you be sure it's the right place?'

'Painstaking research, that's how. Look at the shape of the beach, this rectangle must be the villa, and see here?' he zooms back out and points to a shape on the larger, adjoining island. 'That building there is the Turquoise Grand Hotel.' He takes another sip, looking immensely pleased with himself.

'A hotel,' Tamsin says dreamily. 'It makes it sound so civilised. Like I could just fly over to the Republic, spend the night and get her out.'

They stare at each other. A train rattles past overhead, and the arched roof trembles, a pinch of dust falling from the brickwork, the dangerous cavities where mortar should be.

'Red?' it is hardly more than a whisper, but her smartface is always listening. 'Can you check on that?'

'Checking availability,' says the voice. 'Flights are okay. Hotel… there are rooms… just a second.'

It is not as mad as it sounds. The station reinforcement project is nearly complete, and she could use a holiday. If there are flights, she could even go this Saturday, since the following week will be quiet.

'I'm eighty per cent sure Ted would let me take next week off,' she muses, then jumps as Luka slams down his drink.

'That's your main concern? The bigger hurdle is how to deal with the shit-hot security – they won't just let you waltz in and lead her out by the hand.' He traces a route from the hotel, running his finger along the causeway, shaking his head.

In the breeze, she can smell all of London's restaurants beginning to sizzle, and there it is: the delicate edge of a brighter mood. From years of site visits, of hearing her own echoing footsteps along dimly lit corridors and subterranean passages, she knows there are multiple ways into any building, a requisite number of fire exits, if nothing else. It's always easier to get in from the staff areas, the rickety staircases and service shafts.

'It's worth a try. There's always a back way.' She hears the restrained pride in her tone, and so does Luka, who raises an eyebrow. The last time they all went to the theatre together, some years ago, he gave her a bollocking for wandering off during the interval to look at the under-stage mechanics, though he didn't complain earlier on when his ticket app died and she snuck them in through a side door. Her habit of ignoring *No entry* and *Restricted* signs dates back to before she could walk, almost, when she was with her mum and being left under desks and in the green room at festivals, and later in the laundry rooms and offices of hotels. Even now she tends to get into trouble on site visits because she forgets to pay attention and wanders into some dripping tunnel, only for a contractor to yell, 'Hey, idiot, didn't you see the sign?'

Luka frowns, 'Still a long shot.'

'I know.'

Yet, in her mind, she is already half-way across the Atlantic, tasting the humid, equatorial air.

'It's no good, I'm afraid.' Red manages to inject some regret into the response.

'What do you mean?'

'The cost of a room.' A hesitation. 'I've been through every booking site I can find, and the cheapest is twelve thousand dollars.'

The words aren't really registering. 'For how long a stay?'

'One night.'

'One night?' She is aghast. 'Are you looking at the penthouse or something? What about a single room?'

It might be a glitch. Once, Red had a glitch, and now Tamsin resurrects it whenever the smartface says something she doesn't want to hear.

'There are none. That's for the cheapest double… and it's not even peak season. In fact, we're coming into low season for the Caribbean.' The shock of this price sinks in. Twelve thousand dollars. You should be able to rent a whole mansion for that. She grips her empty glass.

'Can I just go and get a drink at the hotel bar?'

The AI's voice pipes up, not nearly gentle enough to soften these blows. 'The main part of the Turquoise Grand, with the garden bar, is reserved for guests only.'

'VIPs,' says Luka, with venom. 'They don't want the hoi polloi bugging them for selfies.'

Now Tamsin is starting to see why the studio chose this location, an island attached to the garden of an insanely exclusive hotel. Perhaps she was a fool to think it would be anywhere less secure. She joins Luka in his slump.

'We had a plan,' she breathes. 'For one, beautiful second.'

Her imagination was already sketching out the details – how to get Charlotte to a public area, so she would be safe, and then straight to the airport. Soon they would have London, grey and familiar as an old blanket, wrapped around them again.

So much for that.

As if she hasn't suffered enough, Luka comes back from the bar with two apple martinis, pre-mixed in bottles. Oblivious to her narrowed eyes, he smacks wet lips, regaining some of his usual vitriol. 'Maybe we could blackmail her step-mum. She has money.'

'Not that much. And Kathleen… she'd never believe us.' Her cynicism would be off the charts, and she would have the usual things to say about Charlotte's career choices.

Someone in a grubby rabbit costume wanders past along the canal, kicking a can, and the pop-up bar cosies up to the brickwork, lit by faux-paraffin lanterns smelling of hot dust. Luka has been staring intently at whatever his smartspecs are showing him, occasionally dabbing the air with a finger.

'Wait,' he says, popping open a packet of vegan pork

scratchings. 'You really want to help Charl, don't you?'

The answer is too obvious to state. The two of them go way back, further than Luka can possibly imagine. He was not there in school cloakrooms, surrounded by huddles of bullies, looking up gratefully as a tall figure appeared. Charlotte would haul her from their midst, flashing a card at the drinks machine to get an Irn-Bru, 'For the sugar,' before Tamsin even knew she was shaking. The things Charlotte has done for her over the years stick in her mind like the equipment left buried underground when the Channel tunnel was completed, too enormous ever to rust away.

'Good,' he continues, downing his drink. 'Because if that asshat thinks I'm going to stand by while he fucks with her… he's got another thing coming.' The nearest lantern flickers. Luka holds up a curl of crunchy protein in one hand, her apple-scented cocktail in the other. 'Eat me, or drink me?' He takes a sip of the green liquid.

'I thought on your meds you weren't meant to–'

'Eat me, or drink me?'

'Some choice.'

'Eat. Grow.' He hands her the crispy scratching. What is it, mushroom skin or something?

'This tastes like soil.' A strange feeling is stealing over her, perhaps just the dread – temporarily forgotten – of remembering that Charlotte is trapped.

'Disgusting, aren't they?' He empties the bag onto the floor and crushes the snacks underfoot, releasing salty spores. 'Right, so here we are.' He reads: 'Influencers with more than a hundred and fifty thousand followers may stay at the Turquoise Grand on a complimentary basis while visiting the Republic.' He savours the thrill of it. 'Voilà.'

She stares at him, the expectant silence spattered with laughter from the back door of the kitchen. It is like being at work, realising she is going to have to correct someone's calculations.

'I–'

'Just think,' he goes on. 'It's been a week, and what have you given your followers? Nothing. What if you started telling them a story – all the invites you're getting to swanky parties, the modelling agencies wanting to sign you up, the acting jobs… Make out you're living the dream,' it is his turn to be transformed, wire-sprung as his idea takes shape. 'Just double your followers, more or less, turn one follower into two – it doesn't sound impossible, does it? And things happen quickly, especially when you're already trending. Look at that girl with the ugly cat… or the woman who tried to drink a pint of marshmallows.'

The old steel beams and beaten panels muster up a bluish glitter under the lamplight. If she gives his idea wheels, it rolls ahead to some frankly terrifying places. At work, because of the publicity generated, they let her get away with a brief apology for removing PPE before leaving the site. But if they saw her benefiting from the photo, apparently profiting from it, how would that look? She licks dry lips.

'I… I don't think I can pretend to want all that, and it wouldn't work. If you could just wave a magic wand and double your followers then Charl would have done it already, and she wouldn't be in this mess.'

'Yes, but you know the difference here?' he snaps. 'We don't need to worry about reality. The sky's the limit, and we'll go large, fast. No holds barred.' His eyes are watering with excitement. 'You're getting offers every day. You're moving to LA and getting a boob job–'

'Hey–'

'Because you deserve it. And you're meeting celebs and sharing the mad, sexy things they say to you and who gives a fuck if it's true?' He lets out a wild, fluttery laugh, as though releasing an armful of doves. His delight is buoyant, effervescent, unsettling. 'Your mistaken identity as a model is going to become your real identity – it's a dream, a fairytale of fame.'

'But even–'

'If people think you've gone doolally for a few days, at the end we can just tell them it was an art project.' He points with a wedge of lime, writing a zesty scent across the air. 'We'll make a video diary or something, release it once we're done. It's going to be fascinating and you'll love it, playing the role of TunnelFairy.'

Even to think about acting is to reach for a crackling hot coal of an emotion buried in her past. With some difficulty, she finds her voice.

'If you knew… what the last director I worked with had to say about me.'

'Oh,' he flaps a hand. 'That wasn't your fault – they sucked all the fun out of it. Look, nobody remembers that Charl was in that film do they? Because she's done other stuff since. What have you done?'

It has been a while since she last heard someone

mention the film, and it sounds so small and flimsy on his lips, just a fad, not something that has anchored her in the buckled shoes of 'Lucy' her whole life. If you are a child actor there are two ways to go. You ride the wave of fame, finding – or trying to find – the next big high. Or you get out of the ocean.

Luka is still taking aim with his lime, and her face feels clammy, as though it could match the waxy green.

'It's getting late.'

She stands, pushing her chair back under the table.

'Tam?' A cardboard straw drops from his lips as he opens his mouth in astonishment. 'Who cares what a load of strangers think? You've said that a million times.' His voice, as ever, bends the airwaves to its will, so the words follow her along the canal. 'What are you afraid of?'

GOGGLERS (LOVECAST 2309) 'BAD FILM CLUB'

DICK: And look at this – stranger danger. What do you say to the man, darling?
TAMSIN [ON SCREEN, IN FILM]: No, thank you, Mr Faun.
DOC: [LAUGHS] Love it.
DICK: Why do we never grow out of making films that stink?
DOC: The little girl was cute. 'Introducing Tammy May Wilde as Lucy'. Does that name ring any bells with you?
DICK: No.
DOC: I swear I've heard it recently.
DICK: The only good thing about this movie is the soundtrack. Otherwise it makes no sense, and you could cut half the scenes – why does he want to give her an apple?
DOC: No idea. Maybe fauns are keen on their five-a-day.

Twelve

It ain't a misprint, that protein content in your Indiana apple butter, it's a yellow-necked caterpillar... She remembers the pride she felt, towards the end of the second series of *Spill It*, when they stopped scripting these quips for her, when they stood back and let her crack on.

Improvisation is one of her strengths, but right now she seems to be stuck in a stiff old play that morphs from Pinter to Strindberg, or sometimes to Beckett, where she is the nonsense character in the corner, saying her line over and over. It makes her feel lousy, as though she is caught in some humiliating time-loop, unable to extricate herself from beneath the spotlight's 'sticky eye', as Tamsin once called it.

The smell is of melting sun-cream. Is this a reality show? Is it post-reality television? Beside her, Heidi picks up her mug of burnt-roast coffee with both hands, looking like a hamster with a nut. As she spins tales of on-set dramas during her soap opera days, this girl might be improvising, playing a role, trying to worm her way into Charlotte's confidence. Heidi's feet squirm on the sun lounger as though to conceal her slightly bent toes. She talks of scraping for auditions, living on the breadline and buttering up sleazy directors. Charlotte feels herself mellowing and tries to fight it. They've all been there, anyone who takes a shot at acting.

'I know,' she sighs. 'The way they just say "too tall" or whatever, like you've made a rookie mistake.'

'Oh yeah, thanks pal, I'll sort that out next time!'

They smile at each other. Heidi's arms are so thin, and the smell of rocket fuel coffee drifts across and Charlotte wishes they could have met somewhere else and become friends. But she is part of whatever this is. Part of the conspiracy. Charlotte adjusts her sunglasses, allowing silence to fall, and the spell is only broken when a long-tailed bird dives down and, impervious to the chlorine, takes a sip from the pool. Both women instinctively remain motionless until the creature blinks yellow-rimmed eyes, opens its wings and lifts off, trailing droplets.

'You forget wildlife exists, don't you?' Charlotte murmurs. 'The Republic is like a golf course or something, all raked and perfect.'

The flower pots and raised planters only seem to attract hoverflies and scary black hornets. Never any bees.

Although her housemates disapprove, Charlotte's technique at mealtimes is to grab some food and retreat to her room. Today, the smell of pizza coaxes her to the doorway, but hunger makes her careless and she shoves the slice too far down her throat. Her hands fly to her neck, grabbing at the choking lump. Her lungs expand but draw no air, and amid her gasps she is aware of Asher's arms tightening like a belt under her ribcage. What feels like consciousness slipping away turns out to be the walls rising, the floor suddenly unstable.

She tumbles onto the lower level with the bodybuilder still wrapped around her. He has cleared the blockage in her windpipe, but the ceiling has closed and the lights are dim. Flecks dance before her eyes and the dread creeps up, the walls pressing in. She was hoping never to find herself in this room again. What thread will they pull this time, to unravel her?

'Now remember,' comes a mid-western whine aimed squarely in her direction, 'it's all about you, candy pie.' Through her dizziness, she clocks Pacey's mocking smile.

They find themselves looking across a room-sized map of the USA. It reminds Charlotte of those big floating British Isles on which a weatherman would stand, once a minor tourist attraction at Royal Albert Dock. The jigsaw puzzle of states bobs gently, a faint chemical smell emanating from whatever is below. There is a pile of objects — her eye is drawn to a pint-sized Harley Davidson — with toys, appliances, cartoonish cans of beer, and big plastic snacks. 'Howdy y'all,' drawls the narrator, who explains their safe path to the key — glinting across the room in mini-Washington – is to match each product to the state in which it is made. There are groans of 'Fuck me,' and, 'Geography, my worst subject.'

The game begins with the usual flurry of discussion, certain voices dominating. When Spike steps onto Wyoming with a giant taco, it stabilises, but when the others move a coffee cup to Minnesota it bucks and vibrates, and a bucket-load of snow is dumped from the ceiling. Charlotte sits back and takes in the screams as t-shirts are soaked with slush.

'Little help?' someone calls to her. Then later: 'Ever heard of teamwork?'

'I'm not playing,' she says.

Only six of them have been caught in this escape room, so they are short-handed for a team game. She stays resolute until Heidi battles her way back across Idaho and Oregon, shrieking as she moves from a sudden heat lamp to hailstones. She staggers onto the platform and starts dragging at the model Harley.

'Come on,' her big eyes flick up at Charlotte. 'You used to ride one. Where does it go?'

What difference can it make? She sighs and gives Heidi a hand easing the thing towards Wisconsin. Then a blast of sound makes her drop it. A huge, angry face is projected across the entire left wall. 'You pig-ignorant charlatan!' it berates, loud enough to puncture eardrums. Someone puts the wrong product on Arkansas and the abuse is repeated, plus some howling weather, until everyone is drenched and on their hands and knees, clinging to the turbulent floor. There is no mistaking the seed for this game: the flak she received from certain retailers as she exposed shoddy goods on *Spill It*. But it strikes her as childish, this big bullying face. When it bawls again, she screams back. 'Holler all you want, mate! Knock yourself out.'

One step onto Iowa, though, and she is instantly off-balance, bike clattering down. Heidi rushes to help, but is thrown forward as she jumps off another state, face-first towards the Harley. There is a thump that lodges in Charlotte's brain and starts to ring slow alarm bells, but the soap star is up again and, before anyone knows what is happening, there is a shout from Asher in Washington, tearing the roof off the mini White House and extracting the key. At once the rain stops, the states lie flat and, like an assortment of bird cages, six platforms come down on wires. Charlotte clips her harness together and is lifted, her mind easing with every inch. She has escaped lightly, and it feels good. Then she sees Heidi dangling alongside, alternately shielding her face and examining her blood-covered palm.

'Hey,' Charlotte yells at the floor, then upward, not sure where to direct it. 'We've got someone hurt here.'

They are set down in the re-formed living room and crowd around Heidi, who sinks into the first sofa to emerge from the wall. There is a plum-purple line crossing her cheekbone, her makeup smudged, and she is cupping her nose.

'Is it straight?' she whimpers. 'Tell me it's straight.'

But they can't because she won't take her hand away.

'Ey, we need the first-aider. Are you listening or what?' Charlotte slaps ineffectually at the walls, and Asher echoes her. But nothing happens. No one comes. The others fetch wads of kitchen roll for Heidi to press against her face until the bleeding stops, cooing round her in a comforting huddle.

'Does it feel broken?'

'I don't know,' she is weeping a little. 'Is it straight?' The hand lifts, just a fraction so they can hardly see, but Charlotte touches her shoulder.

"Course it is. You're sound.'

There is not much you can do with a nose except allow it to heal, but a brittle atmosphere develops as it dawns on people that no doctor will be appearing to tend to the injury, nor check their housemate has escaped concussion. How can the producers be sure she is okay if they don't examine her? Diagnostic AIs are very smart these days, but even if they analysed the fall it would have been from a distance. Safe in her room, Heidi seems slightly better and is no longer bleeding, but is refusing to come out. Charlotte can feel her distress. It's not so much that she was hurt, although she is probably in shock, but that it was her *face*. Even with surgery an easy, overnight thing these days, it still carries a risk, and a messed-up face might mean a messed-up career.

The housemates talk in hushed voices. As Charlotte leans against the cool wall, she lets her earlier conclusion slip away; there is no hint of artifice in this reaction – they couldn't be good enough actors to fake this sharp haze of fear, like suspended grit in the air. People perch rather than sit on the sofas, fidgeting, probably imagining movement beneath their feet, not ready to face it again. Although the soiled kitchen towel has been posted down the recycling chute, the iron-tang of blood lingers. Charlotte can see a change happening before her eyes, a nascent, shared understanding of what sort of show this really is.

She goes back to the terrace. In a way it is gratifying to have her feelings shared for once, albeit temporarily. They look scared now, but a few beers will diffuse that. They are already working on ways to blot out the unthinkable, whether it is that the show has no regard for safety, or – worse – that no one is watching, that because of some disaster or epidemic in the outside world, the director's chair is empty, and this really has become an abandoned beach house, with dangerous algorithms running its systems.

The thought is horrific. It takes her back to the day she faced this mirror, right here, and told them she wanted to quit, only for nothing to happen. The food and clean laundry keeps appearing, but there is no guarantee that any of this is being broadcast. All these shiny black nubs... are they really fisheye lenses filming, or do they sit inert on the wall? Charlotte climbs onto a bar stool and inspects one. It unscrews, but there is only a bracket behind. Either it is battery-powered and wireless, or it's a fake.

Then there are the mirrors, the suspicious mirrors in all the rooms, and this one by the bar. This looking-glass commands the best view across the terrace. She lifts Heidi's coffee mug, feeling trepidation gum up her arteries, aware this is not going to look good. 'They'll probably make you pay for that,' was Mak's jovial remark when someone broke a hammock. Plus it's seven years of bad luck. But... what the hell?

When she jams the mug base into the mirror, birds rise screaming from the trees. Her whole body is shaking, but as the slow silver peels away, pieces clinking to the floor, she sees a reassuring black-edged lens in the cavity. It is like an anchor, big and dark and heavy in a shimmering sea of shards, and she clings to it. Is anyone out there?

'Lucy, firs,' she whispers, perfunctory, her breath misting the lens.

Thirteen

There is something oddly materialistic about the term 'human resources', as though you might open a store room and find people stacked up like a bunch of IT equipment, plugs and cables dangling. Tamsin waits in an office of sandwich shades: mayonnaise walls with yellow-butter doors, shreds of greenery. Most of the team probably work from home, but there are two HR officers converging around a screen to watch something as they eat lunch.

Their posture reminds her of Luka, hunched like an abandoned puppet. He has messaged her several times, demanding to know what is wrong with his fabulous idea, why she won't even consider building on her unexpected fame, getting the followers she needs to book a room. He can't understand what it is that repels her, that in certain corners of the internet she will always be Lucy, that kid with the cute ponytail who could not act. She rubs her forehead, smoothing away the crust of old rages, anger that arose not because people waved apples at her and tried to get a reaction, but because the mistakes you make as a child are supposed to fade away and be forgotten. The limelight shouldn't be like the sticky lime that people once smeared on branches to catch songbirds, glueing her in place. At university half your social life is online, but if you fear being recognised then it's hard to make friends.

These days, she tries not to care – what does it matter if a stranger makes some silly comment? It was all a lifetime ago – several lifetimes. The shed skins of teenage Goth, perky graduate, theatre denizen, career woman and so many others too subtle to name are piled haphazardly over her childhood, but some emotions stay sharp, pricking her unexpectedly. There is no way to erase *Eternal Winter*. All she can do is ignore it, focus on the things she can control. It has taken graft to earn her place at Ogilby Dobbs which, although not perfect, at least offers grudging recognition, plodding progression and a pleasant push-and-pull of problem-solving each day.

The two office workers open pots of yoghurt, and she can smell the strawberry flavouring, the fragments of translucent fruit. She checks the time, wondering when she will get her own lunch. The meeting itself is not a concern. Ted has reassured her that although she started to remove her PPE too early, the marketing people were equally to blame for not vetting the photos they sent to *Vogue* and failing to give her a heads-up that she would appear on its cover. If anything, this meeting will be to say thank you, or to talk about taking on more responsibility with her next project, even a promotion to grade F. With luck, some of the good feedback she received will have filtered through to these offices.

The door is thrown open.

'Tamsin Wilde?' A man in a salmon-hued suit stands with his hand outstretched, a smile on his lips. 'Sam Ockles,' he says, using the handshake to draw her into the room. 'Tea? Coffee?' She shakes her head. 'Gin and tonic?' He laughs uproariously, only stopping when she smiles and says she'd love one. 'Ah, if only! Cocktails at five.' His office has a large window, and the sun has been baking his beige carpet, giving the room a dry odour. He tells her he needs a holiday, asks if she has anything booked.

'No,' she says, her mind instantly recalling the half-made plan to travel to the Republic next week. She pushes it away, surprised at the prod of guilt it delivers. The leather seat is so pliable her fingertips make dents in its gel-smooth surface, and he has continued to talk while she zoned out for a second.

'Tamsin?' he takes the pencil from his mouth and stares at her.

'Sorry, I missed that. Was it about the photo?'

Again the pencil taps on teeth, a plasticky sound.

'What photo?'

'The one in–'

'Ah, I do want to talk about that… but no, I was referencing your move to King's Cross after that flood incident on the Circle line… rather a stressful time.'

It certainly was. Tamsin remembers the team drafting in every available geotechnician, trying to work out why the substrate kept oozing water like a rapidly compressing sponge. It was a good opportunity for her to get involved in something meaty, learning at twice the usual pace.

'Yes,' she says, wondering where he is going with this.

'I want to thank you for acting up.'

She stills.

'Acting up?' When Ted moved her onto this project, there was no talk of acting up.

'Doubtless it'll make a huge difference the next time you're going for a promotion.'

'But I'm working at that level now.'

'I'm sure you've coped marvellously–'

'Not just coped. Honestly, don't you have my performance notes anywhere?' She curses Ted's laissez-faire attitude towards record-keeping. 'Are you saying I'm not going to remain on band E?' The plaintive note in her voice makes her curl up inside.

'We need grads to get a bit more experience before they reach that level.'

'Salim Sykes is an E, and he came in the same year as me.'

'Oh, Salim? Well, he's one of our micro-vloggers, so…' The HR Director takes another suck of his pencil before replacing it on a desk-tidy labelled *Blood Orange Chewables*. 'Visibility is important, you know.'

'How can you say I'm not visible? Thousands of people have been talking about me in the last couple of days,' her throat is rusting shut with the injustice of it: the way they polished her up as the perfect early-career engineer; the irony of trying to recruit more women with a picture of one whose achievements they won't recognise.

'It's nice that you have such belief in your abilities, Tamsin. I know you'll go far, and I can only apologise that the situation wasn't properly explained to you. I'll make a note of that.' His teeth interlock, a wall of impenetrable enamel.

She hesitates for a moment, then stands. Some internal crack has appeared, and all her joy is draining away. Belief in her abilities? There's no need for belief when she has the figures, the outputs. Even these should not be needed, not when they all know her. What happened to the 'Ogilby Dobbs family'? She turns to leave.

'Wait,' he says. 'You're right, of course. You have got us an awful lot of publicity. Maybe there's a way you can stay at your current grade.' He snatches up the pencil again and rubs it between his hands, like someone sizing up produce at a market. 'Sign up to be the spokesperson at our career events, take part in some videos, and we'll make your grade E official.' He wets his lips. 'A permanent promotion. What do you say?'

The lift doors close slowly over her face, like two hands. She is trembling, hating every chrome gleam. She feels a great urge to hit the emergency button. Emergency! I'm in a metal box, being sent down.

That 'band E' is already attached to her identity, so it hurts to have it torn off and thrown to the ground like an unearned medal. But even if it wasn't such a turnaround, such obvious bartering, there is no way she could accept his offer. It is one thing to be in a few photos demystifying the job for female undergraduates, quite another to be part of a sales team and general charm offensive, the card they play the next time some story comes out about women at Ogilby Dobbs being squashed or sidelined.

She is rattled, as if he turned her upside-down and shook her to see what might fall out. Loose change. Spare followers. Fame that can be spent. A mist of hot tears is gathering and she breathes fast, hoping to dispel it. They will not make her cry. She won't be like the grads who weep in the toilets and then, one day, just aren't there anymore. When the lift reaches her floor she lets the doors open, then stabs more buttons until she is going up, up, all the way to the top floor, where she ascends more stairs and, satisfying herself that she won't set off an alarm, pushes a bar down just below the *No entry* sign.

The high-up air refreshes her. It is thin and cool, and carries the murmur of traffic from below. A weathervane with nickel-plated ship poised above the N, E, S and W swings ponderously overhead. Perhaps this was once a staff roof garden, as two ornamental citrus trees are miraculously surviving in square planters; one has even produced a single, disproportionately large lemon, its skin like cellulite.

How could Ted let this happen? He should have marched into HR and demanded a proper promotion. His quieter approach always seemed like a good thing, not like the snappy bosses she has endured in times past, but now he just seems woolly, like knitted scaffolding, giving no support.

She perches on loose coping stones. Screw the lot of

them. Sam jowly-cold-fish-cheeks Ockles, her useless muppet of a supervisor, the whole shower. Her eyes scrunch closed and she tries to feel her best friend's hand clasping her shoulder, encompassing it; a warm voice reverberating in her ears, telling her to broadcast their hypocrisy on LOVE, not to let them get away with it. Charlotte can be fierce about things like that. If only she were here.

'Red,' she says, 'do we see much of her on today's show?'

Her smartface starts projecting clips: the bodybuilder hugging Charlotte from behind, almost like a Heimlich manoeuvre, and bits of a challenge involving a wobbly USA map. Why do they look so sombre afterwards? Then Tamsin covers her mouth. 'Holy shit,' she breathes. The smash is jarring, shards of mirror clattering down. What is Charlotte doing? The others are drawn out by the noise, and their astonishment quickly turns to rage. They try to pick a fight with her and then leave, rolling their eyes and muttering about what she'll do for attention.

At that moment there is a metallic clang overhead, and a parcel drone falls at Tamsin's feet, its little copters slowing to a standstill, its claws flexing despondently. The weathervane is bent at an angle. Now that it has been slammed down to earth, it makes no sense that this fat metal mosquito was ever airborne. How could it generate enough lift to transport the leaking jar of goo currently rolling along the roof, smelling of fruit and booze? But that's what engineering is all about, isn't it? Making stuff happen. She backs away, her pulse going crazy. *You idiot*. All this time wasted. What does it matter what they think, what anyone thinks, when someone she truly cares about is in trouble? If the situation were reversed, Charlotte would be on a plane by now.

It's time to get her act together and find a solution. She pictures her LOVE profile, all the thousands of people who have checked her out, so the network – which always knows best – has labelled them *followers*. If she has a resource there, a human resource, it is hers to spend. And she is damn well going to spend it on Charlotte.

GOGGLERS (LOVECAST 2338) 'OUTTA CONTROL'

DOC: Heidi? Well she must be out back being patched up.
DICK: For a bump on the nose?
DOC: You know what this lot are like, they'd call an ambulance for a broken nail.
DICK: Well Charlotte will need ten. Smashy smashy.
DOC: Yeah, what was that about? Isn't it seven years' bad luck? I thought the muttering was weird enough.
DICK: She's a devil-worshipper.
DOC: [LAUGHS] Is that it?
DICK: If you listen closely, she's actually whispering 'Lucifer'.
DOC: Uh-huh.
DICK: Seriously, bro. Do you want me to skip back to it?
DOC: It's product placement – she obviously has a deal where she has to say some brand name a hundred times.
DICK: Either way, she's not doing herself any favours.

Fourteen

No sign of Charlotte in the next episode. The rumours about her on LOVE become ever stranger. They say the former presenter is on hunger strike, that she's trying to cast spells, or that she has stolen all the forks from the kitchen. The comments seem to come out of nowhere and only deepen Tamsin's anxiety.

When she rang Luka to say she was up for his plan, he was ecstatic. It was astonishing how quickly he sorted them out with a professional-grade camera and got permission to take photos aboard his station manager's yacht.

Sneaking into the marina via the sailing club is easy, though she feels nervous on deck amid the clinking steel-cable rigging, the upholstered stools smelling of leather conditioner. With no regard for their surroundings, Luka is wearing a t-shirt that says *Eat the Rich*. He is simmering with twice his usual energy as he yanks open a white umbrella and wrestles a tripod. Beneath it all, she can sense the satisfaction of a new role: one of gallantry and derring-do. She can almost hear the clink of his shining armour. With great resourcefulness, and via his directorial debut, he will deliver Charlotte from the clutches of his unspoken rival – the evil Rollo – and perhaps be in the picture again.

He screws a lens onto the teapot-sized Nikon and shoos Tamsin backwards to the starboard rail. Surely someone will appear any minute and ask what the hell they're up to.

'Shoulders back. Don't grin.'

'Red will sort it out. We could have saved ourselves some effort–'

'If anyone detects AI, it'll kill you stone dead.'

'These days–'

'Just trust me on this, okay? We need theatre here, not AI. You have to be a real fake.'

Lilac spots have appeared at the top of his cheeks, so she closes her mouth. He wants genuine, hallmarked photos. For Luka, this is art, and it is serious stuff. It tickles him, doubtless, to think that the power of theatre will be what saves Charlotte, should this plan actually work. He can demonstrate how meaningless it is to court followers when they will trot along after an entirely manufactured influencer, essentially a lie. No wonder he is in love with his plan, that he bends so awkwardly around the camera, planting his big feet in a tendon-fraying horse stance to get the right angle. Tamsin grips her flute of corner-shop Lambrini as he yells at her to look languid.

All at once she hears her mum's voice, bragging about that youthful stint as a model before she got into event management, omitting the detail that it was only raincoats – and old-woman ones at that. What will her mum say, when she hears of this? Tamsin winces, knowing exactly what Maeve will say. She'll have a field day. When she hears her daughter is modelling, the explosion of glee will be visible for miles around. 'It's never too late for a change of career,' she'll quip, and then start toying with the idea as though it could be a serious prospect. Despite years of explanations, her mum is still a little hazy on what engineers actually do.

All credit to Luka's superior camera, the shots and video clips are beautifully professional. He has messed with the perspective, putting objects in the foreground so she is encircled by a giant lifebuoy or dwarfed by a glass of fizz. Better to deal with her height by embracing it, he says, but she discards a few of them, nonetheless. Stepping to one side, she gets her smartface to look at trends and what correlates with follower growth. Luka thinks this is going to be about smoke and mirrors, but she has a feeling they might need a bit of tech down the line, once people believe in her. It's an art project, she tells herself. In a couple of weeks they will come clean and it'll be over.

'Let's see…' He dictates: 'Ending up on the cover of *Vogue* was the biggest shock of my life. But you guys gave me the confidence to come out from under my hard hat!'

'Vomit emoji,' she says.

He throws up his hands. 'It's not you, it's TunnelFairy. Let her be the star, okay?'

TunnelFairy. The name is meaningless, just something she heard on a school trip to the Peak District. She remembers going down puddled steps into an ice-cold cave to see where Blue John gemstone was mined. 'Can you see the tunnel fairies twinkling?' said the guide. Funny how these things stay with you.

They write the rest of the post, the oh-so-secret news that she has been signed by a modelling agency, that it could be New York one week, Paris the next. It feels like a summery story, full of fizz and strawberries and heat rising from airport tarmac. She has become what they mistook her to be. Yet, beneath the cute outfits, she is still an engineer. They'll like that – Luka reckons – the sense of a real person stumbling into celebrity realms. The whole story is just awkward and accidental enough to be believable, to be sought out by people wearied by an internet of slick AI regurgitation.

A few beats pass and then the little *putt* sounds begin, the notifications. A scattering at first and then a hailstorm. What would Charlotte think if she saw her friend's follower count approaching her own, then surpassing it? Tamsin's heart clenches as she imagines this. *Putt, putt, putt.* People are checking her out, but things need to happen fast. Fortunately there are few demands at work just now and, since the meeting with Sam Ockles, she is less inclined to go above and beyond.

Luka's face is twisted against the sun, perspiring but radiating satisfaction. He slings his jacket over one shoulder. 'So, tonight you'll go to the premiere of the new Spider-Man remake.' He pinches his chin. 'What the hell is it called? Spider-Man... goes to Europe? Explores issues of overtourism? Anyway, you're going.'

'I–'

'I couldn't get tickets, but just go to where the red carpet is and the paps will do the rest.'

'What paps? Why would they be interested in—'

He rolls his eyes. 'I'm sure we discussed this. It's a firm called StarSnap, and they'll follow you around for a moderate fee.'

A horn bellows across the water, and she feels it again, that sensation of unreality. Not exactly like someone has pulled the rug from under her feet, but as though it has been given a good tug.

It is all happening so fast. She barely has time to get back to her flat and change her outfit.

'StarSnap will be at the venue in one hour,' Red announces.

A brief curse, and she is diving into her wardrobe. Luka has sent a dozen messages with advice on what to wear, which she plans largely to ignore. There is a slam from the hallway, and she looks up to see her flatmate, Pip, a touch unsteady on her feet and raising her hand in a mellow salute.

'Hey, Tam,' she calls.

Somehow this triggers another, even worse realisation: she can't go for a night out on her own, not without looking like a total loser. As though patching up the blind spot in a visual field, her brain appears to have sketched in Charlotte as her companion. Why didn't she think of this earlier? It's a disaster. As she crumples against the door frame, Pip saunters into the kitchen and peers critically into the fridge. She wears a white mini-skirt, her arm-stockings unladdered. Going-out clothes.

'Pip!' she gasps, 'How about a cocktail?'

'Well, I've just had one. But okay.'

Praise the unlimited stamina of the twenty-two-year-old. Pip is a firm believer in carpe diem, though she is a little pushy about lending Tamsin a different — trendier — dress. Soon they are in Leicester Square, threading through what seems to be a very tall, impeccably dressed crowd, heading for the Odeon.

'Hey, is that a red carpet?' She tempts Pip, nearly tripping over the kerb, which is already syrupy with spilled drinks. Limos are pulling up and security guards stand around menacingly. Where the hell is this pap company?

Then suddenly they are there, Tweedle Dee and Dum, wearing purple bomber jackets with the company logo. Their facial recognition kicks in, and they start calling: 'Tamsin! Tamsin! TunnelFairy!'

For a higher fee, there is an executive package which includes limousine transport, a bodyguard and a publicist to drag the photographers away and tell them the client has no comment. As it is, the two of them snap and yell, and she instinctively brings up a hand to shield her face. Pip is all amazement.

'Tam,' she breathes, once they have taken refuge in a bar across the road, 'are you famous now?'

Nothing amuses her more than this hushed tone. Pip saw the *Vogue* cover, of course, but was not overly impressed. Magazines are for old ladies.

'*Pfft*, no,' she says, and winks.

They watch through the window as gorgeous, gleaming people emerge from cars and manage a languorous wave to the press before sauntering into the cinema. Her personal paparazzi lurk outside, as though the lamppost has fruited two giant plums. Pip is far too lively to stay put, and before long they are outside again, the photographers chasing them onto the red carpet.

'We can't go in here,' Tamsin hisses, as Pip strides onwards, but astonishingly the bouncer eyes their pursuers and steps aside.

They go in.

They watch *Spider-Man XX*.

By the time they come out, the two StarSnappers have gone, but instead there is a whole hedgerow of tripods and white flash-flowers, the genuine photographers having returned, and looking noticeably more professional in their leather jackets and lanyards. Pip hooks her arm into Tamsin's and smiles beatifically, jutting out her hip, and the latter just blinks, blinks until her legs work again.

In the morning she finds herself tagged on several gossip accounts: *And who's this? @TunnelFairy, out from underground!* The praying part of her begs any higher powers not to let her colleagues see it.

Her follower count has shot up, and it is hard even to picture that number of people. It's as though the residents of a small town have decided to look, all together, in her direction.

But it is not enough. Not by a long way.

Fifteen

The knife is awkward to hold. Since she got nowhere trying to lever the mechanical shutters out of their grooves, her attack now focuses on a steel panel just outside the living room, an eight-centimetre rectangle that might conceal electrics. She has a fork ready to swirl into the spaghetti of coloured wires, but getting to them is not easy. There is barely a hairline crack, the knife skidding away. Still, she is proud to have thought of it, to be doing something with the tools available and not just idly waiting. Tamsin would be impressed.

The metal casing bulges. The tip of the knife breaks off, and she swears. Will they bleep it? Despite her irrational fear that this show might not be reaching the outside world, it would be no bad thing if this particular footage got cut. With every scratch, every flake of chipped paint, her reputation sustains damage. She tries not to think about the comments on LOVE. By now the editors have plenty of material they could sew together to make her look a certain way. To stitch her up.

Overhead it sounds like somebody is beating a rug against the roof. The weather has been bad all day, and the housemates have pondered the possibility of early hurricanes. Surely the villa would be evacuated, if there was any danger? The others seem certain their safety would be a priority, but Charlotte is not convinced. When she dug around in the cutlery drawer she found that, contrary to expectations, sharp items were plentiful.

Her knife slides beneath the metal skin. Voices approach, and a bolt of adrenaline rivets her to the spot. The others were deep into a furious ping-pong tournament; she didn't expect them to appear. Although there is no reason to feel guilty, she finds herself trembling like a naughty child, trying to hide the blade.

'What you up to?' asks Shelly, placing her heel high on the wall so she is almost doing the splits. The flapping of flip-flops heralds the arrival of other housemates, who quickly work out what Charlotte is doing.

'What the actual...' Spike grabs her wrist hard enough to make her wince. 'You out of your mind?' The knife clatters to the floor.

'Hey,' she protests, 'I'm trying to make it safe...'
'Safe?'
They are bug-eyed and bewildered. She turns to Heidi and points at the jam-hued bruise on her face.

'Sorry to remind you, but look what it did... you really want the floor to drop again, after that?'

If anything, the incomprehension deepens, like the air between them is furrowing. Heidi steps back a fraction.

'It's why we're here,' she says.

'Yeah, exactly,' everyone is in agreement.

Is it Charlotte's imagination, or is there a touch of fear in their voices? As far as they are concerned, this show is still their ticket to a better life, and they don't want her messing it up. Or perhaps they are trying to convince themselves. Either way, they are on different pages, different planets.

Spike picks up the knife and she finds herself hustled into the living room, right where she doesn't want to be. It has a sort of charge, a magnetic field that drags at every fibre of her being. Mentally she reaches out and clings to the windows and doors. 'Not cool,' they are muttering. She tries to turn on the charm but her smile is like a faulty bulb, no longer able to light people up.

When she was eleven, and a little too immature to understand such things, her mum tried to explain that humans are tribal, 'Which means you're either in, or you're out.' Innys and outys; it still makes her think of belly buttons. Even a child could detect the trace of irony when her mum laid out the rules, when she explained that to succeed – or just survive – in this world, you must love one group and hate the other. Remembering it now, Charlotte wonders if she was supposed to hear the opposite. Or perhaps this stems from being an 'outy' herself now, an outsider looking in. It makes her think of sitting outside the Pike and Pitcher, when she got barred years ago. A bleak experience, like shutters banging down.

Can the others blame her for trying to tamper with the escape room? She is a prisoner here, just trying to do what she can to survive. But perhaps it really is uncool. Normally she can rely on her followers to indicate whether something is okay or not, that hive-mind taking the pressure off her own. She is missing this supportive chorus, relying instead on her own, tentative inner voice. There is no one to tell her whether it is okay to be attempting sabotage. What exactly does 'reasonable' look like, in a house designed to swallow people, on an island made of Florida's construction waste, in a sea of moon-white jellyfish?

The others have formed a huddle and Spike is gesturing furiously, words poorly muffled: 'Ruiner... gotta stop... rest of us.' She doesn't wait to hear the pronouncement. Fuck them. Before they can deliver their verdict, she strides into her room and locks the door.

Who is this person, this non-Charlotte hiding from a bunch of z-listers, ashamed to show her face? Her cheekbones are sizzling hot. She retreats as far as she can, opens her wardrobe and inhales the smell, the layer of wood-dust on each rail. There are no cameras in here. She sinks down among satins and silks, finding a faint coolness cast over her mind, allowing her to think. Has she been missing something? The escape rooms themselves have singled her out – that nod to *Spill It*, for instance. As she roared around on her Harley she left a lot of anger in her wake, yet even if she riled some big American retail company enough to make them seek revenge, it seems vindictive to go after the presenter, a mere figurehead. It could be the lack of sleep, but this whole thing feels like an optical illusion, something that would be obvious if she could just make it out.

The ply seems to pulse slightly, comfortingly close to the outside world, and freedom. *Lucy.* Please get a move on. If you leave something in the wardrobe too long, you forget it exists.

Sixteen

The tiles of Baker Street station glint with their reassuring beetle-shell enamel, as though nothing could ever leave a mark. This is one of the oldest, built before they really knew how to burrow through a city. The Victorians peeled off the street, dug out the tunnel, then put the road back on top. Tamsin loves to picture those early days: the wooden, gas-lit carriages pulled by steam trains, soot so thick that Metropolitan staff were encouraged to grow beards as air filters. It gives her comfort to nestle for a moment into this world, its smoky, clockwork tickery.

This has all been planned meticulously, but mainly by Luka, and it is making her nervous. The passing faces are sweaty, pock-marked, grizzled, bronze-cheeked, frowning or talking loudly into a personal bubble. Some of them are in on it, but she doesn't know who.

When they sketched it out, two nights ago, they agreed

that something big was needed. Despite sneaking into a couple of parties, getting snaps with celebrities and working the rumour mill day and night, the followers just aren't multiplying fast enough. They need something on her feed that will turn a lot of heads, all at once, so she passes that all-important threshold for a free room at the Turquoise Grand.

Luka's idea was to use *Eternal Winter*. 'It's your prior claim to fame,' he insisted. 'Let's milk it.' Hearing this made her mentally curl into a ball. It doesn't matter what strangers think, but she dreads her colleagues making the connection, taunting her with Lucy quotes every time she goes into the office. She should be pulling out all the stops to get followers quickly, but every cell of her body, every microbe in her gut is begging her to leave it be, to keep that bit of her boxed up for as long as possible.

'You said we'd be creating a character,' she told Luka. 'Surely we can sort out a *new* drama for TunnelFairy?'

It came together over ale-soaked beer mats at the Pike and Pitcher, listening to the Aussie bar staff discuss how rammed the Tube would be on Saturday morning, as everyone headed to the free festival in Hyde Park.

As she reaches the platform, her heart pulses so hard that a tremor is sent through her body. Get a grip, Tamsin. Get into place. Get into character. *G'day… Call that a knife?*

At least it is an amiable crush, everyone stoked about the shindig in the park, beers concealed in raincoat pockets. When she reaches the agreed pillar, its smooth iron electrifies her fingertips, dormant magnetism flowing into her. She needs all the strength she can get. Even this, the apparently less-humiliating plan, goes against every instinct.

Think practically, she tells herself, think of Brunel in a different tunnel, two centuries ago, steeling himself to throw an investors' dinner party beneath the Thames, to simper and smile as the band plays *See the Conquering Hero Comes*, when he would rather be in his quiet office. In the name of publicity, even geniuses have to put on a show now and then.

Trains roar and scream to a stop, and then depart with a slice of the crowd. She hears the shout, indistinctly. Heads turn. Their piece of street theatre has begun, and her stomach flips. The desperation in his voice is clearly audible. That short, bleated word. Her name. As rehearsed, she puts a foot on the concrete base of the pillar and hoists herself up so he can see her. He is on the steps. Are they really going to do this?

'Tamsin,' he wails. 'Don't leave.'

'Why not?' she calls, managing the squeak in her voice.

'What?' He puts a hand to his ear. A train sounds its horn and his words are hopelessly lost. She sees him appeal to the crowd. They are too tightly packed to part, but someone turns her way and opens his mouth – by God, Luka's first actor is dressed as a construction worker.

'He says he loves you.'

'He loves me?' She tries to project, but her insides are writhing like a stepped-on snake. It is not her, shouting so ridiculously above people's heads. It is TunnelFairy.

'He loves you,' says the construction worker. His hat is

definitely too orange.

'But... I love him!'

He swivels back. 'She says she loves 'im.'

Someone else, a large woman with an almost operatic voice, helps the message along, bawling at Luka: 'She says she loves you!'

This is never going to work. People are still chattering, awaiting their trains, probably annoyed at all this shouting. She tries to leave her body behind, leave it clutching the pillar, feet on the ground, while she rises above. *We're crammed in like cattle.* Luka peers anxiously from the steps, stretching his twiglet body as tall as possible. The man in the high-vis receives another instruction. People are starting to raise their phones, adjust their smartspecs.

'Tamsin,' one actor calls another, it gets passed along. The construction guy is into it now, smiling broadly, playing his part. His arms spread wide. 'TunnelFairy. Will you marry me?'

She pauses. The whole station is turned towards her. How is this happening? One or two people recognise her, the engineer girl they've seen on LOVE. She feels dizzy already. 'Tell him... Tell him...'

A hot wind blasts out of the tunnel. The train is coming. 'Hang on, I'll tell him myself.' The two skinny guys beside her catch her eye, suddenly declaring themselves part of the cast. Lacing their fingers, they offer her a leg up. Her ballet flats are pristine, brand new with no suggestion of grime. It is a dense crowd, but again she feels that clench of terror: it's not going to work, it's ridiculous even to try, and she is going to fall, awkwardly, crushing people. She beams her desperation at Luka, seeing him half-cover his eyes as she wobbles. But, suddenly, astonishingly, a whole rootstock of hands reach up to steady her calves, her knees, so she can let go of the pillar and begin, one step at a time, to curl her feet over sturdy shoulders. She grasps a baseball cap here, a bald head there, to steady herself. He said he would bring in a few of his Estonian radio buddies to pull off this scene, and she begins to wonder if he has seeded a trail of them all the way to the steps. The trick is to ignore the clamour, the flashes, the tumble of her beret only for it to be retrieved and follow her, passed by willing hands like a small, soft pet. Now she is nearly there and, like magic, the whole station has turned to watch.

Her ankles knock against smartspecs, ungainly close-ups, while others further off will take shots of her pedal pushers, her silvery jumper and the glasses she wears instead of contact lenses – pandering to the cohort who hashtag her as #brainybeauty. She is glad she pushed back on Luka's earlier demands that she bring her hard hat, or some sort of token PPE to help people connect her to what he calls 'the TunnelFairy brand'. Just imagining Ted's face was enough to make her draw the line.

It's enough that she is solving a problem, making a positive out of being petite. One step, then another, moving faster, slipping – but held up, almost crowdsurfing as they deposit her on the steps, someone copping a feel of buttock as she leaves the mattress of hands. They all see Luka kneel, bringing himself to just below her eye level, and she looks at him in awe, then nods, some of them hearing her clear 'Yes,' the smile luminous on her face before he picks her up and swings her round. His dry lips press somewhere around hers – a neat stage kiss.

'Are we done?' she whispers. He nods. The whole station is part of it now, clapping, whooping, snapping and filming. Some people have even forgotten to get onto the train, and it departs, half-full. Apparently it is possible to summon the dusty ghost of a movie and make it your own.

Now that she is no longer swaddled in his arms, she can observe that Luka is wearing a slightly unusual red silk shirt and a touch of eyeliner above powdery cheekbones. His head is dipping into a bow, and she yanks him back. Steady on, Luka. She waves to everyone instead, and they run up the steps together.

'Not too shabby,' he wipes his face, spritzed with euphoria. She almost steps on his foot as they bounce along the pavement in unison, and for an instant she tastes it: the wild positivity he claims is the good side of his condition, that he fears dampening with drugs – the sense of all limitations flaking away. They grab a shady bench to view the clip that one of his minions has already posted. It's rough and ready and real, but it has a bit of didgeridoo music playing in the background, the cherry on an already thickly iced cake.

A *Dundee* cake.

As she sneezes out a laugh, tickled by it all, Luka pats her hand. He's part of the story now. Eagle-eyed followers have already spotted him reflected in her sunglasses once or twice. It is where he likes to be: on the sidelines, sought-out. He is now playing the role of love interest, a childhood sweetheart staying shyly in the friend zone until the threat of her modelling career taking her overseas – perhaps forever – made him chase her to the subway and declare his love. The story will spill out in the wake of the videos and their teasers: *Back to the 80s... You won't believe what this woman does...*

Luckily Luka's career has been too audio-focused and muddied with odd jobs for him to seem like the sort of actor she might hire to play a part. Since his former LOVE profile was deleted, he has produced a fresh one, as her number one fan.

On the bench he fidgets. 'We should have gone further,' he frets. One of his alternatives was to stage an entire pop-up wedding, his radio buddies pretending to be guests, during which the groom would throw a tantrum about the nature of marriage and storm off. She has never really known him well enough to understand how single-minded he can be. It is astounding how much effort he is investing, the favours he is calling in. What she doesn't know is whether he is motivated only by anticipation of Charlotte's warm... gratitude, or by the thought of posting this whole thing on his LOVE account when he is done, as a life-size art project. Art imitating art.

In truth, their performance brought back a long-forgotten joy at abandoning herself to play, just a spark of it. Even if the audience – who didn't know they were an audience – were unfamiliar with *Crocodile Dundee*, they still seemed to understand they were part of a scene, to join in naturally, just as she used to join in at drama club. It was always about being part of something.

'How are we doing?' he murmurs, as they hear the *putt-*

putt-putt of people liking and commenting, while Red goes scouting for other bits of film. The number of followers creeps upward. They drink two sickly cans of Candy Apple vodka that Luka buys from a vending machine, and still it climbs.

'Well?'

The traffic quietens. In the distance, she imagines that strains of music can be heard from the festival, the main event. So much more exciting than her little sideshow.

'Not enough,' she says. 'Not nearly enough.'

'Give it time.'

'We don't have time,' she is startled by her own hoarse growl.

Luka is oddly still. 'Right,' he says. 'Leave it to me.' She can't be sure if it's his grim tone, or the look in his eye, but something makes her uneasy. A bus roars past, drowning out all other sound. Before she can ask what he has in mind, he launches away from the bench, losing himself among the car vapours and drizzle.

GOGGLERS (LOVECAST 2349) 'HYDE FESTIE'

DICK: Look closely guys and you can see my Neck Deep cap, faded blue. See it?

DOC: Yeah we've seen it already.

DICK: I said she was too fit to be an engineer. Didn't I say that? She is genuinely fit. I held her calf and it had a good feel to it. Like a chicken drumstick hot from the pan...

DOC: You're fully loaded with weird, aren't you? I'm pretty sure she is an engineer. Didn't you see those recent posts?

DICK: I like the version where she's a pornstar the CEO hired at a party – that way the drumstick is even more exciting.

Seventeen

In her block of flats an alarm is going off, so distant it sounds like a tiny animal squeaking. Seagulls circle at window-level, trains slink underground, and somewhere out there Luka is keeping himself indoors. It must have been yesterday evening that he made the film and posted it. Now all hell has broken loose.

She puts her toast under the grill and keeps trying his number. When he finally answers, the trickle of relief catches her unawares.

'What have you done?' He has gone too far, she knows that much. The level of trolling is off the charts.

'Have you booked your flight?' His voice is heavy, words grinding past each other.

'Are you okay?' There is no response. 'Luka,' she presses his name into the silence. 'What were you thinking?'

The LOVE network has rallied around TunnelFairy, so

happily engaged one minute, so insultingly dumped the next. In his video, Luka lay on his side, picking at the sofa, still wearing that red silky shirt. His monologue began with complaints that he was having to tag along in the wake of Tamsin's jet-setting. She was getting too full of herself – she never used to be so cocky, showing off her body and flashing herself around. Finally – and this last part made her raise an eyebrow – he admitted he'd started an affair with a reality television star. He was sorry-not-sorry, and this was goodbye.

The rant was a masterpiece: thinly veiled hatred of a woman's new-found confidence and transformation. He managed to get it posted as clickbait across the gossip sites, bringing people flocking to her profile to see her reaction.

'Just tell me, have you booked it?'

'Yes.' Her eyes flit guiltily to the half-packed suitcase by her bed, the sun cream and insect repellent sitting innocently on top of binoculars and supple shoes that will not squeak.

'Good. That's it then. We've done it.'

'I'm worried about you.'

'Oh, shut it, Tam,' a note of his old briskness is back. 'I wanted to push the character to extremes, to see if people would buy it.' Something in his tone tells her that, even so, he was not expecting this level of virulence. He once told her he loves to play a villain, but this time he has been too convincing. Hell hath no fury like people vicariously wronged. The comments foam and spit and offer to tear off parts of Luka's body, to run him over or accost him on his way home, where there are no streetlights or cameras.

'Just tell Charl, when you see her, will you?'

'Tell her what?'

Tamsin paces around the flat, vaguely aware of a burning smell. She opens a window.

'Show her your profile, the whole story,' he hesitates, weighing his words. 'Get her to call me.'

'We could post something where you apologise and send me flowers. Then they'll get off your back.'

A sigh hisses from the earpiece.

'All in good time. I'm certainly looking forward to the big reveal, when we can relax and take our bows.' There is a clunk on the line, and his voice becomes distant, as though he is already removing his smartspecs. 'But it's your show now, and you're on your own. I believe in you, TunnelFairy. Break a bloody leg, all right?'

He rings off before she can tell him she has never found that old theatre adage comforting. In place of the call icon, a confirmation from the Turquoise Grand Hotel pops up, its booking assistant flickering with delight to be welcoming her to the People's Republic of Love. How formal it looks, written down. Charlotte often encouraged her to visit, and now it is happening – under circumstances neither of them could have predicted.

The SOS replays in her mind, that desperate message for her ears only. Luka is right: she needs to get her act together, both to make his sacrifice worthwhile and to justify pissing off Ted with a last-minute, non-negotiable request for holiday. She clears her dry throat and continues packing, the gulls outside shrieking as she folds a sundress. After a moment's hesitation, she picks up her tattered

Brunel biography and presses it into the suitcase. She has just reached the part where the investors get cold feet about building a railway line all the way from London to Bristol – men and shovels versus all those hills, valleys and rivers – and Brunel just says, 'Why stop at Bristol? Why not add a steamship taking you onwards to New York?'

Bristol seemed so far away, deep in the West Country. Did Brunel ever feel this same emptiness, this mine-shaft drop in the stomach that she is feeling now, thinking he would never get so far?

Of course he didn't.

The airport is a tarmac-covered lozenge of land, connected to the main island by a causeway. As the plane tilts, engines at their loudest, she gets a view of other road bridges, of dusky islands in the distance. Back in the eighties, they used soil and chalk dug out from the Channel Tunnel to extend Kent a few hundred metres into the sea, which seemed revolutionary at the time. Now it is common to hear that the concrete from demolished apartments will be used to build up an island's coastline. Down below, the reclaimed land is recognisable by its geometric shapes, islands that are perfect circles, triangles or heart-shapes, everything bracketed by breakwaters. Tamsin is an experienced – if unenthusiastic – traveller, having lived abroad with her mum, but she has never visited a country as man-made as the Republic.

Her flight booking also triggered an email from the Foreign Office, warning her that the island nation is *Highly unregulated* and her travel insurance is unlikely to be valid. The more she reads, the more it becomes apparent that other countries see the Republic as a rogue state, a tax haven thumbing its nose at international law, only extraditing criminals who aren't considered cool, or who don't have enough cryptocurrency jingling in their digital wallets. Articles on dark money and shady deals abound. *Exercise due caution,* warns the FO. With all this in mind, she only hopes Luka's research holds water, that she won't reach the relevant location to find empty buildings, or locals staring at her and saying, 'Film set? What film set?'

Maybe it is just the light-headedness that comes with two flights and poor hydration, or the way her stomach reaches up to her throat as the aircraft descends, but she feels pathetically grateful to step out of the ratty little plane. The breeze that reaches her is warm, suggestive of buttery croissants in the terminal building. She is just pausing on the steps when a voice says,

'Hey.'

It sounds like some kid testing the airport's PA system. Then she looks up, and the lurch backwards is so involuntary that a passenger on the step behind grudgingly pushes her back to vertical. It is a giant hologram, a colossus towering above them, head higher than the cockpit, feet the size of sun-loungers. The projected figure wears a black vest, and his aviators glint with a reddish hue. He aims a playful finger in the general direction of the disembarking passengers. Tamsin feels a tight thrill in her stomach as she measures the proportions.

'Y'all right? I'm Rollo Boone, and I'd like to personally

welcome you to the Republic.' The apparition's hand turns ghostly as it reaches up to scratch the dark, distinctive jawline, and of course there are inky scribbles on his arms. The voice, nearly coming from the right place, continues,

'I love my country, and soon you will too. Welcome to living *life*!' His arms spread, and the last two words boom around the tarmac. A few passengers applaud the welcome message, but others ignore it and walk straight between the hologram's legs, intent on being first through passport control. As the restless figure glitches and vanishes, all Tamsin can hear is the rush of her heartbeat, before a voice behind her mutters a pointed 'Excuse me...' and she hurries on down the steps. So this is the man in charge, with the power to set up cruel new TV shows and cancel any critics.

Her wheelie case is heavier than usual. As well as the usual items for a long weekend she packed a dress belonging to her mum that would fit Charlotte, plus an extra travel bag of essentials. She drifts through the terminal amid a medley of American accents, before emerging at a line of neat maroon cars which open their doors enticingly. In his narrow sunglasses and black waistcoat, the guy who is feeding people into taxis has the grim lips of someone managing a fairground ride, impatient to get each car full and rolling away. Soon her knees fold into the front seat and she is off, palm trees flashing overhead, tinted glass muting the dazzle of a stunning sea. It is like driving along the horizon.

'So, what brings you to the Republic?' The car is programmed to make small talk, or it is collecting marketing data, but Tamsin's throat goes dry and she rushes to answer.

'Just a holiday! Work's been so crazy.' A bark of parched laughter follows the words.

'Sounds great. Hope you enjoy yourself.' The car's cool, robotic tone makes her feel like an idiot.

She shivers, the air conditioning bringing back the atmosphere of the plane. What if she can't do this? It sounded so easy when it was just a case of staying at a certain hotel, slipping down some back stairs, as she did throughout her childhood. Now, with the sea lapping either side of the causeway and a well-spoken West Coast accent still ringing in her ears, she feels like some tiny mouse hoping to steal a morsel from beneath the nose of a massive predator.

'Stop,' Tamsin says. The car does so with surprising promptness, so she is thrown forward. The internal cyclone of fight-or-flight is making her tremble. What does she know about this country? The arrival experience proves there is nothing normal about it. Law and order are replaced by whim and personality. There will be no respect for international agreements, no rules except Rollo's. A little research turned up tales of his vindictive nature, of people being humiliated at parties, exiled or even 'Bermuda Triangled' – some half-humorous euphemism for getting them downgraded on the LOVE network, though nobody quite understands how he does this. She has travelled here on a magic carpet woven of lies, and if anyone finds out she has no modelling contract, no sponsorship offers or celebrity contacts, what consequences will she face? She could be in big trouble.

Her sweat dries cold. The car's voice drones into her hearing,

'Ma'am, may we continue your journey?'

She wants to make it reverse. In her mind, the foundation for this venture, into which she and Luka put such effort, has become quicksand. They are not supposed to be talking now she is in the Republic, because the government has free access to all communications – part of the 'nothing to hide' school of thinking on crime prevention – so she can't even message to tell him she has stage fright.

'Ma'am, we aren't permitted to remain stationary on the bridge.' Her car is insistent. She closes her eyes and feels her skin prickle, as Luka must have done as he logged on and saw that he'd played the bad guy, the arsehole, a little too well, and that pitchforks were being sharpened. Her fingers twist the flat blade of seatbelt. No matter how small she feels, Tamsin has to let the car take her onwards, into a country where visitors are greeted by a fifty-metre hologram. The land of giants.

Part Two

THE ISLANDS

Eighteen

They used to be private islands, these cays, before they came together as a brand new nation. The rows of luxury villas make it look as though someone peeled Malibu off the edge of California and pegged it down with palm trees. From a geotechnical point of view, it is coral limestone bedrock, topped up with waste rubble and sand where the land has been reclaimed, but what sticks in her mind is the more general consensus: the Republic is built on money. This is the part she hasn't quite understood, the inherent deception of the place. It is one of the smallest countries in the world by landmass, but has a population of two million digital citizens: people who live overseas, who have registered businesses here.

The coastal road undulates around gated estates, occasionally passing a little waterfall made from paving blocks. Everything is mown and clipped and managed, like a high-end holiday resort. It has the opulence of Monaco and the bland heat-haze of Miami Beach, a sense of exclusivity behind wrought iron, of private landscapes within a private country. Even the clinic is gated, along with two casinos and a sailing club. Chunky cars pass her taxi, but there is no one out walking until she reaches 'the Strip', a line of cafes, bars and boutiques – like portals to shiny, otherworldly realms. They advertise the world's rarest vodkas, the most botanical of gins and the finest champagnes, all resting in troughs of ice. The harbour is the only place that looks remotely like the Caribbean, with a couple of fried fish and plantain shacks tucked away behind a car park.

Her panic has abated somewhat, now that the car's muzak has reached her veins. It suggests refreshing drinks it can vend for her, and she chooses a locally produced papaya shake, sprinkled with brown sugar crystals. There is something reassuring about how clean and organised everything is, how the car sends puffs of fragrant air towards her forehead and the hotel broadcasts welcome messages in between the adverts, describing how comfortable they will be making her.

'It'll do you good,' Luka declared, when she told him the special treatment would go to her head. 'Plus you can be a complete dick and no one will notice.' If he ever went to the Republic, it would be to observe the filthy rich in their natural habitat. He is already looking forward to recoiling at the tales she will tell.

They pass a semi-artificial lagoon, whose bed has been seeded with LEDs. The light shows are solar-powered, different every night, and give a shareable backdrop to the famous yacht parties that happen there – it's a shame she won't have time to see it. Finally, the car takes a right and begins spouting an unusually rich torrent of praise. 'It's been so great driving you today, I really hope to have the privilege again soon...' This means they are about to arrive and, sure enough, the hotel's unmistakeable turquoise cladding atomises the sunlight. Brassy cages on wheels wait by the entrance, and a man wearing a grass skirt over his neat trousers takes her bag. The humid air touches her skin only briefly before she is inside the lobby, where the air conditioners are heat-seeking and blast her as though she is a fire to extinguish. Keep breathing, she tells herself. She has been in and out of a zillion hotels like this. Even though she is expecting to be welcomed, it is still rather overwhelming to have three reception staff rush towards her, one with a pale yellow cocktail on a tray.

'Delighted to see you, Ms Wilde!' they chant.

'How was your journey?'

The place is decorated with burbling fountains and live butterflies in silver filigree spheres. Everything is fragrant, spotless and infinitely shareable. The cocktail is probably the most refreshing drink she has ever tasted, like liquid primroses – a house-blend lemon sherbet with vegan foaming agent. The main Welcomer describes all the things you can do on the archipelago, talking as though she expects Tamsin to extend her three-night stay, but not being so unsubtle as to suggest it.

The room can't possibly be hers. Prim sheets on a four-poster bed, crystal chandelier above a glass dining table, plus a machine that will produce almost any drink on demand, to which the bellhop encourages her to say 'caramel latte,' because it's the best. There are bamboo toothbrushes and essential oils in the bathroom, and her flight-addled senses are telling her to make the most of this luxury, to get out of these stale clothes and into the pool.

One frothy coffee later, the smack of guilt hits her: the real reason for this trip. What is she doing pissing around like she's on holiday? Somewhere out there Charlotte is alone, trapped, with no idea if help is on the way. Tamsin throws the balcony doors open, drapes billowing. What if there is no sign of it, their research somehow flawed? The hotel's tropical garden extends towards a glowing beach, lapped by glassy waves.

And there it is.

The causeway looks too narrow for vehicles, though a small van is even now progressing along its length. It leads to an island, a blue-green smudge in the distance. Is she really so near? A surge of emotion liquefies the view, and Tamsin blinks it away. Strains of music and conversation filter up from the bar, and beneath it all is a vibration only she can detect: a sense of Charlotte, her heart beating somewhere on the horizon.

The rubber paths through the garden are translucent as wine gums. Her purse swings with calculated nonchalance as she lets herself be enveloped by twittering birds, oar-sized banana leaves dipping into the sky. The walkway leads towards a beach bar on the right, the causeway over to the left. Now she is closer, she can see what looks like a one-man bus shelter, a member of staff sitting in the shade, wearing a turquoise cap. She narrows her eyes and her smartspecs zoom in, giving her a clear view of the security guard's excessive black moustache. With the location so secret, the hotel so exclusive, they might not be expecting a guest to make a beeline for the island. This could work to her advantage.

The causeway begins at a sandy bit of service road where recycling bins cluster. Her eye is drawn to the neon wristbands worn by someone jogging along the coast. The turquoise cap moves, the guard standing up as the woman approaches. He intercepts her, has a word, and gives her a friendly salute as she skips inland a few metres to avoid cutting across the base of the causeway. Damn. He must have orders not to let anyone set foot on it.

A heaviness encases her heart. She watches for a while longer, then walks down the beach, fine as flour under her toes. The water is shallow, the swimming area marked by a line of buoys. She wanders as close to the causeway as she dares, until she can see its piles driven into the seabed, slicked green. They would be tricky to climb, but it might be worth a try, especially if she swims out far enough to avoid being seen. How quickly does it deepen? By the boardwalk a sign informs her that the bathing area is also protected by a net. Protected from what? It is not until she scans down and finds BEACH DANGERS that she reads about blooms of *Aurita booneo*, sometimes called red heart jellyfish, which have apparently invaded these waters. There are some stark warnings about them, and reassurances that the fine mesh should prevent even a single stinging tentacle floating through. She regards the opalescent sea with alarm. What can she do but trudge back to the hotel? Back to the drawing board.

In the lobby, the air is coconut-scented. Two women in identical suits call to her from a display stand, after that pregnant hesitation that indicates facial recognition is taking place.

'TunnelFairy! How are you?'

The blood rushes in her ears. Part of her has already dropped this persona. She needs to keep it up, to remember who she is at this hotel.

'I'm okay, thanks,' she carries on walking.

'It's such an honour to have you here,' they gush. 'Would you like to try the latest Anylocks hair polymer for free? It retails at around sixty-five Luvcoin.'

She is still getting her head around the Republic's cryptocurrency, but that sounds like a lot. It wouldn't be right to accept freebies. These sales reps think she is a rising star, when actually she's an illusion, a passing sparkle. It unsettles her to imagine what they are seeing, this whole TunnelFairy flash-in-the-pan. Are they thinking she looks smaller in real life?

'No, thanks,' she says, stepping into the mirror-lined lift and watching them narrow to a strip as the doors close. How long before someone discovers she's a fake, that nobody has asked her to be 'the face of' anything, and the drama with Luka was a sham? It makes her feel fragile, like a carnival float of flowers heading into a storm.

GOGGLERS (LOVECAST 2360) 'KICKING IT'

DICK: Who was he, some voiceover guy, not even a celeb?
DOC: Yeah, his LOVE account is pretty new. Luka 'the phoenix' Loxley.
DICK: Dumping your fiancée on LOVE… that's not cool. I wouldn't do it, would you?
DOC: And he's basically just body-shaming and hating on her success.
DICK: Hope someone's checking in on my little chicken drumstick.
DOC: Literally everyone is. She's being amazingly positive.
DICK: Well, he's really getting it on LOVE. Ouch. Martian345 says, 'I hope someone hurts you as much as you've hurt her'. Then there's 'You jealous prick, you despicable specimen'. Oh, and here's 'Stone him to death', of course.

Nineteen

When is a door not a door? This is from Tamsin's repertoire, and the answer is: when it's ajar. If your whole life depends on getting through a door, you start to notice what a strange thing it is: an opening designed to let you through, but blocked with a rectangle of sturdy wood, yet equipped with a handle, then beneath it a lock, but a lock must have a key... controls within controls. Even passing through the living room makes Charlotte's feet tingle, like the beginning of pins and needles. She manages to get a scoop of curry, a spoon of rice, and then she is safely in the corridor, plate in hand. What started off as a luxury lifestyle could now be described as scavenging.

In the kitchen, something about the shiny work surfaces and chairs makes a flash of Old Sally's come back. Her fork slips. The chickpeas are too bulbous, their loose skins like flesh. Her stomach has a wobble; it is some sort of rubbery white fish rather than chicken in the meal, and she slides the plate onto the kitchen counter, leaving it to go cold.

Outside, the palms are flapping their leaves like green birds tethered to the earth. On the edge of hearing, a clang sounds, then a clean tapping, almost like a metronome. Perhaps the fence could work itself loose in the wind. It is a seductive image: the metal barrier wrenched free and lolling forward to kiss the scrub. She could just nip through and stroll back to civilisation.

Fluctuating pressure makes the door tight as a suction cup, and when she gets outside she has to zigzag across the terrace, buffeted as she descends the steps. A wicker chair rolls lazily across the beach. Sand stings her ankles. Which side of the perimeter should she check first? It is hard to see beyond her own whipping hair until she wrestles it into an elastic.

There is exhilaration in the moving air, the clean zing of extra oxygen forcing itself into her lungs. Perhaps she could take one good leap into the wind, let it carry her up and over the fence. The leaf litter would mesh into a mattress and cushion her fall, and it would look great on camera. She glances back towards the house and is surprised by how little distance she has covered. Pressed up against the folding doors, like a crowd observing a car crash, are the rest of her housemates. It does not encourage her to go back. Now she is out here, the weather doesn't seem so bad. Gusts and counter-gusts huff their airy harmonies. The sea whips up around the rocks but curls only low, lacy waves across the sand. Perhaps the tide is going out. She tastes salt on her lips, though there is no discernible spray. The waters are thick with dissolved shadows, reflecting the sky. Then she sees it, something large and yellow, bobbing upon them.

Twenty

Long ago, in another large hotel, her mum once left her in the corridor for ten minutes while she went to get a conference client who had arrived early. Tamsin followed the *ting* of hot pipes to the laundry room, fascinated by the huge washers pounding round, opening their glassy mouths to be force-fed dirty sheets from a tube. The air was dry and starchy and, when she tried to leave, the door had re-locked itself. It makes her shiver to recall it, the fear that no one would think to look in this room and she would never be found. The thunder of the machines became terrifying. What if they hiccupped, choked on their washing, and began to vomit soapy water? She would be pressed against a sealed door, gargling detergent as bubbles filled her lungs.

After that Maeve gave her a skeleton key, so it would never happen again. The hotel manager might not have been pleased to know that a seven-year-old could get into any room, but Tamsin felt much better with this secret weapon in her pocket. As she explores the lower ground floor corridors of the Turquoise Grand, she wishes that this key, or its equivalent, was to hand. It is proving tricky to find the entrance into this hotel's underworld, its service areas and laundry rooms, where fresh sheets and toilet paper might be loaded onto the little truck that shuttles over to the island. Unlike the silent, automated hotels in which she sometimes stays for work trips, the Turquoise Grand has a lot of staff. It likes to flaunt them, to give the place a premium feel. But it has not skimped on technology either, not least in the facial recognition locks on these doors.

No fewer than four housekeepers have asked if they can help her and, when she meets a maid for the second time, it makes her worry they will become suspicious. She returns, defeated, to ground level. Outside, the grey, greasy sea resembles Ted's mushroom cup-a-soup. What the hell is she going to do?

'I'm afraid there's a spell of bad weather coming,' a voice rises above the panpipes of the lobby, and she turns to see the smiley manager.

'Oh, well,' says Tamsin, caught off-guard, 'it's still better than London.'

'Can I show you to the restaurant?'

Is it lunchtime already? It's frightening how time just drains away, with nothing to show for it. She tells the manager she'll just grab a snack in the bar, having barely enough appetite for a packet of peanuts, but when she checks the menu there are no simple options. The green salad she orders is laced with truffle oil and garnished with sapphires of sea-salt.

The wind has got up, and is snatching all the napkins from the terrace tables, waiters helping to move guests indoors. She is not sure what draws her gaze to the group of men by the bar; perhaps she looks over because others are stealing glances that way too. They are laughing, lolling across the marble to observe a woman pulling pints. Two of them wear high-end smartshirts that show misty images moving across the fabric. If the tattoos on his forearms were not so distinctive, she probably wouldn't spot him, facing the bar with that yellow leather flat cap on his head. Perhaps it was the hologram that made her anticipate someone taller, yet he stands out due to an unmistakeable aura of celebrity, a magnetism that means everyone in the room is subtly aware of him.

Something icy drains into her stomach as she realises the governor of the Republic must be at this hotel for a reason. Does he know about her plan, that she is here to disrupt his little game? She took precautions before she left, making use of Charlotte's well-worn password formula to hack into her account, finding and erasing any stray photos, any recent connection between them. Precision engineering didn't seem necessary, because how could Rollo guess her intentions?

Her neck vertebrae contract as she shrinks a fraction more, making herself as small as possible. The governor's voice rises, and he slides a monochrome pint back across the bar, 'Bruv, can you believe this?' The others make noises of shock. 'There's a foam burner right there, and she has the rocks to serve me a Guinness without my face on it. What's your name, girl?'

Tamsin wants to dash out of the restaurant but forces herself to take slow, unhurried steps past one table, then another. When Rollo turns to face his friends she flinches, terrified he will look a bit further and she will hear a querulous, 'Hey, don't I know you?' Every hair prickles at the root as she narrows the distance between herself and the exit, certain she is about to be stopped, trying to stay out of the various filming that people are doing, VIPs and non-celebs alike, all in awe of the man with the most followers. Each rasp of laughter is abrasive in her ears, and her breathing becomes quick and shallow.

At last she emerges into the mood music of the lobby and refills her clenched lungs. Maybe Rollo's presence is just a coincidence. He seemed fully engaged in what he was doing, not looking out for anyone in particular. She massages her scalp, pretending to read the list of hotel activities projected on a wall. Tennis and Boules, Chinese silk painting and cocktail-making. Comforting, meaningless words. Before she is quite calm, a man blusters out of the bar behind her, and for one terrifying instant she expects to see Rollo. Instead it is a thick-set guy with his earlobe stretched into a metal-rimmed hole, one of the entourage.

'Hey,' he grabs a passing manager, the friendly woman who spoke to her earlier, and points to the nearest door. 'Does this go behind the bar?' he starts pumping the handle.

'Yes, sir, but it is staff only, I'm...' a hesitation as her eyes flick to the silver VIP pin on his shirt pocket, and then her voice is both mild and faintly nervous. 'Sorry Mr Rees. Yes, that's the way.'

Miraculously, the door opens for him, and the manager is frozen in an awkward pose, clearly wondering whether she should follow.

'He doesn't work here, does he?' Tamsin asks, curiosity getting the better of her.

'No,' she shakes her head, fidgeting with her earpiece.

Tamsin swallows. 'That's the governor in there?'

Finally focusing, the manager flashes a practised smile. 'Correct. He's been here a lot over the last few weeks, and obviously it's great for the hotel to appear on his feed.' A note of strain belies her breezy tone. Inhaling, she turns and takes her sigh away to a safe distance, heels blunting themselves on the polished floor.

Tamsin wanders towards the lift. The two 'Anylocks' product reps, perky as ever, call out greetings, intercepting her. It is less convincing to pretend she is in a hurry when they have just seen her loitering outside the bar. 'Are you aware that this is the world's first smart-hair?' they ask. 'It's hair unlocked! Create any colour or style on demand. Look completely different with one click of the included earrings, or by using the app.' One of the reps touches an ear, and her chestnut bob fades to blonde. 'Try it,' they are like excited children, pushing the pearlescent box into her hands, 'post a picture and tell us what you think.'

'Completely different?' she echoes, thinking of Rollo in the bar.

Any on-site project comes with hazards, even if they are ones she never imagined. It would be unwise not to make use of whatever personal protective equipment is available.

By the time she is finished with the gloopy polymer, her hair has doubled in volume. The drapes are being sucked outward by the wind, and the banana trees outside are giving each other a good beating. White-toothed waves bite at the beach. Such a ridiculously tiny distance to the islet, yet she cannot find a way across. Two nights have passed, and the situation is urgent; she just needs to do something, *anything*. When Charlotte helps people, she is almost on autopilot; her values run on rails. It is a quality Tamsin has always admired, and now she desperately needs to channel it, to stop calculating and recalculating. The idea of getting on a plane tomorrow, alone and with a suitcase full of failure, doesn't bear thinking about.

But what can she do? Down below, the guard has removed his cap to stop it blowing away, but he is still sitting on his plastic chair, probably enjoying the wind through his moustache. Bar staff are rushing to remove cutlery and condiments from tables, to stack chairs before the wind picks them up. But they are not going fast enough: furniture is toppling over, skittering across the patios. Then Tamsin sees something that sharpens her focus, puts her whole body on alert. The guard rises, no longer able to sit by while his colleagues struggle, and goes to help catch the flying chairs.

The towel drops from around her shoulders and she dashes to the lift – too slow – and then patters down the stairs, emerging near the terrace. She leans into the wind, whipped by her own vest-top and shorts, stumbling as she reaches the grove of cacti. The causeway guard is right here, talking in a calm, pleasant way to a young gardener, even as the wind tries to wrestle a canvas parasol from his grasp. 'This is nothing,' he chuckles, 'just a few gusts. Wait till October hits.' His tone is reassuring in the face of what she assumed was a full-blown hurricane, but it means he won't leave his post for long.

She takes a shortcut through the foliage, twigs scratching her arms and leaves blowing into her eyes, crouching slightly to keep a low centre of gravity. A plastic chair flies through the canopy and smashes to shards on the path. Arms covering her head, she runs the gauntlet, cutting across a corner of the wave-lashed beach, now having to contend with the wind sandpapering her calves, her eyes full of salt that feels like pepper spray. The causeway is just metres away, a one-lane strip of concrete with crash barriers either side, very exposed. She was afraid the sea would be flooding it, but the waves are travelling in the same direction, curling round the piles. If she can just be quick. Her rubber shoes grip well on the damp tarmac, but she curses herself for having worn such bright colours. This is all reckless, unscheduled – not her usual style. A few more steps and she will be on the causeway. It should be possible to hurry along if she stays low and central, so the gusts can't knock her into the sea.

Then, a shout. 'Hey!'

He is running towards her, waving his cap. It must be obvious what she is doing. She veers away, but he is too near and her steps falter, the impending failure making her clumsy. She trips, stops, bends forward, trying to calm the storm raging in her chest. The man is wearing a t-shirt with the hotel logo, his thinning hair wet with rain. Amazingly, he is not even out of breath. His arm comes out, loosely encircling her shoulders, and she is so wired she tenses up, ready to fight him off, but he is bracing himself against the wind, guiding her back towards the relative shelter of the wooden slatted bin store. Briefly, she wonders if she can pretend to be someone else, or claim to be lost, jogging, drunk, anything… Anything to stop him escorting her away to get her stuff, to be thrown out of the hotel, expelled from the country.

'I–'

He hushes her. 'It blinds you when the wind is blowing into your face,' he says. Then he stops. A huge goofy grin breaks out beneath his moustache, plus a whiff of spicy meat. 'Hey, you're the London girl, aren't you? Oh my god, you're so cute. My little daughter just adores you. She's a #brainybeauty too. Please… can we just have…?' His cap has a pin-thin line suspended below the peak. He holds it at arm's length so the camera can detect their faces.

For a moment she just wheezes, unable to fathom what he wants. Then it sinks in. Her lungs are still exploding, but she ignores them for a few seconds more and bites her lips into a wan smile.

GOGGLERS (LOVECAST 2400) 'ALL THE OLD SHIT'

DICK: *The Bare Boones*? Of course I watched it. Are you trying to get me sacked?
DOC: Like *The Kardashians*, only with men – that's how she's describing it.
DICK: And Rowena.
DOC: And Rowena.
DICK: That massive LA penthouse with the hot tub on the roof? I could have slummed it there, man. Why doesn't a film crew want to come and shoot my family…
DOC: That sounds…
DICK: Ah, yeah. [LAUGHS] Not like that.
DOC: I guess it started with the gym documentary, didn't it, with the dad, Baxter?
DICK: *Pump Up the Gym*.
DOC: He was a real tough nut, Boone senior, but funny with it. He'd be like, 'here are my reprobate kids…' Rollo would have been, what, nineteen? Twenty? Adrian was the golden boy and Rowena they'd basically ignore. Did the mother just bugger off back to Jordan?
DICK: Rowena is still super-hot. She can guest it on this show anytime.

Twenty-One

Do not pass GO... and do not pass the lagoon, you don't deserve to go sightseeing. Ironically she will be leaving the Republic with more followers than when she arrived, all because of 'Anylocks'. The reps loved how she looked in their product. What could be more on-brand for smart-hair than a smart model with an engineering degree? They handed her an ice cream and swirled her hair up to match, and the image did so well on LOVE that they offered her a sponsorship deal on the spot. No wonder people strive to become influencers, with so much money sloshing around. Of course, they were inconsolable to hear she would be flying home that afternoon.

The car seat presses into her back like a firm hand, ushering her across the island. Leaving doesn't feel like a decision; it is just happening. She is inert and following the path of least resistance. If she does not check out, they will begin charging her twelve thousand dollars a night. If she does not get on this flight, she won't be back in time for work, having left herself barely a day to get over jetlag as it is. Ted will be impatient to tell her what bids they have won, what their next project will be. When she planned this trip, three nights seemed like more than enough.

Unlike the bland airports back home, this departure lounge has quirky art on the walls, fabulous views of lime-green islands. Mirrors with the LOVE logo encourage you to record a video snippet about your visit. It is possible she underestimated the level of visibility in this country? Everything seems to have eyes. The most practical option for reaching the villa was to slip unobtrusively through the hotel, but she was always so damn *seen*. She was out from underground, glowing and reinvented, but what she needed was to be small and savvy and able to get behind the scenes.

The airport bustle is not enough to drown out the wails of her inner voice, asking every other minute how she can be leaving empty-handed, why she has nothing to show for all her sacrifices and all the trolling Luka endured. A hot spring of shame is poaching her insides and she fans herself, barely moving the air. This feels like a cruel, unnatural end to TunnelFairy's story.

Charlotte will forgive her, of course. She values good intentions and will be suitably impressed that Tamsin travelled all the way to the Republic. But no matter how touched or tearful her friend is, Tamsin's failure will leave a dark little bruise on her own soul. Good intentions are just blueprints, filed and forgotten.

All she can do now is trust that Charlotte's own resilience will get her through. She is the tough one, after all, the one who got the terrible news about her mother's death right at the start of secondary school, but survived it anyway. There was something almost unnaturally strong about her back then, something rich and warm-blooded. Her spirit animal, if she had one, would be a huge, powerful, glossy bear. Tamsin needs to remember this.

Airports stretch and compress time. When she closes her eyes, the smell of floor polish pulls her backwards through the years to the Liverpool hotel where her mum once worked. In the ballroom, she and Charlotte would lift the thick, pinkish tablecloths and hide underneath – two little kids building a den. She still thinks her mum engineered it somehow, knowing her old friend Kathleen had a house just around the corner. 'Oh, she's much the same age as your step-daughter, maybe they could play together...' Maeve is one of those people whose plans usually work out.

So, instead of being left with janitors or reception staff when her mother worked late, Tamsin found herself in a home where whole rooms were designated just for 'games', or 'drying clothes', and there was unlimited smoothie in the fridge. The adults joked about Tamsin running wild, but seemed happy enough leaving her to entertain curly-haired, dreamy-eyed Charlotte, who was otherwise rather lonely. Tamsin struggles to remember what they did all day, skinny imps running about the place. In her ear, a high, childish voice says, 'Sharklotte?'

Her eyes flicker open. The sound sits lightly on the humid air. Two fellow travellers, a woman and child, are almost back-to-back with her. The girl is snuggled up against her mother, who holds a basic tablet at arm's length. 'It's a combination of two words,' the latter murmurs, kissing her daughter's forehead. 'Shark and Charlotte, because she is swimming like a fish, see?'

'Like a shark,' says the girl, pleased.

'Yes, sweetheart. Or maybe a flounder,' she swivels her rings so the gems are aligned, and turns her smirk into a nibble of her daughter's hair. Tamsin finds this nonsense intriguing enough to remain twisted awkwardly, watching *Outta My Room* on the tablet. A motorboat marked COAST GUARD bobs its way up the beach, nosing over choppy waves, and then a woman in uniform helps a bedraggled figure over the side. Right at this moment, the mother becomes aware of Tamsin craning over.

'Sorry,' says the latter, automatically. 'I was just curious – I haven't seen this yet.'

'You haven't missed much,' the woman says, softening. 'Spike and Pacey have a spat, and Charlotte has to get rescued from the sea.' She clocks Tamsin's disbelieving stare. 'I know. Desperate, right?'

'Desperate?'

'For attention.' She flashes a flat smile and clasps her child. Several tiers of princess dress crinkle noisily.

A completely surreal conversation. Tamsin wonders if her ears are slightly blocked. She adjusts her smartspecs and tunes into the show, and, after ten minutes of rewinding, her mouth drops open. Has it been faked, this footage of the coast guard closing in on her friend's flailing limbs? There is no way she would do this, not a hope in hell. 'Meanwhile,' says the narrator, 'Charlotte decides a massive storm is the perfect time to go for a swim.'

'Bollocks,' she says aloud, making the woman look round.

The camera cuts to a row of housemates watching in horror. Then there is the bun of Charlotte's hair bobbing above the waves like a burnt cottage loaf. She swims in short, frantic breaststrokes, half the energy lost on upward thrusts, keeping her face above the waterline. It looks tiring. How long did they let it continue?

The next shot shows a damp woman wrapped in a towel, surrounded by concerned faces. The narrator is talking about her antics, and is taking much the same view as the mother who explained the 'Sharklotte' remark. It was a ploy for attention, a dollop of drama. The show is making it seem as though she's fine, framing it as faintly comic, so viewers won't look too closely at the haunted look in her eyes, the fork-shaped mark on her calf that might be a jellyfish sting.

'Flight AE 2953 to Miami…' The announcement is from some other world, barely registering. She is submerged in these scenes: the sped-up swimming, the leg-tremor as her friend climbs unsteadily from the motorboat. It dredges up discomfort in her belly. Something is very wrong here, as though a section has been edited out. There is just no way Charlotte would go swimming, not in a million years. On beaches, the most she will do is mess about in the shallows, nervous of being lifted off her feet, fearful of fish and crustaceans. Even if she somehow found the courage, the bad weather would surely put her off. Couldn't she tell the storm was just getting started? Tamsin shudders, her throat a dry lump, as though she has swallowed a tissue. Without the coast guard on hand, would Charlotte have drowned? If things are so desperate, how is she going to last several more weeks?

Tamsin stands too fast. They have called her name, telling her to 'make her way urgently…' There is no point staying here, but what if she lands twenty-two hours later in London and sees headlines red and raw across entertainment news: *Charlotte Hardey has…* She can't even think it. The rest of your life, she tells herself, the rest of your life is how long you'll regret it if you leave and something happens. It doesn't matter if there is no solution in sight. You need to look harder, think bigger. To even consider leaving was a mistake, a moment of weakness.

When her name booms around the airport once more, people inevitably trace it to the woman with glazed eyes and open mouth, bathed in sweat and gripping her wheelie case. One or two start filming as she drifts away from the gates and towards the exit, pressing herself into the hot sponge of the afternoon.

From overhead, a voice reverberates through the wings of stationary planes, 'I love my country, and soon you will too.'

Twenty-Two

A bowl of salad. They are determined not to offer foods she can preserve. That can preserve her. If Charlotte brought back a tub of the salty ocean, could she pickle things, make them last longer? Even the thought of seawater unsettles her. It has seeped into her memory and wrinkled it, smudged the clear vision she had at the time: that she would use this handy yellow dinghy to paddle round to the causeway or the hotel district – it couldn't be that far away.

The idea seemed so practical. She only had to get her ankles wet to reach the inflatable, which was big and buoyant, resistant to being tilted. The grey blade of an oar nestled inside, convenient for scooping out the puddle of lukewarm water. Where had it come from? It didn't matter. A tourist's cast-off would become her salvation. It ballooned up as she tumbled over the rim, the squeaky plastic of childhood holidays.

Getting out of the cove was no problem, but then the wind wanted to take her far from land. *You don't want to go back there*, it howled, *come with me instead*. The inflatable became like old skin, not bouncing back. As it flattened into something no sturdier than a wet anorak, the rain came, drowning her slowly from above. The temperature dropped, the plastic collapsed and Charlotte tried to swim, her panic growing. Beneath bulbous, thunder-thickened clouds, her world shrunk to nose and mouth, and keeping the saltwater out, her energy like a guttering flame. When she heard the chugging boat, and strong arms nearly wrenched hers from their sockets, it felt surreal – like an act of God or an alien abduction.

'Please,' she gasped to the skipper, a swarthy woman with a nose ring. 'Don't take me back there.' The stern was bucking, sounding a rhythmic *plash-plash* as it squashed the waves. The harbourmaster didn't seem overly thrilled to be out in this weather.

'What you playing at?' she grumbled. 'An' I'm sorry but it ain't my call.' To her dismay, Charlotte saw the cube-like rocks closing in. 'An' why wouldn't you want to go back, anyway?'

She told her.

They are kind, swaddling her in fluffy towels and pressing a hot chocolate into her hands as she huddles on a kitchen stool. Hardly anyone hangs back; it is touching, a little unexpected.

'Thanks,' she says, when Shelly attempts to drape an entire duvet around her. 'This is so unlike me.' Mortified, is the only way to describe how she feels. Asher, who rushed out to help drag her half-numb body up the steps, pats her heavily on the back.

'Girl, if you're gonna try anything stupid again… don't. Or at least come get me first.'

'It was stupid.' She covers her eyes, then pushes back her wet hair. How could she have been so blasé about the treacherous waters of the archipelago? *Boat*, is all she remembers thinking. It just appeared, as though fate had provided a life raft, impossibly tempting. She did not think of checking for punctures. As her feet slithered on seaweed, her judgment slipped too.

The contortionist hands her a third towel, and puts the bowl of salad within reach, smiling before she retreats with the others. Charlotte clutches her hot mug, sorry to see them go. They might be crazy for playing along, but these housemates aren't so bad. Her duvet slides to the floor. It is like being in an airing cupboard, everything so dry and snug. She fingers the claw of a bottle opener, a shiny chrome crab. There is actually a sea theme to this kitchen, while in the cosy corner it feels a bit Latin-American, all rainbow-weave rugs and cushions. A thought unfurls slowly, uncomfortably, as she starts to translate this interior design. These objects, these choices… they are not the result of sponsorships. Yes, the producers must have used AI to plan the escape rooms, crunching and regurgitating her data, but what about these personal touches? The Bolivian fabrics are a particularly low blow, so subtle that she didn't even realise until now why they bugged her. All those colours woven relentlessly together. They were in the photos, in those last few months of her mother's life, snaps taken in villages around the field hospital. Involuntarily, Charlotte feels the velvet of a warm cheek against hers, remembers an embrace in which all her fears would melt away.

There is a ripple of laughter from the living room, like the warble of strange birds. A captive canary, she once heard, can eat its own bodyweight in food every day. She must not forget the hunger of these people, that gnawing need to make a success of it, to come out of this so-called reality show bigger than they went in. If only they could know how it feels to be the butt of this unfunny joke, for their skin to crawl, as hers is doing now, because the escape room is leaking into the whole house, in ways nobody else would recognise. Through the doorway, eyes flash her way and she can guess the topic of conversation. Her stomach caves in and she turns back to the window, to a sky still bruised from the storm and waves spitting gobs of foam. Her hair smells rancid, sludgy with salt.

The harbourmaster. Will she say anything? She said nothing at all in the boat, as Charlotte marshalled her chattering teeth to tell the story. After all the effort of shouting into the wind, she closed her eyes, just briefly, and the next thing she knew her body was cocooned in a foil blanket on the sand, which instantly blew away. She pictures it flapping like a punctured hot air balloon, landing in the gardens of the Turquoise Grand.

Twenty-Three

The marina boardwalk is uneven beneath her sandals, the air briny with the scent of freshly caught shellfish. Three days have passed since she deliberately missed her flight, and she still hasn't managed to speak to the security firm's 'coast guard', its lone harbourmaster. The stern-looking woman who plucked Charlotte from the waves didn't look like much of a talker, and it's unlikely she knows anything, but it might be worth meeting her just in case. Having had no joy on the phone, Tamsin is now standing at the door to the harbourmaster's office – only to find it full of young guys who shrug and pick their teeth. They have no idea when their colleague will next be doing a shift, or where she is.

There is a small ray of sunshine on the way out, however – a bunch of motorboats bobbing together, available to hire. Tamsin was beginning to despair of finding a rental. These are weedy things, their sun-canopies overloaded with fake flowers and fairy lights, anything that will give pizzazz to a picture, but they will chug along at eight knots or so. She probably still has the muscle memory to handle a small outboard motor, some left-over confidence from those working summers on the Med.

As she pauses beside a suspiciously neat stack of lobster cages, a golf buggy pulls to a halt beside her.

'Gorgeous isn't it, darling?' the greeting is so unexpected that for a moment she just stares at the beaming face, the tight ponytail and coral-rimmed sunglasses. It is Dee, a slim, impeccably dressed woman, originally from Singapore and now married to the famous James Baltimore. After Tamsin decided she would stay longer, the Anylocks hair reps not only provided accommodation but also an image consultant. Dee showed up at her condo in a chartreuse suit, neat as a pin, excited about her first client. She is clearly a bit of a socialite, an incorrigible name-dropper, but Tamsin is finding it useful having someone to answer her questions.

'Have you been out on the water?' Dee asks. 'We have a little cruiser over to the right, do you see it? The "Milky Moon", it's called.'

Tamsin smiles, shading her eyes to look. 'Very sporty – I like the flybridge.'

Let people think her a boat enthusiast. It will be less suspicious if she is spotted out on the waves later.

'Are you heading back now? Can I give my favourite client a lift?'

In the rear of the golf cart, Dee's eight-year-old sits in

what looks like an incredibly uncomfortable position, one high heel tucked beneath her bottom. The child averts her eyes from Tamsin.

'It's fine, I can walk.'

'Walk?' Dee's voice leaps in pitch. 'That's crazy talk. Get in.' The door swings open and Tamsin reluctantly climbs into the buggy, which lurches off the promenade and onto the coastal road.

It is hard not to enjoy crossing the lagoon bridge, seeing the water glinting on both sides, jade green where the yachts cluster, already cranking up their sound systems. There is a touch of butter in the air, caterers baking their quiches and vol-au-vents. Tamsin is distracted by two extra bridges over the lagoon, wiggles of metal looping elegantly over the water. They are closed to traffic, but nicely frame the banana-shaped ridge behind the water, which is planted with yellow flowers. Never before has she seen such a well-executed vanity project. In her day job, the work is always to a purpose: fixing cracks, patching holes, shoring things up and making them strong. Millions of people use the Underground every day, and the aim is to keep things running so smoothly that commuters never have to look up from their devices. Engineering just to make the world more shareable is an entirely new concept.

Ted was not pleased when she called and asked for more time off. There are meetings she is supposed to attend, reports to complete. He argued just enough to get her blood up, and she fired back a tirade about Ogilby Dobbs taking advantage of her, then having the gall to knock her down a pay grade. She could picture him pushing his glasses up his nose, softening and retreating into himself. 'One week or two?' he said then, and she felt awful. Of all the managers at Ogilby, he is the good one, the one who trusts her and lets her get on with things. 'Just one,' she said quickly. 'Honestly, I'll catch up when I'm back. I'll be better after a break. Sorry.'

His voice was back to its measured, querulous timbre when he said, 'I guess I'm surprised you like it there. In the Republic, I mean. Anyway, enjoy yourself.'

The call left her desperately hoping that Ted has stayed away from her LOVE account, though no doubt other colleagues have seen her recent posts and are saying all sorts of things about her. A devious corner of her brain instructs her not to care. If she were to leave Ogilby Dobbs, would anyone even keep in touch? Her hand strays to the book peeping out from her diamante satchel; Brunel's biography is a dog-eared stowaway. She has just reached the 1850s, the building of the world's largest steamship. It led people to say that Brunel had bitten off more than he could chew.

'You're so lucky to have snagged a big pharma company,' Dee declares, interrupting her thoughts. 'They'll put some serious resources behind you, and I think Anylocks is going to be really popular once people get the hang of it.' She adjusts her ponytail, obviously remembering she is supposed to use the polymer herself.

As an Anylocks influencer, Tamsin will have help with styling and publicity. Her seaside condo will be rent-free in return for a steady stream of content, which must be 'as magical as possible.' By now, she is almost used to the weird tug on her scalp as her hair coils up into an iced-gem swirl, or slowly fades from lilac to white. An app is used to create different styles, and the reps were astonished at how quickly she mastered it. She touches her frozen locks, grateful to be looking like someone else.

As the golf buggy whines its way up the hill, Dee points across the bay. 'See the glass sundeck? That's our place. The pink turret is Bethany's princess annex.' She lowers her voice, 'not exactly classy, is it? It'll come down in a few years. Then all the money we spend on glitter and unicorns will go on therapy.' She laughs, stepping on the accelerator.

Despite reading an article about Princess Therapy as a growing and lucrative specialism in the Republic, Tamsin remains incredulous. The aim is to undo the 'princess complex' that parents so indulgently cultivate in their little girls, which becomes irksome once puberty hits and it's embarrassing to have your teenage daughter strutting around in a crown.

'So we're having a party tonight,' Dee goes on, 'I wish I could invite you but the Hamilton gang are coming and it's all ridiculously vetted.'

Tamsin feels only relief. 'Not a problem. Someone mentioned you can see phosphorescence in the sea at twilight, so I was thinking I'd take a boat out.'

There is a hummed acknowledgement, but faintly quizzical, as though her stylist finds this an odd motivation.

'Get some good shots,' Tamsin adds, 'you know, with the hair and everything.'

'Oh, I see. Wonderful, darling. Well done.' She yanks the buggy left to avoid a parakeet dustbathing in the road.

Being an image consultant, or perhaps employment in general, seems a slightly new experience for Dee, but she is full of enthusiasm. No doubt her impressive 'little black book' of contacts helped secure the job. 'I've got my work cut out for tonight,' she goes on. 'The governor is coming.' Her tone indicates this is quite a coup.

'Is he?' Tamsin keeps her voice level, training her gaze on the iridescent, peacock-green bay.

'His sister – you know, Rowena Boone? – she's followed my husband James for years. With the governor there too, literally anything could happen.' Dee emits a jittery giggle.

It is still a mystery why Rollo, a corn-fed bully, is so popular. Is it possible he brings a saleable kind of danger to these events? Tamsin feels doubly glad not to have been invited.

'Cheers,' she says, climbing out nearer to Dee's gates than her own, and watches her neighbour continue, like a doll in a battery-powered car, up her sticky tarmac drive.

Fairy lights come on with the ignition, but she turns them off as she furrows the brandy-hued water. The boat handles beautifully, its battery full of solar power. Her sunset silhouette is crying out for a photo, but she prays that no one will see her.

Following the coastline brings her level with the Baltimores' mansion, which is drenched in a syrupy light, its private beach decorated with paper lanterns. Dee has outdone herself. A small blues group is striking up a tune –

something Charlotte could probably identify – the trumpet surprisingly loud across the water.

As Tamsin is steering her motor round the headland, she gets a sudden premonition that this is not going to work. Logic falters in the Republic. Perhaps her evening would have been better spent trying to get hold of the harbourmaster and finding out what she knows, instead of being seduced by the idea of taking a boat out herself.

The grey smudges are sandbanks, so she puts a little distance between her vessel and the shoreline, pleased to see other boats still out. When the slant-roofed rectangle of the Turquoise Grand rises up ahead she slows, looking out for the causeway so she can follow its line of lights. She keeps the motor on its lowest setting, and embraces the deepening of the evening. A tepid, mineral haze rises from the sea. It is best not to think about what might be below, as the water oozes and sucks at her keel, smearing it with seaweed.

Her throat is dry and she didn't think to bring anything to drink. Here is the causeway at last, and it leads her to an islet with a breakwater of cubic rocks, the interior mainly palm trees. She has to go round to the seaward side before the white-sand cove appears. This must be it. In the weak light, she can detect hammocks, a squat building with glowing windows.

It's the place all right.

Breathe, Tamsin. You only get one shot at this. In and out. There will be cameras, and the only ace you hold is speed. The tourist boat has a shallow draft, designed for picnics on powder-white cays, and will be easy to beach.

Her hand, hot and sticky, adjusts the throttle. She allows herself a fleeting image of Charlotte – her face as the shock registers, as she catches sight of her old friend. The boat purrs onwards.

And turns left.

She didn't touch the wheel. Quickly cutting the power, she corrects the course, feeling the graze of a rock as though the boat's outer skin is her own. She tries again and this time the boat turns right. It is disconcerting to have the steering develop a fault just now. Instead she tries the oars, bruising her forearms against the gunwale, but nothing will propel the hull forward. She rows to one side, and then the other. It can't be a sandbank. She leans down and dips a hand into the water. There is nothing; the barrier is completely invisible. Could it be electromagnetic, if that is even possible, something they can turn on and off?

She tries again, scraping the hull several times when she is careless and gets too near the rocks. Finally there is a crunch that scares her, makes her feel exposed. If they have this kind of barrier technology then there could also be infrared surveillance. The boat bobs for a moment longer, the beach whitening as the moon rises, so ridiculously near that she could cry. If Charlotte happened to be outside, Tamsin might get her attention. If these tourist boats had anchors, she might consider swimming the last few metres, but the boat would drift away and in any case it would be slow, far too slow. If they caught her it would be game over – a speedy deportation from the Republic. Or worse.

The prow encounters resistance again; it is nudging the barrier, maybe even setting off alarms. She doesn't want to give up, but what choice is there? The motor splutters as she turns and heads back out. Every bump of the boat makes her spirit dip. Was it naive not to expect state-of-the-art security? This is supposed to be a film set, after all, not Fort Knox. Rollo's well-trimmed beard comes to mind, his face smug at how efficiently he has confined his ex-girlfriend in her prison. He doesn't do things by halves.

Mansions crouch along the shoreline like monsters blinking their yellow eyes. She can tell from the music and voices that she is approaching her neighbours' beach. It is coming into view closer than expected. Guests are running down to the water's edge, though she is not sure why. There is no way they could have seen her, but a cold sweat breaks out along her back, and the boat rucks up a wave as she accelerates.

Everyone is pointing and waving at two figures on a sandbank. She hears little screams, gaspy and terrified. What are the children scared of? They are not far from the beach, the intervening water fairly well-lit and obviously shallow. She glances down, and her first thought is that she has found phosphorescence after all. But it is a far more lumpy and sinister glow, that of jellyfish massing, soaking up the early moonlight.

The boy and girl huddle together, their dinghy bobbing just out of reach, their evening adventure misjudged. They are surrounded by a glutinous, dangerous soup, all threads and blubber. Perhaps the creatures were swept in suddenly by the storm. Her boat might be seen if she gets any closer, but she can't tear her gaze from the children. They stagger with every lick of the encroaching tide, unstable on the shifting sands. Her hand is on the throttle, and she fully intends to motor onwards, but instead finds herself swearing and adjusting her course.

As they hear her, the children turn fearfully, wet hair straggling across their faces. They start backing away, ankle-deep in stinger-water, until she flips the switch on the fairy lights.

'It's just a rental boat, kids, here to help,' she ploughs its hull into the sand, then helps them aboard, their little swimsuits clammy despite the warm night. With comforting words in her best child-friendly voice, she wraps them in the towel she brought for Charlotte.

The launch circles round and approaches a shore jostling with partygoers, all straining to see what is going on. Tamsin motions them briskly aside as she beaches the boat. Then willing hands grab hold and drag it from the surf, sparking momentary concern about how she will cast off again.

Before she can pinpoint her neighbour, the night turns inside out with fierce flashing bulbs. It is utterly unexpected, almost like something inside her is igniting, spewing out light and energy. Then the press-size cameras come into view, like the ones used by the paparazzi company when they followed her around London, and a spurt of adrenaline zips up her lungs. This is the last thing she needs.

From the corner of her eye she sees the kids snuggle into Dee's embrace, arms closing over them like cupboard doors, strangely satisfying to witness. Tamsin swings a leg over the gunwale to shove the boat backwards, but the partygoers misinterpret this and catch hold of elbows, wrists, to help her out. Sequins crunch against her collarbone as people hug her, women in dresses that rustle, and then a guy in a velvet tailcoat claps her on the back, smacking a dry cough from her lungs.

'We heard them yelling and we had no idea what to do. Our other dingy's with the yacht...' His baritone turns breathy as he recalls the distress of seeing his children surrounded by so many venomous creatures.

'Glad I could help.' She tries to make her excuses, to return to the boat, but James Baltimore is used to getting what he wants, and he wants to toast her with a bespoke crystal chalice almost as big as her head. What amazing luck that she was passing.

Twenty-Four

All she wants is to get back to her bungalow and burrow into bed, but TunnelFairy must drink at least one glass of champagne, as their honoured guest. Strings of moon-lamps hang across a violet pool, and in the gardens there are – as described by Dee – misty-white statues and amphorae, denoting James's love of ancient Greece.

'Tamsin! Tamsin, over here!' At least five people are trying to talk to her as she drifts through this dreamscape, accepting a canapé and then forgetting why she is clutching half a quail's egg. The drinks sparkle so vigorously they fleck her cheek. It doesn't feel wise to be here. Every air-kiss and brush of fabric seems to erode what little anonymity she has left.

'Hi,' says a woman in a crimson crinkle-dress and matching glasses. Her voice is musical. 'I'm Fanessa. You're quite an action hero, a great role model. I'd love to have you on my show. Is that Anylocks hair?'

Everywhere Tamsin turns there are smiles, words of praise. Here is a glass of thirty-year-aged tawny port, here is a cashmere wrap for her shoulders, a pineapple perfume, an invite to someone's upcoming premiere. All that remains is for the ground to gently detach from her feet, as the bubbles in her drink lift her to a new plane of existence where everyone is rich and famous and fawning. She presses a palm to her throbbing forehead. Was she ever on a dark boat, scudding over waves? Her sandals are already dry and the warm night breeze is pleasant on her ankles. Flawless, rainbow-hued people bustle around, all wanting to congratulate her, and surely Charlotte is just in another room... isn't she?

Dee, still rather breathless, takes Tamsin's arm and steers her into an inner sanctum filled with melting black leather chairs and men watching a wrestling match on a big screen. The faux-fur rugs seem to moult into the air, dust motes mingling with the fug of perspiring bodies.

'I want to thank you,' she says. 'I've never been so scared.'

Before, when they spoke, it always sounded like Dee was addressing someone just beyond the top of Tamsin's head. Now her voice is low, full of emotion. With the furtive air of someone about to share something precious, she guides her client and neighbour further into the forest of shoulders. Too late, Tamsin realises that Dee really does want to thank her, and is doing the nicest thing she can think of. Voices rumble overhead, and she sees him in his own little clearing, people leaning in but then stepping back, as though his personal space could sting them.

Her whole body is reticent, but Dee pulls her on, determined to introduce her to the guest of honour. There is something calculated about his appearance, certain parts of his arms revealed through artfully slashed fabric. With half-closed eyes he distances himself from the earnest, white-shirted man who is standing opposite and talking politics. Dee waits in the sidelines, one forearm tense and horizontal as though she might need to hold Tamsin back.

'Look at the Agnatov affair,' the man is saying. 'If that cohort of criminals get in again…'

Rollo is standing beside a sharp-looking woman who faintly resembles him, her figure encased in an almost see-through dress. It rustles as she steps in to interrupt,

'It's not that we're sick of hearing about the election… we just can't get excited about the US till ours is done.'

'And ours is like a zillion times more fun,' Rollo adds, 'more honest too, since it's all on LOVE. No debates, no slogans, no bullshit.' He bares a set of perfect teeth. His face, seen only on screen and at a distance, is strange this close. As he turns, light falls on the waxy follicles of his skull, newly shorn. At the nape of his neck, a stylised eagle spreads inky wings, red-edged and fresh.

'Governor,' says Dee, stopping short of touching his arm. 'I'd love to introduce our new neighbour, Tamsin Wilde.'

Rollo's eyes land on her, cold and with no discernible interest.

'TunnelFairy,' Dee adds.

'Oh, T-Fairy,' he brushes the businessman away and opens up a space for them to come closer. 'You are so hot right now.' His air-kisses come with a dry vanilla aroma. Every instinct is telling her to back away. Transparency is such a fundamental part of the Republic that maybe her skull has turned glassy and he can see right through and know she is here because of Charlotte. He takes a sip of his smoky whisky and says, 'This is my baby sister, Rowena.'

The woman grips Tamsin's shoulder and plants a single salty peck on her cheekbone, somehow snagging a hair. 'Crazy, but hot,' she remarks, smiling.

'London, right?' Rollo goes on. 'Cool place.'

'Have you been?' Tamsin tries to silence the road drill that has replaced her heart. Perhaps it drowns out her words, as he doesn't seem to hear.

'So the story is you're an engineer. Is that for reals? Say something smart...' There is a pause as he peers at whatever is popping up on his contact lenses. 'Oh dang, check you out in the boat. At night?'

Their eyes meet, perhaps for the first time. His are mostly pupil, dark grey with an uneven glitter, like iron pyrite. She is among sleek, powerful animals, and has lost the ability to tell whether she is merely a lower-ranking member of their pack, or a whisker away from becoming prey. To her enormous relief, Dee chooses that instant to wedge herself back into the conversation.

'Looking for a killer shot, of course,' the hostess laughs. 'Apparently there was some phosphorescence.'

'The sun sets so quickly here.' Tamsin is perturbed to find a squeak in her voice.

'That's the equator for ya.' Rollo is all charm, giving her a pat on the elbow. His sleeve, as it brushes past, is cool to the touch. It must be made of some clever fabric with an inbuilt refrigeration effect, his well-cared-for body protected even from the climate. 'Those jellies are kind of a ball-ache. What can we do about them?'

'The jellyfish?' she is tentative, unsure if he expects an answer. 'You could replant the reefs, get some natural predators back?'

Other people within earshot seem to step back, just a fraction.

'Or people could just swim in swimming pools like God intended.' He laughs and waves impatiently to someone across the room. 'Maybe we could hold a derby, like they do with lionfish. I wonder how many jellies you can get on a harpoon...'

The sportsmen around him raise a low roar as a wrestler flips someone on screen. Her sensation of temporary comfort begins to evaporate, as she watches Rollo's face, his amusement-seeking eyes. Her fear for Charlotte's wellbeing gathers anew, like a pressure on her airways, but she must not show it, must not even think her name.

Just as she is about to make her excuses and leave, a photographer with a moist face and lanyard appears beside the governor, who mutters, 'Where were you?' Rollo's arm encircles her like a smooth bronze serpent. 'Right then, TunnelFairy,' he says, rotating her towards the camera, its flash reflector an oversized cocktail umbrella. From the corner of her eye, she sees him grinning and pointing to her with both hands, before narrating a quick video. She isn't required to say anything, just to smile. An alarm bell sounds, somewhere at the back of her mind, but there is no time to ponder it. Then the governor is retreating, taking a last sip of whisky and wiping his mouth. He calls to someone, raising his tone past the level of her head, and people fold into the space so that, without consciously moving, she is on the outside of a wall of shoulders, and Dee, who is taller than her, looks equally small.

Still in her dressing gown, she becomes aware of a scratching at the front door, an occasional knock, awkward and irregular, as though someone is bumping into it. Outside, she finds a dozen drones all circling stupidly because there is no room on the front porch for what they are carrying. Even the swing-chair is groaning under boxes and, with the knife of a headache trying to lever her skull apart, she can't face bringing them inside, though of course this means the banging will continue. She closes the door and goes back to the kitchen, where a tall golden fridge has been newly installed, the delivery man wheeling it in at eight am this morning and proceeding to fill it with *cuvée de prestige* Champagnes.

In between the beats of her throbbing brain Dee's voice comes back, explaining to her, just as she was leaving last night, why she goes around the island in a golf cart. 'You see, we've just purchased a monster truck,' she said, pointing it out on the drive, wheels up to Tamsin's shoulders. 'We said to our oldest that he could choose the family car if he did his exams this summer.' The vehicle crouched threateningly as they walked past, no doubt impossible to manoeuvre into any of the island's car parks. 'Wow,' she remembers remarking, 'He must have got amazing grades.' Her earlier impression of Dee as someone who did not demand too much of her kids was to be set aside only momentarily. 'Oh, not exactly – we're thinking of having words with his teacher – but the important thing is that he took the exams.' He tried, and that's what counted. Now he has a monster truck, and Tamsin has the world at her feet, and neither of them deserve it.

This time the knocking is definitely human, and she drags herself back to the door, wondering what luxurious gift will be waiting. Instead she finds her image consultant in a neat tan suit, beaming as though she has won the lottery.

'Do you like the fridge?' Dee asks.

'I–'

'On top of everything,' she goes on excitedly, 'you've smashed my engagement targets overnight. I could kiss you. Do you want me to kiss you?'

Tamsin stares at her blearily and waves a hand. 'That's okay.'

'Fourteen million impressions. A dozen major influencers have you at the top of their accounts, and you're pictured, right there, with the governor himself.' She leaves an incredulous beat before continuing. 'The head of brand is over the moon. They've sold more product this morning than in the last month.'

Tamsin skulks by the breakfast bar. Her back might break if it gets any more patting. Dee brings up several LOVE accounts on the digital wall, all of which use the word 'engineer' in the same way that you might use 'leprechaun'. She looks over, a new reverence in her gaze.

'Can I fix you a drink? Anything you'd like?'

'Maybe a bloody Mary?' Tamsin says, and hears the words repeated as her stylist bawls them at the voice-activated cocktail-maker.

All these photos of last night's heroics. It is like looking at *Vogue* all over again, her arrival on the boat captured with a finesse and perfection that would be difficult to stage. Her eyes have the supernatural, light-dappled look of an anime character, and her mist-blue hair – chosen to blend into the twilight – is framed by fairy lights as she brings the children in safely, one hand on the throttle, upright and serious. Even her black clothes add to the effect, and Dee is effusive in her praise of Tamsin's decision to 'let the hair do the talking.' There is a whole galaxy of comments about TunnelFairy as a bringer of good vibes, a mysterious, beautiful soul. Everything, as usual, has gone too far.

Luka messaged at some point last night, though she was almost too tired to read it. Just a comment about her being away longer than expected, wanting to check everything was okay, telling her he still believes in her. Beneath it, she could sense the pent-up desire to give her notes, just a word or two on how to improve her performance. In her reply, she reminded him they are not speaking. As far as the world is concerned, he is the man who recently dumped her. Keep it together, Luka, she remembers thinking, in her exhausted state. Don't get impatient.

'Here you are,' Dee hands her a lava-coloured drink, appealing in its frosted tumbler. 'It's the Republic's national breakfast – did you know that? We serve it with horseradish-flavoured protein powder.' There is something nervous about her chatter, and the way she is standing in front of the screen. Tamsin realises her LOVE feed is stuffed with offers from sponsors, the makers of other hair products. 'We'll automate some responses for you,' Dee announces, 'get the emojis flowing.' With a quick command, she switches the digital wall to display Rollo's profile, then relaxes beside Tamsin on the sofa. 'How great is that clip with you and the governor?'

She should be feeling relief at how it panned out last night, how he made her into a prop and then let her go. But it is hard to shake off the touch of that supernaturally cool shirt. Rollo's eyebrows are raised as he points at what his arm is encircling, as though she is catch of the day. Dee shows off the caption: *She be lucky I think. WANNA RUB HER HAIR.*

Tamsin wants to die.

'We can use that,' Dee says. 'He definitely wants to see more of you.'

'Are you having me on?' She clicks her earring to let her hair unlace from its French plait and settle on her shoulders. There is something disconcerting about the image on screen, something cartoonish and cute.

Her image consultant smiles and places a soothing hand on her arm. 'He's constantly being spun this way and that by an army of stylists. You can't expect a normal conversation with someone like Rollo.' She leans over conspiratorially. 'I think he enjoys anything a little…' she waves a hand, 'like you.'

Tamsin stirs her drink with its celery garnish and takes a gulp of the fresh tomato juice. She does not feel deserving of whatever Dee is trying to imply.

'No pressure of course,' her stylist adds. 'All I'm saying is that Anylocks pays a premium for a VIP badge… So whatever gets you closer to the governor is worth it.' She taps her smartwatch, 'anyway, your diary is maxed out for the week, and apparently you agreed to go on Fanessa's show this evening.'

'I did?' Everyone thinks TunnelFairy is a real thing. This is like *Vogue*, but different. This time the offers really are pouring in. She is caught up in some hellish circling of life and art, real and fake.

Beyond the condo, the sea is being combed into gentle waves. Her friend is still out there, boxed up in a place so artificial that only its makers know the way in. Something tugs at a corner of her mind. It is the thing about a VIP badge, that pin she saw on the man's shirt as he grabbed the door handle, asking the hotel manager for directions not permission.

'VIP status gets you… what?' she says, cutting Dee off mid-sentence, so she has to fumble for her smile.

'Oh, loads, darling,' she enthuses. 'A follower boost, invites to every party… the freedom of the Republic.'

'Are you sure?'

A nod. 'Unless Rollo changes his law. He wants his favour to mean something. And Anylocks…'

Tamsin zones out as Dee runs through the company's next-level sponsorship package. She recalls Rollo's vanilla-with-an-edge aftershave, his yellow leather cap and celebrity gravity, and once again she interrupts,

'He'd never pick me, though, would he?'

'He might. You're the latest thing, and he'll want to be associated. Especially this near our election.'

The world of influencers is a fickle one, like birds stealing from each other's nests. Rollo's image is carefully feathered. Even Dee has confessed to noticing certain gimmicks: the couple of Einstein quotes he brandishes whenever he needs to look intelligent, the ruthless human accessorising. He has a solid following, having built something almost cult-like on his reality-show foundation. Plenty of celebrities sell fitness and wellbeing, but to this he has added a whole world of 'head health', which is mental health in cooler language. When he gets another ten thousand sign-ups to his 'Trust it' campaign – trust your instinct, that is – he will reward himself with a new tattoo. *Baby, I'm gonna be so good to me,* was the caption of his latest post on LOVE, which Tamsin read with narrowed eyes. Somehow he has made himself into a guru of self-esteem. If people follow him, and follow him right, they will never feel small again.

She blinks, tracing a tapping sound to Dee's fingernail on her watch. The image consultant has an encyclopaedic memory for celebrity, a fame-based filing system in her mind. Boones and Fanessas trip off the tongue, but what have they done that is noteworthy compared to someone like Brunel – whose name would be met with a blank look? She sighs, just as Dee laughs triumphantly. 'What was I just saying? You've been invited to the governor's Me Day party.'

'Is that International Me Day?' It is little more than a hashtag in the UK. Tamsin wipes condensation from her glass and inhales the spicy scent of her drink. Maybe she has been going about this all wrong. The Republic does not work like a regular country. You can't get under its radar because the radar goes all the way down, and you can't find the holes in its security systems because there are none. The only way to get anywhere in the Republic is on its own terms. You need the right clearance. You need a backstage pass.

When one door closes, another opens, though it is unclear why this one in particular should evoke such dread.

GOGGLERS (LOVECAST 2420) 'TATS'

DOC: I hear Rollo has added to his tattoos again this week. A bird, wasn't it? He's shaved his head to show it off.

DICK: Ouch, back of the head.

DOC: And the neck – that's gotta hurt. Is it to do with getting his beloved Mynah bird to talk? He's being kind of cagey about it, which is weird because–

DICK: The thing that people with tattoos love best is explaining their tattoos.

DOC: Right. He's piled crazy on crazy this week, hasn't he? Starting to take it all a bit seriously.

DICK: Now you can buy a drop of his sweat–

DOC: With authenticity certificate! He also reckons he's invented a new style of tattoo, and is calling it 'modern hieroglyphics'.

DICK: Oh yeah, hieroglyphics – brand new.

Twenty-Five

Charlotte lies on her bed, fingers twitching as she plays Schubert's *Impromptus* on an invisible instrument. It is dangerously quiet. In her mind, silence is a sort of fog that makes things disappear. Hopes. Dreams. People. She was never afraid of the dark, but the silence – that was a different matter. Back in Liverpool, her dad and Kathleen could at least be depended upon to make a lot of noise, whether it was the squabbling, vacuuming, or just hustling her stepbrothers out to football. 'Best for Lottie we all carry on as normal, ey?' In those first two years of secondary school, since she was not ready to play the piano again, all she could do was plug her ears with podcasts and music, warding off the creeping hush that always threatened to silence her too, to make her vanish – just as her mother had in a field hospital not far from La Paz.

Her mental image of Bolivia was a blur of snowy peaks.

When it happened, Charlotte was too young and distraught to have much to do with the arrangements, the complications of repatriation. Her mother's woodland burial eventually took place on the outskirts of Liverpool.

It is the little things, the lighter things, that she remembers: a blackbird offering a few bright notes just as the spade scraped on stones, spider threads floating down and touching her unexpectedly on the cheek, and springtime flowers masking the musk of fungus. The beech tree had leaves like green tissue paper, and Charlotte was pleased to have this marker, to always know where her mum would be. You could hear the traffic too, but everyone said this was no bad thing. What Charlotte's mother had loved the most, apart from her daughter, was the open road. Only her failure to get custody had forced her into spending more time with one than the other.

The next time Charlotte visited, she was dismayed to find the woodland pervaded by an irritating hum, which was apparently the sound of fans from a newly opened data centre. It spread thickly over the forest soundscape, stifling all the whispers and trills. She stood beneath the leaves and felt the vibration creep up through her body, a numbing sensation that somehow made it impossible to cry.

They probably put in a skylight to illuminate the bedroom more effectively, with all these hidden cameras. She stands on her bed and examines the wooden frame, the catch. The villa is like a theatre turned upside-down, yet she never thought to check the ceiling for trapdoors. This is where her hope lies: where they underestimate her. She sweeps the hair ties and bottles off the bedside cabinet, crouches to get it in a bear hug and hoists it onto the bed, laying it sideways for stability. A pillow on top gives her an extra inch or two of height, then she climbs precariously, reaching for the wooden frame, her head almost level with the ceiling. Take relationships out of the equation and it is pretty useful being tall. She undoes the catch. If she unhooks a little lever the skylight opens fully and she can flip it all the way over, till it makes a squeaky crack like it's broken.

Quickly, lest something should stop her, she grabs hold of the frame and pulls. Her arms are too weedy, the result of a patchy diet and minimal exercise. 'Pull with your mind,' is what her personal trainer used to say, 'it's the strongest muscle.' This is her ticket to freedom. With every fibre straining, she gets an elbow through, then the other, her head and shoulders, the pine rim scoring a cruel line across her ribs as she folds over and scrabbles to get a knee up; a scrape of shin and she's through, her cheek slamming down on tar-scented roof felt, abrasive as an emery board.

There it is at last: a breadcrumb-trail of stars. She draws in her legs and sits clutching her grit-pocked knees, panting. The startling freshness is not just the night air, it's also the novelty of being out of sight, beyond the cameras – a sort of out-of-body experience. The skylight window, lolling back at too wide an angle, is alarming. She just climbed onto the roof. This isn't something she does, or not these days anyway. Was she channelling Tamsin's approach to off-limits areas? Maybe a little. But there is some trace of an earlier self in this, of striking out to explore on her own...

The entire thought lasts only the time it takes to catch her breath, but it makes her keenly aware of the gathering chill of night, the odours of metal and glue and seagull droppings – so thick under one nest that they form crusty grey sculptures.

She must keep moving; this is her great escape. A few screws roll around as she gets to her feet, the dents in her flesh aching with the promise of bruises. On her right, a higher section of roof is crowded with the fittings for solar panels. From here, she can either go towards the swimming pool terrace – no use – or the back of the villa. Shuffling in this direction, a sunken yard comes into view, with a truck parked on a dirt track. A dotted line of lamps marks out the causeway. Her head spins, not with vertigo but because, across the water, the lighted windows of the Turquoise Grand are irresistibly close, even closer than she imagined.

Then, abruptly, her level of roof ends. Although she could easily get over the waist-high panel that blocks her way, it is a sheer drop beyond, not so much as a windowsill or drainpipe to provide a foothold. Is there really no way down? The ball of hope in her stomach won't unclench. She touches the grooves on top of the composite panel, some sort of lightweight, interlocking material. Would her feet find any purchase on the vertical sheeting… or perhaps she'd survive the drop? But no, there's no damn way. It's a bitter blow to end up perching here, like a bird exploring the confines of its cage.

A slight quiver runs through her hands, presumably from a generator nearby. The yard is well-lit, with a lean-to of corrugated iron. There is stuff on a workbench – a few tools alongside dirty plates, cutlery and two crushed beer cans. Her breath catches as she recognises a pair of her knickers hanging from a wooden crate. What is this, souvenirs from the show? That looks like the Stetson hat from the USA escape room – the one Spike accused her of taking when it vanished. Before she can identify more items, someone hurls open a side door. The man who emerges is completely unremarkable, a man in a slobby t-shirt with brown hair thinning on top, but Charlotte stills, gazing at him in awe. Someone from outside the bubble.

The man is chewing stretchy gum that he tugs away from his teeth and wipes on the underside of the workbench. He settles in his chair, facing away from her, and then a projection lights up the wall. Charlotte's fingers tighten on the panel. It's a glowing green pitch, a match between Liverpool and some team whose colours she doesn't recognise. The man holds a can of beer out from his body before cracking it open, then takes a long slurp.

It is so comforting to see the tiny figures running around, her first view of the outside world for weeks. She watches the whole match, and then, as the man begins to potter around, wonders if she could get his attention. Her fist bangs on the panel, but the sound is obviously not enough to reach him. She thumps it with the flat of her hand for a few seconds, before something makes her pull back. It is clear by now that this is a prison. This guy could be her jailer, and the first thing he'd do would be to seal off this little crawlspace. Don't be too hasty, she tells herself. Watch and learn.

Eventually, the maintenance guy crushes a can of Red

Stripe and flicks to a different show. She is excited to recognise the infinity pool, glowing like a blue marble, the water sloughing off Asher's tanned limbs. This must be from a week or so back, before he let Jake cut his hair. The camera flits from scene to scene so quickly that she struggles to keep up, taking pleasure from every glimpse of her daffodil-yellow dress. She drinks it in: the drone views from above, the scenes she never saw, of the chef kissing Shelly in the shallows, of escape rooms she avoided and post-challenge celebrations she missed. This must be how the maintenance guy keeps up with what is happening just a couple of thin walls away.

He gets up and clears away his plate and empty cans, leaving the projection running. So considerate, she thinks, folding her legs beneath her. The ache is worth it, as she watches the end of that show, and then the beginning of the next, obviously just cycling through the season. By the third episode, she has seen enough of herself to feel thoroughly humiliated. The Charlotte on screen looks robotic, her usual posture stiffened into awkward movements, and she has not worn enough makeup for the cameras – a rookie mistake.

Her cheeks are warming – maybe she should stop watching – but then something draws her forward, so her chin rests on the barrier. She knows this footage. The only time she wore that sky-blue top was the day Pacey made fun of her for having an imaginary friend. And there it is: Charlotte writing in the damp sand, her lips moving. They have captured it. *Furs not firs*. The message is out of the bottle.

Beneath the velvet sky, fireworks go off in every part of her soul. Her words are out there, and Tamsin will decipher them. Nothing has ever felt so definite, or so wonderful. Her friend is a machine which, once set in motion, will not stop. She will kick up a fuss on social media, or make long distance phone calls to the studio until she wears them down. She won't care what it costs. Charlotte can almost picture the two of them joking about it when this is all over. 'For your next birthday, Tam, no escape room, okay?' Her gaze reaches beyond the truck, sketching in a small figure ready to sneak her out through a side-door. There would be a knowing smile, a bit of fringe, unless she has grown it out. Too many months have passed since they last saw each other. The whirlwind that led up to this show gave Charlotte only scraps of time in which to miss her friends, to worry that she was neglecting them. Her fingers grasp the top of the barrier. Tamsin will have seen the message, won't she? She will come.

No fir trees… A lump gathers in her throat. When they were young, Tamsin slipped easily into the role of naughty little sister, often overdoing it so she got into trouble. Even now, her friend seems to nurse an odd anxiety about their relationship. Tam thinks she is the only person in the world who ever felt like a needy child, and has forgotten all the times when she had to be the strong one, when Charlotte was crying down the phone at her, lonely and sofa-surfing and penniless, and certain she was wasting her life. Tamsin has been the adult more often than she realises, and right now, curled up on the roof of this hellish playhouse, a grown-up is exactly what Charlotte needs.

Twenty-Six

Fanessa lets the images rest on screen for a mercifully short moment. Already the audience is sharing her giggle, and Tamsin's hand is floating up to hide her face in shame.

'Very sexy,' Fanessa says, milking it. 'Where did you find trousers with so many pockets?'

'I think it's just called *Workman* catalogue.'

'That's so cute.' She addresses the audience, 'Isn't she cute, though?'

Whoops, and cries of 'Yeah!'

Cute – it just rolls right off her back these days, as though TunnelFairy is protected by her own iridescence, by tight, interlocked feathers.

'And you wore those... items?'

'All the time.'

'But you – *you* – were invisible!' The host is fascinated by the emergence of this stunning butterfly from its PPE cocoon. 'So let's go back to where it all began,' she says fawningly. 'Were you blown away the day that front cover appeared? Did you totally die–'

'I *totally* died,' says Tamsin. 'I am dead. One minute I was sloshing through mud in a tunnel, the next I was on a boat drinking champagne, discussing contracts…' Hopefully Ted isn't watching this. *Sloshing through mud –* he'd be thinking, as he turned off the lights in their comfortable office – *what is she on about?*

Fanessa speeds up the questions, hurtling onward so the tight waistband of Tamsin's skirt begins to feel like a seat belt. Only the tiniest crab-apple of a blush finds its way to her cheeks when she lies about all the offers she got, her brief engagement and life ramping up to breakneck speed. The auditorium aches, the audience salivating for her story. With every selfie they take on their way out of the studio they will secretly hope for a similar curveball, a glitterbomb of unexpected stardom.

'And it's not just the way you look – you really were that other person. And you didn't ask for this… In fact, whenever you've had setbacks you've done extraordinary things with them.'

Tamsin touches the silky firmness of her hair, hearing again how she climbed over a subway crowd, doubled her followers after being dumped – and zipped out in her motorboat to save some kids. There is a tingle of transformation. Could she be stepping into role model territory?

TunnelFairy's LOVE profile explodes onto the screen: two children in a boat, framed by fairy lights, a photographer's filter making it dreamlike. The excited burbling of the audience, the sheer delight flowing her way makes Tamsin wonder, for one crazy moment, whether she could just ask for anything she wanted and they would grant her wish. Alongside the photo, comments appear in real time, praise and heart-emojis, and then:

I don't fucking BELIEVE in you, TUNNELFAIRY.

At first the words do not register. The intense velvet of the sofa nibbles at her legs, and her glass of water is just out of reach. Are those capitals – all sharp corners and edges – really appearing in front of everyone? Why are they still on screen? She is dimly aware of Fanessa trying to gloss over it, muttering about trolls. In the Republic trolls can be well-resourced and dangerous. Her mascara-fuzzed eyelashes afford all the protection of a broken umbrella against the spotlights – roaring blowtorches that make her clothes swim on a film of sweat. Fanessa is talking, but Tamsin's mind is far away, trawling the Republic, wondering who on earth would say this, who might be jealous of all this attention. Then she realises. Like a cruel, unexpected pinch. It hurts like hell.

Even as she smiles and waves, feels the faint wetness of Fanessa's kisses on both cheeks, a part of her is seeking him out, watching his thin fingers typing the words, the racket of a coffee shop zoned out with industry-standard headphones, his lips matching the space-bar – a thin line of nihilism. He probably isn't sleeping well, kept awake by too much caffeine and his inability to vent his frustration except through these tiny virtual fist-shakes.

Of course, to Luka it must seem as though their plan has failed. She made it to the hotel, but has not emerged with Charlotte as promised. There has been no payoff, no grateful phone-call. From his point of view, Tamsin has soared up to dizzying heights, shedding integrity and friendships like the icy fizz of a comet. She is having an awesome time, while he – the maestro – has been discarded. Ever since she appeared on Rollo's feed, snide comments have been popping up. Words on a screen lack the potency that his voice bestows, they are skinny and scratchy. *You look good together,* he wrote, but she barely read it, borne away by the next appointment or appearance, the endless product posts and vlogs.

Not for a minute did she think Luka would stop trusting her, that he would threaten so openly to pull the plug. It's a whole new flavour of fear, to imagine her followers finding out she hired her own paparazzi and faked a whirlwind engagement. It scares her to remember the things they invented: that her hard hat sold for thousands, that she partied on a private jet for days – then fixed its engine, plus she's neurospicy and survived several accidents and got lost underground and saw angel wings… anything that would be a talking point. There have been fakers before, and to be found out is to be thrown to the lions. Fans hate the idea that they have been taken in by lies, that they've lavished real emotion on a fraud. In a world of disinformation, trust is the currency that matters. There are campaigns urging people to be honest online, and even at school she was hearing about *authenticity,* like a new sort of moral code. Without truth, without real people, there can be no global community, no netizens. If it became known that Tamsin broke this sacred bond, especially here in the Republic, she dreads to think what might happen.

Her knees are unsteady as she climbs into a limo. This was all so much easier back in London, when she and Luka were working together. Now he sees her from afar, her posts framed with Anylocks branding, her skin and hair infused with an otherworldly glow. It obviously bugs him that she is making money, judging by some of his comments, but what does he expect her to do, refuse it? The Republic requires all transactions to be in Luvcoin, and if she hadn't let Dee set up an account for her it would have looked suspicious. Has he forgotten how she got here in the first place? Part of the strategy has always been to pretend she is drowning in flowers, jewellery, and designer clothes. To prove you are a success, cash must be flashed. In any case, the fancy cars and yachts and wine-tasting via helicopter were all lined up by Anylocks as fleeting photography backdrops. Luka is, of course, unaware of this. He might see the silver bracelets and the thousand-Luvcoin handbag, but not the blisters from these impossible heels.

The car grinds to a halt on the gravel before it has exited the studio gardens, flashing up an error message. She gives it a minute and then gets out, looking back towards the sound stage. Having said her goodbyes to everyone, she is reluctant to face them again, and it is pleasantly cool among these box hedges, fragrant with juniper and the sand underfoot. While the car reboots, she goes to examine a dry glitter fountain, strangely silent. A clever magnetisation causes all the sparkles to be attracted into the bowl beneath, ready to be squirted up into the air in three dazzling plumes. It is not as crazy as it seems: water is a limited resource on the island, so glitter makes more sense. If Luka had a little patience, a little imagination, he might see that she has not abandoned the plan, only altered it. *I don't believe in you, TunnelFairy…* To think that Luka would do this, when there is so much at stake. Doesn't he realise that his every acid remark eats away at her safety?

She takes a look at his recently created 'phoenix' LOVE profile, and is dismayed to see that most of the comments are still abusive. Her followers are growing, and that means more people are reading her story, scrolling down to see how it started. He has tried to delete the video message in which he dumps her, but others have already copied it and posted new links.

An alert flashes up – a reminder for later. She keeps forgetting that today is International Me Day and she has only a few short hours to get ready. Rollo's invitation forbids anyone to arrive late. Back at the car, she leans against the hot metal. It is easy to picture Luka in London, in the corner of some post-industrial pop-up bar, wearing a hoodie, a scarf pulled above his nose, anything to thwart facial recognition. Life is no beach when you are getting trolled. But if he were to spill the beans it would not only put her in danger but also undo her progress. She can still fix this – all she needs is time.

Luka is lashing out, unsurprisingly, but he would be mortified if she let him ruin everything. He wants Charlotte back safe, as much as anyone. Maybe more. There was that evening at the Pike and Pitcher, red wine on everyone's breath and Charlotte mucking about on the battered old piano… Luka was draped against the instrument and couldn't hide his expression, the joy softening his face. Later, when Tamsin joined him for drinks while Charlotte was away filming *Six on the Beach*, he launched into a sort of praise-rant about her: 'Why is she so fucking nice, so tolerant of this bunch of lolly-brained losers? Is it in her blood or something? Type A – adorable…' and Tamsin saw, clear as day, that Luka is haunted by a missed opportunity. The official line, admitted only under duress, is that he's not quite 'over' Charlotte. But it goes way beyond that. He is nuts about her. He would move mountains, swim oceans, or even face the wrath of the world wide web.

She sighs. He will have to wait a little longer to be appreciated. The trolling, at least, is a problem she can solve. She gets into the car, which thankfully purrs straight off, taking her out through the studio gates. Instead of replying to Luka's last message, she gets Red to order flowers.

'How many?'

'Lots of them. Like we need to outfit a garden. Maybe some chocolates, too.'

'And to whom are you sending them?'

When the director storms off set, you have to take matters into your own hands. She picks a fleck of glitter from her tongue.

'To TunnelFairy, of course.'

Twenty-Seven

A year ago, there was the man who filmed himself sieving the fish from an aquarium tank then eating them raw, fins bristling from his mouth. There's the guy who wears his entire wardrobe, passing out repeatedly from heat exhaustion on the humid island, and a woman who got her cat and dog pregnant at the same time so she could film a cat suckling puppies and vice-versa, and say, 'We never thought it would happen.' There's the man who crashed his car spectacularly into a wine bar while his mate filmed it, and the guy who planks on public highways, along with people who eat for a living, or starve, or who have their bodies altered to match their favourite filters. With cosmetic tweaks so readily available, beauty is a choice, but what gets more hits is punishment surgery. Charlotte's former neighbour, Patrick, could only win back his estranged A-lister boyfriend by agreeing to have something disturbingly akin to a tiny penis surgically attached to his forehead for a fortnight, though in the end he only managed a couple of days. When Charlotte met him in the lift, he faced the corner, his usual, 'Hi babe,' replaced with, 'Don't say it,' though of course she never would.

It was being up on the roof, with its solar panels, that made Charlotte recollect a particular housing development in the Republic – the estate with the 'solar ceiling' overhead. It's a cul-de-sac with a faintly chemical odour, where children make mazes from the zig-zag light, and it's full of wannabes and has-beens. Tourists who reach the end of the Strip walk a little further to gawk at the twelve-foot fibreglass shark sticking out of someone's window, the silent disco garage and the gnomes doing bad things to each other. *Competitive housing*, is what residents do if they can afford it, each tiny domain working hard for its owner. For these 'chasers', life is like stabbing at the elevator button, never sure if it's coming. Unpredictable, and closely watched by the Republic's security service, they are tolerated only because they have a reasonable number of followers, and every now and again one will rise above the others and join the ranks of the genuine influencers.

And who are these people? They are barely a rung below the contestants Charlotte can hear screaming on the other side of her door, as she drifts fearfully towards it, uncertain if the escape room is just particularly stimulating this evening or if it is tearing them limb from limb.

Earlier they were talking pointedly about how she is wasting her place here. They are afraid Charlotte is damaging the show's entertainment value by staying in her room. What these people should be worried about is another water-filled deathtrap, or mechanics so violent they can break a nose. No first-aid. No help. But that is what sets them apart from other z-listers. She sees it now. It explains Pacey's outrageous foreplay with Spike, Mak plugging his perfumes and Asher flashing his six-pack day and night. They are a motley crew, but with one thing in common: their need for fame burns like an Olympic torch. They are all hyper-aware of that lower circle of hell into which they could be cast – like the one beneath the solar panels – and will do anything to stay out of it.

It hurts that she must also have been in this category, picked for the purity of her hunger, for the likelihood that she would fight tooth and nail for another series win. She sinks against the door, hearing machinery kick in and trying not to imagine the escape room beyond. Her bare shoulders press against wood that is just another part of her skin, calcifying into walls white as bone, the more terrifying parts hidden on a deeper level. Like her, the villa and its island are beautiful on the outside.

Sunset has gilded the roof, every panel shimmering with warmth as Charlotte climbs out of the skylight. To be crawling across a rooftop looks pretty desperate, but everything inside is designed to drive her crazy, even the people. So she sits on hot felt, rubbing the bruises from her shins amid the gutter-scent of rotting tropical leaves.

When she reaches the barrier, she fears he will not be around. There is no one in the battered chair, no projection on the wall. But then, to her delight, a side-door opens and he emerges with a gigantic pizza overhanging its plate – her mouth waters to see it – and two cans of Red Stripe, stacked one on top of the other. He puts down the feast, settles in his chair and fires up the projection.

No football tonight, apparently. He scrolls through shows, hovering here and there, and then swipes the lot away. His head lolls back, his bald spot aiming straight at her. On the screen, a talk show begins. The set is familiar, as is the host – Fanessa – a rambunctious, voluptuous woman who asks chisel-sharp questions and always gets the best gossip out of her guests. Charlotte has appeared on the show twice: once with Rollo, when it was filmed in LA, and later a short interview in between the two seasons of *Spill It*. For a moment she enjoys the taste of that memory: a car whisking her off to the studio, people bringing her Blue Mountain coffee as the host twirled her trademark shades. Fanessa was really sweet that second time, and remarked on Charlotte's step-change in self-assurance following the presenting job. Heady days. Who'd have thought she would end up here, crouching on dirty roof felt, watching telly instead of being filmed?

That's when it happens. The next guest has huge heels and pale blue hair. Charlotte blinks. For no particular reason, she finds herself warming to the woman on screen. Then they show a close-up of her face, and the warmth is converted into an acidic queasiness. It is not the first time she has doubted the evidence of her own eyes, especially in recent weeks. Maybe this woman is just a lookalike. Yet the way she speaks, the way her lips slide back for a smile... All of that is one hundred per cent Tamsin.

There are no drones overhead, no buzzing. It does not look as though they are watching, but has this all been set up to mess with her? Do they want a reaction, as she observes her best friend, who she last saw on a grubby station platform, re-cross her legs and sparkle to the camera? Nothing about her rings true, except that every close-up reinforces that it really is Tamsin. This is a person who gets excited about bits of rock and bridges, who rarely wears makeup. Charlotte rubs her aching brow, not daring to look away. The longer she watches, the less sense it makes.

Is *Fanessa* filmed in the Republic? She is pretty sure it is, unless they have shifted back to LA. That would mean Tamsin is here on the archipelago – her heart leaps and flutters at the thought – and there is only one thing that would bring her such a distance. She must have got the message. It worked.

On screen, Tamsin smiles a bit more than usual, as though at a job interview or on a date. It is hard not to be impressed by how perfect she looks. A grain of doubt enters Charlotte's thoughts and it is unpleasant, like sand marring the silk of an oyster. She knows her friend inside out, and any plan of hers would certainly involve slipping through side-doors, unfastening windows, and generally making use of being small and handy with a screwdriver. Becoming this visible, this recognisable, is not going to make that easy. She tries to read something – anything – in Tamsin's face. Have her plans gone awry, scuppered by some act of God that has made her unexpectedly famous?

If only there were subtitles. Fanessa points to an image of a tiny woman in a yellow hard hat, obviously back in London, posing as though to take the piss out of posing. Charlotte stares so intently her eyes dry out. All those years staying out of photos, and now her friend is on the cover of *Vogue*? Is this some alternative universe she reached through the skylight-trapdoor, where everything is topsy turvy?

No fir trees, Lucy. But who is Lucy? The back and front of the wardrobe switch, and Charlotte is desperate to escape Narnia. She lifts sore fingers and finds them coated with grit. When she was a nascent celebrity, she expected her friends to be understanding. Perhaps this windfall was something Tamsin could not refuse, an unexpected, irresistible opportunity to rekindle an ember of her identity that had not quite gone cold.

Charlotte bites her lip, savouring the sting. Her friend would have come to help. There is no doubt about that. But something has changed, the wind blowing in a strange new direction. If she is busy giving interviews, for whatever reason, there is no way Tamsin can be aware of how serious things have become on *Outta My Room*.

The chat winds up amid clapping, air-kisses. This bitterness tastes unpleasant, and she tries to swallow it. Tamsin deserves her support. She has done what anyone would do, what Charlotte herself would do, if presented with a once-in-a-lifetime opportunity. For years she has been telling her friend to stop overthinking everything and go with her instincts. When life gives you lemonade, don't freeze-dry it into lemons. 'Go for it,' she was always urging, and now Tamsin has gone.

Sections of roof loom up on either side, solar panels sharp against the nebulous sky. Tamsin is the one viewer she needs and, with awful timing, her friend is distracted. Who else sees her plight? Even the stars are clogged by a dirty grey cloud.

The maintenance guy reappears, wearing a baseball jacket. Perspective is the thing. It's all about perspective. Now she knows this is definitely a show, reaching the outside world, the man down below looks less like a thug and more like an ordinary crew member.

'Hey!' The shout bursts from her lungs before she knows it is coming. 'Up here!' she thumps on the plastic. It is obvious he can't hear her. She casts around, finds a vent she can use as a toehold, grazes her ankle on the flap, then hauls herself upward, the ball of her other foot lifting onto the top edge of the barrier, which digs in cruelly. She hangs onto one corner of a solar panel.

'Hey!' She is yelling as loudly as she can, but the night sky is a big sponge.

He pauses, looks up and sees her.

Twenty-Eight

When she was at school, Tamsin remembers having to take a couple of filler subjects, but she is amused to hear about Dee's kids doing 'Me Studies'. They are all messing about on the beach when she hears them testing each other on their likes and dislikes. The little girl is solemnly explaining to her brother that she no longer likes the combination of cheese and peanut butter, therefore her answer is still correct.

'That must be some exam,' Tamsin remarks. 'Can you get anything wrong?'

The children stare at her with big, disdainful eyes. Of course you can't. The whole point is that everyone aces it.

On International Me Day, it is customary to get yourself a gift. After all, it's not about your mother or father, or anyone else. Today is about you. Don't you deserve a day? Even right before the party, there is still time for Tamsin to get her chipped tooth fixed, if she wants. 'We can get a dentist over in half an hour,' Dee has already explained that the Republic is a place free of red tape, that you can call an ambulance as easily as a taxi, if you have the money. Although she speaks glowingly of the system here, Dee's dream is to move the family nearer to her native Singapore. She is tempted by their revamped 'Forest 2.0' artificial island, which will offer a dazzling marina, ultra-smart condos and a semi-managed micro-climate. Or so the brochure says.

Tamsin needs to hurry up, dust the sand from her feet and finalise her choice of outfit: an opaline playsuit, or a dress with foldable wings, whichever will feel less plasticky against her skin. A car has arrived to pick her up, but Ada, the grouchy neighbour who lives opposite, complained that it was too large to be parked on the road – it ruined the look of her frontage, hindered the filming of her one-woman interior design channel – so the driver has manoeuvred it awkwardly onto Dee's flowerbed.

'You know what Rollo is doing for Me Day, for the party?' Dee zooms in close, fake eyelashes fluttering like ragged moths. 'He's face-matching staff. They've all had light surgery and latex so they look like him. You'll see it tonight.'

'What? Why would you—'

'He did it last year, too, maxed out the island's surgeons for two full days.'

This sounds like a wander into wind-up territory. Mentally, Tamsin takes a step back. Thinking outside the box is something she understands, but this is just unthinkable. Her whole body aches with the desire to skip this party.

At least she no longer has Luka worrying at her heels. The stunt with the flowers seemed to do the trick. When the bouquets started arriving, she vlogged herself reading the labels, which all said things like *Forgive me, I was an idiot!* Then the mystery was solved as the signature emerged – *Luka Loxley* – and she turned to the nearest webcam: 'Of course I forgive you.' Perfectly staged. If TunnelFairy accepts his apology, so should her fans. If he has any sense, he will post something to complete the reconciliation, a heartfelt *I feel terrible*, or any warm remark to cement the idea that they are friends again, but there is nothing yet.

It strikes her, when she runs back through the message thread, that she never for a moment considered doing what he wanted: dropping the whole charade. All her focus has to be on the evening ahead, on keeping her character watertight. He should understand that.

In the mirror, she looks with satisfaction at the foil-winged dress, which will go well with her ice-blonde hair. She is feeling a little better about the party now, and aims to make it pay off, to make Rollo notice her.

'You know what?' she says. 'Let's send the car away. I'm going to travel in style.'

It is bridled and waiting, not a speck of dirt on its fleecy white coat. A shimmery horn splits the light into pinks, purples and blues. It shakes its mane and releases a smell of fresh hay.

'Ever ridden a unicorn?' The young groom's tone is playful.

'I've read the manual.'

In the Republic, reality is not as important as shareability. If you can book a convincing unicorn, why wouldn't you? If Rollo is always going to go too far then she needs to keep up. The horse's flank quivers as she mounts. Set against the sunset framed by candy-floss clouds, her reflection in the window is languorous and Pre-Raphaelite, like an illustration from a book.

'Sweetie, you should get going. I'll see you there.' Dee climbs back into the car. The stable is barely a mile from Government House. Tamsin nods to the groom and they set off via the north harbour, to give the people lazing on their yachts a glimpse of her glamorous steed. Her hips rock pleasantly from side to side, the odour and warmth of the horse bringing back memories of riding in France as a child.

The evening is delicate as a flower. Unlike Rollo, she has novelty on her side. She is brand new, hugely influential, and still mysterious. There is no need to feel intimidated by him. He might like to think of himself as a giant, towering over the lesser beings who arrive on his territory, but when they met at Dee's house his larger-than-life persona wasn't perfect. Small things were undermining his performance: the clumsy slurp of whisky, the awkward conversation as he waited for his photographer. He asked what could be done about the jellyfish, seeming to forget that he himself had protected them earlier that year, after noticing the species was called *Aurita booneo* – like his surname. Most of all, it struck her that Charlotte must have had to wear flats when they were together, because he wasn't as tall as he seemed.

'Excuse me, ma'am?' The attendant tugs at his man-bun. 'Should we trot? Only it's nearly eight-thirty.'

It takes a second for his words to register, to ignite defiance. 'Don't worry. We'll be fashionably late.'

The groom nods, but looks tense as he leads the horse onto the windward coastal road. They are nearly there, but this last stretch seems to be closed to traffic. A couple of cars are doing three point turns and a boxy ambulance is parked on the verge, the driver having an argument with Rollo's security men. 'How am I supposed to get this patient to the clinic?' He is furious, but it is having no effect on the guards. At first Tamsin is fearful of being delayed herself, and then deeply embarrassed as the staff check her face and wave her through. The ambulance driver glares up at her, in all her finery, and it makes her want to sink into the earth. *This is not me,* she longs to tell him. *I'm not one of them.*

Rollo's event includes a spectacular parade, which is even now progressing up the driveway of Government House. The trampled grass gives off a summery, humid scent as people gather, watching, and the boom from speakers vibrates up through her mount, making the animal whinny and snort. There are drummers and bass guitarists, dancers in Rollo's brand colours, leaping and spinning between fountain-sparklers. But the main event is the gigantic 'Rollogram' she saw at the airport, accompanied by a little projector-truck. It dances up the driveway: sidestep,

sidestep, fist-pump, booty-shake... It wrings a faint admiration from her – being so content with your figure that you can make it house-sized and know people will applaud. Charlotte always says you have to love yourself before you can love other people. If that's the case, Rollo Boone should be the best lover in the world.

The crowd pulls back to let the hologram pass. The music is becoming almost too loud, and the groom renews his grip on the bridle, placing a hand on the horse's flank. The animal totters, jittery.

Rollo stands on a balcony above the portico. 'I can really see myself in those shades!' He roars, then hi-fives his effigy, for what seems like a long moment, until it vanishes. His arms spread, bouncing, taking in the crowd. 'Aren't we the greatest?'

The guests scream, their applause louder than tropical rain. Anyone who can fit onto the balcony floods out and mobs the host, straining for a touch of his arm, his smooth scalp, his shirt.

All of a sudden, now the parade has dispersed, she realises she is the only person arriving, and everyone is outside to see it. There is that imperceptible shuffle of feet, as people take in the unreal vision she is presenting, the sense of devices zooming, recognising, snapping. She clip-clops forward on her unicorn, an eerie quiet having followed the crazy-loud boom. Almost involuntarily, she allows her wings to unfold.

Hesitantly at first, people begin to call out to her, to wave furiously. She is aware of the green lanyards that denote paparazzi, then the cool hand of the groom as she dismounts. Her arrival at this party, the Me Day ball, is every little girl's dream. The only thing troubling her is the way that Rollo meets her eye, staring out from within his nest of congratulatory arms.

Twenty-Nine

The near-invisible selfie stick gives Dee the air of an insect missing one of its antennae. Not wanting to enter the mansion alone, Tamsin latches onto her with relief.

'Sorry I'm late,' she says, noticing her stylist is half-way through her drink. 'Nice dress, by the way.' It is white with pom-poms. Dee flashes her small teeth.

'Thanks, doll. My daughter chose it. The whole look, in fact.'

Tamsin nods, recalling the unsettling catalogue on the Baltimores' coffee table, which included this *Snow Mommy* ensemble. It was one of many mom-looks a child could choose, some requiring more work than others.

Although people refer to it as Government House, it is obvious why the mansion's official name is Gilded Springs. Beyond the dull-gold Doric pillars of the foyer, chlorinated water runs down a bronze feature wall. If Tamsin stares for too long it looks like the floor is rising. Woody scents coax her into a walnut-panelled lounge where people sit on high-backed chairs, razor-thin lines of powder glowing brazenly in the lamplight.

'TunnelFairy.' She hears it under people's breath as they recognise her, or more likely she is registering on their devices. Dee moves off, absorbed by a group of similar-looking women in flawless attire and, before Tamsin can follow, she encounters an enthusiastic mob, desperate to meet a hot new influencer. The unicorn was obviously the right call, and maybe it was no bad thing to have arrived slightly late. Her stock needs to be as high as possible right now, and that means making herself the number one topic of conversation.

A tray of drinks appears, held by one of the many unnerving clones. Up close, the waiter's face is grotesque, like papier-mâché with stubble glued on, just fractionally too large for his neck. As he turns, the bird tattoo looks like a biro sketch. Tamsin fights the urge to flinch. She wonders what this poor guy really looks like, whether he'll get his face back intact, and how much he was paid.

'Gives me the willies,' whispers the guest next to her, and they both back away with their drinks. This man has a youthful, American sort of look, spirals of chestnut hair a messy counterpoint to his black silk tie. His breath is faintly botanical.

'Right?' she says. 'It's the craziest thing I've ever seen.'

'And it must have cost a fortune.'

'I'll bet.'

The man lowers his voice. 'Comes in handy, being in

charge of the central bank.'

Tamsin stares at him, pausing mid-sip. 'Who is?'

'The governor.'

'You're saying…?'

'Nothing, obviously. It's actually AI-controlled.' He grins, his eyelids flickering, as though not quite permitting themselves a wink. Some sort of conspiracy nut, yet she is grateful to encounter a guest who is not utterly mesmerised by all this spectacle. She tastes the drink, a champagne so pale it resembles sparkling water, dry on the tongue. The hubbub swirls around them.

'So, what are you known for?' she says, wondering if she should have worn smart contact lenses or similar. Dee normally takes care of the introductions.

'Oh, nothing,' he says. 'I'm an unknown.' He allows himself another grin before cutting straight through it. 'My name is Joss. I'm an image consultant.'

'Nice to meet you. Do you know my… Dee Baltimore?' She looks around but Dee is nowhere to be seen. 'I think she's avoiding me.'

He laughs. 'If you're cramping the style of your stylist… well, they're not doing their job right.'

As he lifts his drink, there is the promise of muscle up his sleeve. Sometimes old emotions flare up, like willo-the-wisps. In her teenage years she would be suspicious of someone so far out of her league wanting to talk to her.

The tinny smash of dropped crockery makes them both glance towards the buffet, where sweating servers carve slices from a chunk of lab-grown meat. It has been formed into the shape of a suckling pig so large that the red apple in its mouth looks like a cherry.

'I've never met a Joss before,' she muses.

'My parents kept swapping my first and middle name. Mom calls me Josh, and Dad prefers Ross. I couldn't handle it so I compromised.'

'You finally made Joss stick?'

A very satisfying and uncontrolled laugh bursts out of him, making people look over.

'Just so you know, I'm incensed you made that joke.'

She rolls her eyes. 'Just so *you* know, this is the most ridiculous conversation I've had since arriving, and that's saying something.'

He clinks his glass to hers, and a little more of the self-consciousness lingering around her wings evaporates. Ever since dismounting she has been aware of the rustle from behind, the silvery fabric folded into an angular cloak, and has been on the verge of apologising for looking so ostentatious. 'Own it,' says Charlotte's voice in her mind. A touch giddy, as though her heels elevate her to a thinner atmosphere, Tamsin tucks her long pearlescent hair over one shoulder.

'So, do you have a client here?'

'Not right now. But it's good to finally get a look inside Government House. Are you hungry?' He inclines his head towards the buffet.

Although she does not feel like eating, she moves closer to where plates are being filled with slivers of 'meat'. Her instinct is to queue. When they were driving through the Strip the other day, Dee announced that there are no queues in the Republic. Here, everyone is at the front.

Tamsin directs a half-smile at her new friend, nods at the pig, and raises her voice above the clamour. 'I'm surprised it doesn't have Rollo's face too.'

Certain he'll appreciate the quip, she is not expecting to see his jaw tighten. There is a cackle of laughter from behind her shoulder.

'OMG, he's going to love that.'

Tamsin turns to see Rollo's younger sister in a gauzy wrap, her dress black as the sea at night. With strong hands, Rowena seizes her shoulders and lands kisses on both cheeks. Tamsin feels perspiration spring up on her neck. All she had to do this evening was keep a lid on her dislike of the man.

'I was only messing about.'

The response is a laugh of childlike glee; the woman seems to have a sense of humour at least. But before Tamsin's muscles can tentatively unclench, Rowena has swooped over to the pig and snatched the apple from its mouth.

'I'll let you off,' she says, 'if you show me the way to Narnia.'

Does everyone go quiet, or is it time stopping? There is the blushing fruit, smelling faintly of apple but mainly of the roast-pork juices and vapours that have been sizzling up around it. At a distance, she can sense the usual scene approaching, as it has before in bars and at college and even, once, in a bus station toilet. *Take my apple, Lucy*. With this size of audience, she would expect the embarrassment to be acute, even overpowering. To her astonishment, the moment passes with no rising red mist. Is it her imagination, or does Rowena look faintly disappointed when, with a lightness that lifts the corners of her lips, Tamsin takes the fruit – rather bruised and soft – between finger and thumb.

'That's not how it works.'

Those who have been listening sense a punchline and chuckle politely. Rowena retrieves the apple and tosses it back to the chef, grinning.

'Attagirl,' she seizes Tamsin's hand, not giving her a chance to say goodbye to Joss. 'Come on, Roland will kill me if I don't share you.'

The guests they pass wear everything from sheet metal to cling film, grabbing as much attention as possible within the confines of the 'monochrome to the max' dress code. Tamsin holds a lungful of air and then lets it out slowly. This woman is a stranger, yet she knew exactly where to prod. Perhaps Rowena saw comments on her profile about *Eternal Winter* – probably something about the faun and his apples. There is no reason to assume she watched the movie, yet this is all a bit close for comfort. Tamsin's safety in Rollo's domain depends on him never winkling out her secret, never realising she is a close friend of his ex, and not putting her under any heightened surveillance. To this end, she has tried to avoid even picturing Charlotte since landing. Their relationship, at her insistence, has always been so offline that there is no real trail to follow… unless someone looked closely at the cast list of that damn movie. But – and she takes another deep breath – that was decades ago and, unless Rollo got wind of a plan to help Charlotte, such a coincidence would hardly raise eyebrows.

Tamsin allows herself a flush of pride at not having freaked out at the mention of *Eternal Winter*. Is it the Republic itself that is numbing her to this old embarrassment? Here, people will do anything for attention; they will bare any part of their body or soul. It makes what she did, aged ten, seem lightweight by comparison. Strange that she has carried it around for so long.

After a moment's indecision, Rowena takes her through the largest door, into a lofty, dimly lit room. 'House, where is my brother?' she directs this question to the ceiling. Tamsin wanders over to a wall of books.

'Neat, huh?' says her host, pausing to let her look. They have the dusky covers you might see in the library of a stately home, though without the dry, papery scent. Tamsin thinks of the Brunel biography in her bag, like the antidote to all of this. She is struck by a sudden urge to be back at the condo, picking out some scene from two hundred years ago, losing herself in the quiet, measured language of engineering.

Rowena's black-gloved fingers glide across gilded titles, until she grips a copy of *The Grapes of Wrath* and tilts it outwards a few centimetres. A section of the library slides out at chest height, becoming a bar, and clumps of book spines – only spines – move aside to reveal backlit bottles of whisky and rum. 'Fooled you,' she says, yet there is something conspiratorial behind her grin, as though she doesn't often have someone on hand who will appreciate the mechanism.

Rowena's lips are sharply defined, her black hair swirled into a comma. She has the same shadowy beauty as her brother, but is more bright-eyed, as though life is worth waking up for. Her online sportswear shop includes some stylishly outrageous self-defence accessories, including peppermint pepper spray and some sort of knuckle duster made of chunky gold rings.

She pours them both a shot of caviar-infused liquor, and Tamsin feels the warm stroke of her fingers as a glass is put into her hand. As if it were not enough being taken under the wing of the cool girl, there is now this nascent mood of seduction. She follows Rowena's silent motion to drink, and the clear, salty liquor makes her cough. Then a photo is taken, and all at once it becomes clear that she is just a prop, like the faux-library and the shiny bottle. Predictable, she supposes, but it is hard to stop the little sag in her chest.

When they return to the corridor, she is reminded that Rowena is one of the famous Boones. Guests look their way, falling over themselves for a word or a selfie, and many of them recognise TunnelFairy, too. Rowena's hand presses on the small of her back, positioning her for filming, and soon her palm is tingling from all the hi-fives and fist bumps. Her mind is equally jarred. Does showing off now carry a faintly positive moral charge? Even back at Ogilby Dobbs they wanted her to do it, and here the approval washes over her, rinsing away her fears, the lingering bad taste of *Eternal Winter*.

They go into a courtyard through a rainbow-smeared waterfall which parts into two streams. There is a moment of coolness, but not a speck of liquid lands on their faces.

'AI-controlled, like everything,' says Rowena.

'Very neat.'

'That's how he likes it.'

On the grand staircase she finds herself out of breath trying to match Rowena's long strides. At the top, folding doors lead onto a terrace where black rattan chairs and tables are arranged. On each side there is a bar, and above the music she can hear the *chip-chip-chip* of someone attacking a block of ice. Beyond are the floodlit grounds, the tops of palm-trees ghostly grey, with yachts moored below. The two wings of the house jut out on either side, each with a slightly higher sundeck on top. Rowena emits a cry and goes over to a display table by the bar. 'Who put these away?' she demands, and the staff look at her blankly. Opening a silk-lined box, she takes out items that resemble tiny, flattened torches. They are lime-green, tiger-striped, fuchsia, coral and gold. 'My new range,' she explains, picking up a cerise one dotted with roses. 'Personal tasers, great for getting back safely, don't you think?'

Each device has two metal prongs at the end, like blunt fangs. Tamsin's eyes widen.

'Are they legal?'

Ignoring the question, Rowena clips a taser to her belt and marches them both over to where her brother is sitting.

'Look what I found,' she purrs, fondling Tamsin's wings.

Thirty

The governor's obsidian silk shirt crackles and surges up around his body, revealing triangles of golden flesh. His face is full of colour as he absorbs adoration from the attractive people on either side, and the table jostles with cocktails and champagne coolers, plus a small pot of cocoa butter.

'Oh, hey, great you could come, T-Fairy,' he says.

Mildly encouraged, Tamsin takes a seat, and Rowena perches on the arm of her chair, somewhat invading her personal space. She shifts, putting another few inches between herself and the taser's bared teeth. Now she is closer to a caged bird on a pedestal, preening dark plumage. An acrid smell rises from the layer of chalky droppings.

'Mynah,' Rollo says, a tenderness in his voice. 'The smartest. Wait till you… look at this, right.' He crouches before the bird, who eyes him beadily. A nut appears in his hand. 'Alec, come on Alec, what day is it?' With a squawk that could be anything, the bird produces two syllables. 'Me day. Me day!' It receives the snack with a brisk crunch, and Rollo laughs happily, obviously enjoying himself. A certain brilliance right in the centre of his eyes makes her suspect he is also getting an internal pep-talk from some chemicals. 'Only took, like, a week,' he says. 'Anyway, how do you rate the party?'

'It's amazing,' she says, not exaggerating. Every window frames a vignette of chandeliers and beautiful people. The east sundeck juts out over the sea, and has been furnished with a pirate theme, or perhaps its Jolly Roger flags and cannon are the remnants of a photoshoot. The other wing is in a different style, an infinity pool on top and the floor below full of gym equipment, several people jogging on treadmills. It seems odd that they are sweating away up there when there is a party in progress. Rollo follows her gaze.

'Oh, them. They love working out.' He waves towards the glass walls. 'The gym is twenty-four seven, y'know? Keeps the place lit.'

'They're generating?'

Rollo hesitates, as though he didn't expect her to get her head around the idea so quickly. 'It's a power workout. Get it?' He smiles. 'Guess you wouldn't expect us to be leading the world in sustainability, hey?'

Surprisingly no, Tamsin thinks. 'How much electricity do they actually generate?'

The words are hardly out of her mouth before his eyelids sink, his smile dies.

'Plenty. But everything starts small, Tinkerbell.'

He snaps his fingers to summon a waiter, who hurries towards him like a human mirror. The cocktails smell of melon liqueur, a sickly haze that adds to her mounting panic as Rollo's attention shifts to other favoured individuals, who laugh and adjust the bikini-clad women on their knees. Rowena catches her eye, very briefly, just a cold glitter without any message behind it.

'It does,' she gushes, 'but it's all about that first, killer idea, right? *Your* idea?'

There is a stillness and then, to her huge relief, the compliment reanimates him like a coin in a meter. His eyes brighten with pleasure and his shoulders settle into a more relaxed gradient.

'Right.' He stands to embrace a young man who is approaching, putting him in a headlock and knuckling his hair. 'Bruv. This is the face of our new wellness campaign,' he explains, as the guy struggles weakly, delighting in the attention. Here and there, adorning the bland, beautiful people, Tamsin catches a glimpse of a silver VIP pin. The mark of the favoured few, and her door-opening ticket out of here. His 'cabinet', as Dee calls them, are like the half-asleep kids at school, blank-faced and incurious when unplugged from their phones. Yet they have clearly learnt what she is only now discovering, that the only conversational tool you use with Rollo is flattery. He wants nothing but lubricant, no spanners in the works.

Now he is telling some story about his youth, snapping at a minion when they helpfully add his brother's name. He wants the tale to revolve around his dad, his lips smacking around 'Baxter', name-dropping his own father so repeatedly that Tamsin starts to wonder what it means. A luminous drink is thrust into her hands, and he turns back to her.

'Rowena showed me your mum's photo site – helluva lot of old guitar-lifters.' He gives a throaty laugh. 'And who's your pa? Is he even on LOVE?'

Old guitar-lifters? The language throws her, until she remembers his aversion to celebrities too traditionally famous to bother with the LOVE network, footballers and rock stars comfortably ensconced on other social media, with followers in the millions. His level of research has taken him further than she would like, as far as her mum's pride-and-joy collection of selfies with everyone who played Glastonbury back in the day. This is way too much investigation. There is every chance he could find something to cast doubt on her fairytale ascent, or – worse – link her to Charlotte. A low-level dread kicks in, as she wonders what other questions he might ask.

'I don't know,' she says, distracted by her accelerating heartbeat.

'Be honest with me,' he begins, but there is a sudden rapping on one of the windows. A woman's voice reaches them, tremulous and bent around a thick New York accent.

'He-ey!' she calls. 'Can we talk, sweedie? Sweedie?'

When she hears it, Tamsin is starkly reminded of her geographical whereabouts, so near the US and so far from home. The woman feels her way unsteadily to the French doors, holding her tiara in place. She is stick-thin, with unnaturally large eyes, plum lips and a matching cocktail dress.

An undulation of Rollo's jaw tells Tamsin the interruption is unwelcome. He tilts his head resolutely away from the woman, who is trying to step outside, impeded by the thick fingers of a security guard clamped around her arm. Her face is slightly familiar; it has appeared beside Rollo's in recent weeks. He dates only beautiful women, yet there are stories of him turning down a supermodel because she lacked a decent following.

From the corner of her eye Tamsin can sense Rowena awaken from her reverie, flexing an ankle and touching the rose-pink taser on her belt. It is not so far from the colour of the woman's dress. Tamsin basks in a fleeting sense of superiority – even as a newbie she managed to come up with something monochrome. Rowena raises an eyebrow at her brother, then gets up and goes to meet the woman, smooth as clockwork, taking her off into the party somewhere, as though steering a child back to bed.

'Can you believe some people?' Rollo murmurs. 'This isn't her Me Day party.'

'Was that Petra Zielinski?' Glad he is so easily distracted, she is keen to keep the tangent going. 'Your girlfriend?'

'Not anymore,' he says, with a certain relish. He dips a finger in his drink and sucks it, before downing the glass in one. Half of his movements are sudden, half in slow motion. 'Super-good swimmer, Petra,' he adds. 'Did it professionally before she got her acting break.' He exhales a gust of sugary alcohol. 'Love is like charity, you know. It begins at home. You asked me earlier about the power workout? Well that wouldn't happen without love.' His voice softens around the word. 'I love myself, so I also love my home, my country, my planet… so of course I'm going to think of ways to care for it. It just comes naturally, so long as you have that bottom layer of the pyramid, the solid foundation that supports the rest. If people are a bit fucked up, it's usually a problem with their…' He trails off.

Tamsin suppresses the urge to say *bottom*. 'Foundation?'

"Zactly.' Lifted by the energy of his argument, he motions her over to the balustrade. A band is playing, down in the garden, but it is just possible to hear waves below, licking at the rock on which the mansion is built. The air is full of mingling perfumes, a hint of gunpowder from the spark-fountains of the parade, and beneath it the moist breath of the ocean. He turns to face her, leaning one elbow on the elegant railing. The quieter his voice, the more articulate he becomes. 'That's why Me Day is so important. It helps remind people of this,' he touches his heart, 'the place where all love begins. Those gym machines power this mansion, but love, and believing in yourself… that powers the world.'

She mirrors his posture. If he really is powering this mansion with gym equipment, then at least one positive thing has sprung from his strange passion. His conviction is what keeps the followers rolling in. It is human nature to look up to anyone who seems to know what they are doing. Rollo's certainty condenses from the air, so concentrated it makes her want to bottle a tiny dose of it for when she is next unsure of herself.

This is like a sort of initiation, an induction into his way of thinking. It is important she doesn't mess it up, though a part of her is impatient, wondering how long it will take to charm a VIP badge out of him. In the distance, there is a faint slam of wood on wood, chased by a single echo. Her eyes stray to the sundeck with the pirate-ship furnishings. Beyond the figurehead, on the seaward side, she is surprised to see a plank being run out, like a springy diving board. There are two figures now, very blue and indistinct. One has shimmied out on the wood.

'Up there,' she points. 'I think there are a couple of kids playing walk-the-plank.'

It doesn't look safe. He remains with his back to the balustrade, appraising her in a way that makes her aware of the different joints and elements of her body, the shape of her face beneath its sculpted hair; that up-down look that strips off the makeup and accessories, that rates her on a scale of nobody to somebody.

'I thought you were faking it, but my AI couldn't find any AI. You really were on those red carpets. Must be luck, I guess. Are you a lucky charm?' He takes a shot at a London accent, managing a Cockney squawk that makes her squirm. He pinches her hair. 'If I rub, will the luck come off?' She tries not to pull away, though a sickly feeling is creeping beneath her ribs. His fingers are small, boyish, a red welt of hangnail on one thumb.

Way up high, the figure on the diving board totters, arms flailing. Someone skinny as a pole. That spiky, gem-dotted hairline, a flash of plum-pink… Tamsin's breath snags in her throat. She can almost feel the flimsiness of the board beneath her own feet, the desperation to catch hold of something. The woman falls – swiftly, shockingly. Beads of moisture make Tamsin a tiara of her own, and she is listening so intently for the splash that she hardly catches his last words. What is below? Does it overhang the private harbour, or are there rocks?

'Seadog Studios did a great photoshoot,' he says, 'but they shouldn't have left the set up there, it's too tempting. Y'see, it stops people sneaking back in, if they smell of seawater.' His eyes are cold embers, all charm burnt away. 'She's always in the wrong place at the wrong time, y'know? So long as she doesn't hit anything on the way down...' he tilts his head from side to side. This feels as staged as the parade, as any other aspect of Rollo's perfect party, and as wrong as her calculations. It is not an initiation. It is something quite different. The ocean breeze turns chill, as though full of ice chips from the bar, and the railing in front of her is too low, so she backs away, dizzy. Her wings don't work – one of them is torn – and he could swat her down.

'Anyway, time for my speech, if you'll excuse me?' A lazy smile plays across his lips. 'Nothing worse than being late.'

Thirty-One

Rollo must be the best lover in the world. That's what she thought, seeing him wash sand from the smooth concave of his torso with handfuls of seawater, seeing the care he took over himself, and how it extended to her. He touched her cheek as though discovering a rare and delicate shell. He would ease apart the ties of her wraparound dress, only to do them up a shade tighter, teasing her. He would bring her cubed pineapple on a banana leaf for breakfast, sticky and sweet, licking his fingers.

When they won *Six on the Beach*, she kissed him, and it was the most real kiss of the whole series. At that moment, she believed in the two of them. They could make it work, despite the craziness of coming together for entertainment purposes, of embarking on a love affair without being sure which bits of it were real.

When a relationship ends, Charlotte is not one to cut

off all ties with an ex, unless there is major hurt involved. Some, like Luka, she counts among her closest friends. If you are bound to someone, it makes sense that one or two threads will remain – values or understandings you once shared. The present moment aside, you will both continue to exist in each other's past, even if they use an app to erase you from photos. Perhaps it is vain to imagine her fingerprints left on people's hearts, but she cannot help it. Especially with Rollo who, in quiet moments, may remember that he once told her a secret.

Even after their triumphant win, the performance continued because people thirsted for it. Heads were turned when he showed up at her apartment in a stretch limo with built-in hot tub, apparently naked, sloshing water until she came downstairs, threw off her sarong and joined him, in a bikini that she was being paid hundreds of Luvcoin to wear. Drones shone spotlights upon them both, and the car could scarcely get through the crowd. Being so much in demand was an all-over physical experience, her senses so overloaded by whistles of excitement, strobe-like flash bulbs icing her skin, that it was like tasting sherbet as a child: that impossible, saccharine foaming. And she hadn't even popped any pills – it was all him.

Rollo liked it when she was on form. He was happy to be with her, especially the side of her that was game for anything, the 'fuck it' part that sometimes needed to be put back in its box. Although she was also hitting it hard, there was a whisper of unease, the faintest beginnings of humiliation each time she saw, in the morning, the images of what he had done after she left the party, blurry shots of her boyfriend kicking peanut trays off the bar, or pouring fizz over a frieze of topless women.

It came to a head the night before they were due to go on *Fanessa* together, not long after their big win. She wanted to know why he was doing this, why he was so obsessed with furiously growing his followers when they were both fending off sponsorship deals like kids playing dodgeball. It was never enough; he was trying to fill a hole that kept getting deeper. 'What is it you're looking for?' she had asked, taking Rollo's hand as they sat amid the honey-yellow flowers of the ridge above the lagoon, their selfies all taken, the sun almost set. 'Because if it's not... us... that's something I need to know.'

Normally, communication was not a problem with Rollo. He praised anyone who was good at expressing their state of mind. But this time she could barely get a word out of him. He rubbed the back of his neck and sighed.

'I love that you love me,' he said, finally. 'But here's the thing... that's as far as I can go, y'know?'

'I don't understand.' Yellow petals bruised between her finger and thumb. He made her affection sound like a trinket. 'So you can... nearly love me?' The pain involved in getting these words out, especially in a measured tone, did not seem to register with him. When they walked up here, hand in hand, she was so certain they'd be moving forward, not back.

'It's not you,' he said, with a brief grimace at the cliché. 'I don't have a good track record of success in relationships. Even if I find someone amazing, I'm not able to give them my full and undivided love –'

'Why not?'

He flicked a flower from its stem. 'I'm not ready. Got to reach a certain point with myself first, and I'm not there yet.' His finger stroked a red-hot line across the top of Charlotte's shoulder before travelling to his own arm, the earliest of his tattoos, raised and charcoal-grey: eye, boat, star, the zig-zag *M* and *W* of a crazy spring break in Milwaukee, his childhood passions and prides – all the things that made him. 'Have you heard the thing about your body being a temple?' He began to take her on a tour of his tattoos, but the words blurred, barely heard as she focused on the way her skin desired the warm attention of his fingertips. She knew all the tattoos by heart – everybody did – so why keep going on about them? It was not easy to muster a good-natured tone with which to soothe him.

'I think you *are* there,' she said. 'What's not to love?'

Even this did not make him turn to her. He muttered some limp reassurance that he would make it eventually. The way he slid down the bench, legs splayed, reminded her of a cheap fabric doll she had as a child that had lost both arms and all of its hair, a toy she hid when friends came round. Then their car appeared on the road below, and it was time to brush the pollen from their clothes and go down into the hill's shadow.

Only later did it occur to her that they had both just assumed, throughout the conversation, that she loved him. Maybe she should have shared his hesitation; of course she was still working on her own self-love – who wasn't? But there were other reasons it would have been difficult to say those three punchy words, if it had come to that. She had loved plenty of people before, after all, it's just that, with Rollo… the feeling was different.

The next day she couldn't bring herself to be happy, chirpy and loving on *Fanessa*. The 'aw's of the audience grated on her sense of honesty. She would not be true to herself, to her straight-talking brand, if she played along. When the time came, she stopped short of blurting out the real reason why they would not be staying together. In the car, on the way home, Rollo had looked a little vulnerable, saying, 'That was a bit of a share, okay?' It was a secret that didn't fit his brand, so she skirted around it, being as honest as she could without pretending there was any hope.

And did it really make any difference, ending their relationship in public? They did everything in public. Though she felt bad after the show wrapped up, when the host and other guests formed a cradle around Rollo, hugging him. From within the comforting arms, he shot her a look that has lodged in her memory. But afterwards he used the whole thing as a springboard – sprang all the way to Governor on the strength of those headlines and his ensuing carte blanche for misbehaviour. He got his own talk show, and his personal channel gained thousands of subscribers. She was happy not to have to worry about him.

Besides, he gave her no option except to end the relationship. It was understood, wasn't it, given what he'd said? At least he valued her enough to make her one of the few – perhaps the only person – who knew how he really felt. Even as he built and fortified his temple, and promised enlightenment to anyone who could love themselves as much as he did, there was still this tiny qualm, this faltering that meant he could only play at being in a relationship, nothing more. No doubt he regretted being lulled by the warm nectar haze of the evening they shared, and revealing more than he had intended.

It elicited just the faintest tug of compassion, as she watched his antics, as she saw him burn through women and summon a gilded – but steely – personality for the cameras. It also explained why he was so desperate to be Governor. When he won, almost a year ago, she sent him a quick message of congratulation, a real paper card with a yellow daisy pressed inside, proper old-school. *Enjoy it,* she wrote. If he is officially the most popular person in the Republic, if everybody loves him, then his long journey is over.

Thirty-Two

Is she only imagining the hum? It is just on the edge of hearing, yet persistent. It could be the back yard generator. Her inner cynic has to entertain the possibility that they are piping it in, trying to remind her of a woodland burial plot where she tried to block out the *thrum* of the nearby data centre. But that would be ridiculous. She never filmed it, never even mentioned it to anyone except Tamsin, and that was only to beg for company as she wandered among logs disintegrating into gingery splinters, wisps of vent-burnt air mingling with the smell of wet leaves.

At the worst possible time, right after it happened, Tamsin was whisked away abroad. She could send only virtual hugs, tears frozen by glitchy video calls. She was with her mum in Monaco for so long that, on her return, she had the look of a traveller: braids in her hair and a well-embedded tan, excellent French and a complete lack of social skills. After wanting to be saved for so long, Charlotte ended up with a friend who, at that school, was in real danger of being eaten alive.

Now, as she starts pacing around the room, Charlotte wonders if she dreamt it, that image of Tamsin on screen. Her friend's cheeks were unnaturally coral with blusher, her freckles shimmer-washed, and she wore a dress of dazzling gauze. Someone must have styled her. What could she have done to become so famous, so quickly? It is baffling. This is a woman who is happiest a hundred metres underground, who has, over the years, become deadly serious about her career. Charlotte has needed to prod and tease her a little, just to check she can still be silly, that work hasn't smothered her inner child. What could have changed? There are too many questions right now, and Charlotte can barely trust herself to answer them.

A tremendous clatter makes her jump, and it becomes clear that Spike has set up his improvised drum kit again: a punch bowl, some pots and two metal trays, which he hits with wooden salad paddles. His frenzied percussion seems to jar the delicate bones of her ear canal. She opens her door.

'Hey, Ringo,' she shouts, but he is facing away. Cursing, she takes two strides into the room and taps his shoulder.

As though it is waiting for her – and she instantly assumes this is the case – the floor begins to move, knocking them all off-balance. There are cries of alarm. Already the shutters are almost closed, and her dive goes nowhere; the floor grates downwards until she slithers onto the lower level, pummelled by rolling pots and pans.

Her elbows and shins throb where the bruises will appear. How easily they have trapped her. Before the regret has properly set in, she notices the smell. It is an incongruous, fresh-mulch odour of real soil, replete with bacteria and detritus, black and damp – more like the stuff back home than the sandy grits of this cay. No expense spared. 'Oh God,' she moans, dread twisting her stomach. The others are sniffing it too. The room is dark, and their voices bounce back from fuzzy, spindly shapes. A blue spotlight falls upon an old-fashioned shovel leaning against a tree. There is a hole in the ground. An owl hoots. She has a bad feeling about this.

'A terrible curse has fallen upon this beechwood,' intones the narrator. 'The bones of the witch have been disturbed, and you must return them to the grave or never again see the light of day.' Gradually a monochrome wood is revealed, the digital walls making it feel much larger, yet dense with overhead boughs and peeling grey bark, mushy with rot. Charlotte is a statue. If she does not move she is not here. Rope-thick spider-webs stretch up to the canopy, a hint there will be items hidden above as well as below. The chef lifts a hollow log to peer inside. Shelly finds arrows marked on black toadstools. The others start to climb trees as the owl flutes: 'Hoo has one?'

Charlotte closes her eyes, blocking it out. A foulness has overwhelmed her senses. The fresh green leafy bower drenched in decay, the grave exhaling dank spores... is this really happening? Just breathe, she tells herself. These are universally spooky images, a horror theme. She shouldn't assume they're trying to depict one particular burial, even if it feels that way. Then, beneath the rustle of leaves, just above the level of hearing, it is there, unmistakeable: a hum. She can't look at the hole in the ground. They needn't send spiders; nothing could crawl so deeply under her skin as this.

A nudge. She almost screams, but it is Asher's warm shoulder. He clocks the tears streaming down her face.

'You want to sit this one out?' His tone is low. This is an individual task, so she could lose it, just stay still and let the ceiling close. But then she would be in this lightless hole alone, and at their mercy. Her neck crackles as she shakes her head. 'Okay then, let's get it over with,' he points to the top of the nearest web, a nest in the tree with a couple of bones poking out. His fingers lace and slip beneath the arch of her foot, giving her a boost. She clutches the rope, clambering slowly, catching a glimpse of bulging calves as he overtakes. On her right, Heidi is climbing a different web, but there is a scuttling noise and suddenly coarse-haired spiders appear, about the size of rabbits. It is almost too shadowy to tell, but they seem to be holograms with convincing sound effects. Heidi screams and slips back down. Spike, higher up the web, cries out in annoyance when its angle changes, so he is climbing horizontally rather than upwards.

Below, Pacey and Shelly pluck keys from the bones they have found before tossing them into the hole. A line of light, as the ceiling opens, gives Charlotte hope that this will soon be over. The ropes beneath her hands and feet wobble like crazy. Whatever they have used to make it glisten smells like old Halloween costumes, of face paint and joke shop 'goo'. She forces herself to climb a little more. The web trembles as Asher reaches out. Then he brandishes two bones in triumph. 'Here, catch,' he flings one down, and of course she misses, feels it brush her fingers, unpleasantly realistic, as it falls. The rope trembles as though considering whether to continue bearing her weight, and it takes all her focus to get to the ground. When she reaches through, the gaps widen and narrow around her arm. She pulls her sleeve over her hand and uses that to grasp the bone, detaching the key as though robbing it of a piece of jewellery.

Almost at once, to her great relief, a wire descends, the seat butting her thighs. As she clips the harness together, she turns, wondering if Asher is down yet, but he is still up near the nest. At first he seems to be wrestling with the ropes, messing about, but then she sees them move of their own accord. A hologram snake slithers from the tree and he bellows. His whole body topples sideways through a brand new gap – she can almost feel the rope burn – and suddenly he is caught by the neck. His large face flushes red as he plucks ineffectually at the ropes that are criss-crossing at his Adam's apple, fibres bristling.

'Asher!'

He only gulps in response, as though trying to talk through his nose. The other housemates are being lifted, and her wire seat is also starting to rise. All her strength flows, concentrated, to her arms, and she grabs onto the ropes, shakes and yanks them as much as she can, though it is hard to tell if her efforts are making any difference. He grunts and drops free, with a face-scrape that must have hurt, but the thin layer of soil is no cushion. When he hits the ground, his cry has a high-pitched break, right in the middle, a note that a voice like his should never be able to strike. As she is borne upwards, Charlotte sees him sprawled, a line of dirt up his arm, one leg clearly broken, though there is no blood. Not yet. A stone-cold lump has lodged in her throat, her body wanting to throw up but too appalled to do so. The tendons in her arms ache from trying to hang on, and as the wire pulls her upwards she hates it, this sickly, wholly conditioned relief-response singing in her veins.

'Asher,' she yells, and all the housemates are yelling too, twisting as they rise.

'Hey buddy, you okay?'

'He's hurt, man.'

This is Asher. The guy with the toddler-naughty grin, who has braved unpopularity a dozen times to stick up for her. Now the grey leaves that brush her legs are blotting him out, the floor closing, and she can't do a thing about it. The last she sees of him is a pale, crumpled shape, his Inca-cola vest bunched under one armpit, the furze of his hair as his head lolls down. Charlotte is trapped like a child in a swing, blinking wide, helpless eyes.

As soon as she has wrestled off the harness, she turns to the others. 'Safe, is it?' Her anger is white-hot, wildly satisfying. 'How safe are you feeling now?'

Thirty-Three

Town looks shabbier today, as the detritus of International Me Day revelry is swept from the streets. Tamsin wears her sunglasses indoors. The traditional headscarf of the incognito celebrity is replaced by a setting on her hair app called 'natty grey' that makes her look twenty years older.

This cafe faces a vacant lot, whose flat, sandy earth, tattooed by tyre-tracks, is like a patch of Rollo's skin, coarse grass bristling through like stubble. It's all him, from the beaches to the Strip to the lagoon to the dozens of islands and causeways. The Republic stretches out like a web, Rollo at its centre. If he wants, he can know everyone's movements, every second of the day. Him and his creepy sister. He is clearly pulling the strings of her waitress, who reappears to tell Tamsin the Genoa cake is no longer available.

'Sorry, but it's just been outlawed,' the woman says, tugging at her grass skirt. 'Clause 3.2 – it's new – Fruit Cake is Nasty. You still want your tea, ma'am?'

The election is coming up, and that means lots of new laws to keep the governor's followers entertained. It is the first time that Tamsin has really noticed this aspect of the Republic, really felt the breath of the governor down her neck. He gives with one hand – declaring free beer on Fridays – and controls with the other, ensuring via people's pulse-monitors that no one skips their workouts. Then there are the laws that really get the headlines, like when he banned boiled carrots because a girlfriend hated them, decreed the 'dickhead defence', or enabled citizens to report any visitor who – in their view – falls short of the Republic's sky-high beauty standards.

'Ma'am?'

Parts of the previous evening come back to her in bruising little jolts. How could she not have noticed that she was being singled out for all the wrong reasons? He was toying with her like some feline with its prey, Rowena delighting in the show, until the opportunity arose to make his point.

The vision of Petra plummeting from the sundeck is like something from a dream, yet a word to her smartface was enough to bring up footage of a dripping wet woman picking her way around the outer wall of the mansion, a car finally rescuing her from sodden humiliation. One other post that caught her eye, on Rollo's feed from a week ago, showed Rowena messing about with her among the cannons while Rollo filmed them, muttering something about 'Bermuda-ing her.' His sister coaxed the other woman onto the plank and then berated her, 'Don't fuck about, Petra!' So the incident was not as spontaneous as it appeared, the ground prepared. For some reason, this is even more frightening.

'Sorry, no.' All at once the booth is stifling, and Tamsin exits swiftly to the street. Everything in the Republic seems to be made of compartments, of private islands and estates and McMansions with masking greenery. You can only move from one to the next, never really get outside of them. SUVs with tinted windows glide along the road. People meander in the wake of their head-mounted selfie sticks, bubbled in conversations or filming themselves as they go, or ramping up their music to drown out other people's playlists. Her face tenses as she walks through clouds of drum and bass, garage and yacht rock, the damp wind blowing strands of coloured streamers round her ankles, each step taking her deeper into loneliness.

There really is nowhere to go, except back to her beach house. Following this road would only lead to the artificial 'pleasure island' set up for cruise passengers, a glorified waterpark with pools and fake beaches. The only square of greenery among these cafes contains the famous vodka fountain, pungent and burbling, from which you are allowed to drink your fill. It features in countless tourist videos, usually just before the part where they vomit. She perches on its adobe wall, taking in the strong odour as the crystal-clear liquid evaporates. Everything is a bit unhealthy – how did she not see it before? And to be on the wrong side of Rollo is to feel like an enemy of the state.

It makes her wonder how Charlotte could ever have been in a relationship with this guy. There was always a certain intensity in the way he fawned over her on screen, looping her own sarong around the back of her neck to pull her into his bedroom. At the Me Day party he was simultaneously thin-skinned and prickly, taking an adolescent delight in his throwaway remarks about Petra being a terrific swimmer. If he can arrange so casually for his ex to be thrown into the sea – luckily without harm – it is easy to believe he would throw Charlotte to the algorithms. Until now, there was a tiny part of her that still thought this too ridiculous to be true, that Luka had just blamed the governor out of jealousy.

She sees Rollo's tanned hand, rose-gold rings nudging the knuckles, gliding up to blot out the person he didn't want to see. His machinery, how he works, is only just starting to make sense. If he can't deal with a person, his preference is to get them out of his sight, to cancel them. There were those three wrinkles, an eye-scrunch as the woman appeared. It was straightforward – and somehow not assault – to make her vanish.

The vodka smells like paint-stripper, yet she takes a shot glass from the stack and dips it into the flow. That interview. It was a long time ago, but she remembers it being excruciating. Charlotte was asked straight out whether she and Rollo had a future together, and since she couldn't in good conscience say yes, she had to say no. *No.* A hole punched right through his ego. He thought he'd snagged the most popular girl in school, but it must have made him feel like a spotty loser to be dumped.

Considering what he did to Petra, just for being a slight annoyance, it is hard to anticipate the scale of his revenge against Charlotte.

She shivers, and the glass slips from her fingers, vanishing with a *plop*. As if she could have charmed her way into his band of influencers. The fantasy of getting VIP status was withered instantly by the look he gave her, that remark about being late. When she arrived at the party, eyes falling upon her like summer rain, it never occurred to her that she was stealing his thunder.

Has she been lucky and gotten away with it? There is no way to be sure. She takes a second glass and tastes the vodka, toxic on her lips. After coughing, she tosses it away, full of regret and a faint queasiness. This can't be hygienic. Her smartface, complying with the rules, has shared an image of the glass, and already her followers are sending their laughing emojis, their warnings about that messed-up fountain, comments that it's a bit early in the day, that they like her style, that it's probably a mistake. She agrees. In fact, for the first time it feels comforting to have them around, these few thousand invisible people, always there. Her close friends are steel beams, her family more like timber, and these names on a screen, previously little more than dust motes, have clumped into a sort of amorphous cushion. She is grateful to have a buffer, something that makes it worth Rollo's while to exhibit her and leech off her popularity. Around here, it's the only thing that offers any kind of protection.

GOGGLERS (LOVECAST 2461) 'OUTTA MY ROOM'

DOC: No jumping to conclusions, I mean, this Jerónimo guy is probably shitting us…
DICK: Just read it.
DOC: Okay… 'I hear this sound above me. I look up and it's Charlotte Hardey, in her PJs, really high, hanging on to the solar panels. If she let go she'd fall flat at my feet.'
DICK: How did she get on the roof?
DOC: He says he yelled up at her not to jump, but the generator was too loud, he couldn't tell if she heard. So he goes inside to turn it off, and by the time he's come back out, she's gone.
DICK: He's making it up.
DOC: Hope so. I mean, we'll report it to the producers, just in case…
DICK: Oh, look…
DOC: Oh my giddy aunt.
DICK: So he's maybe not as concerned as he sounded, since he's also taking bets on whether 'suicide girl' will try again. What a charmer. I hope they hurry up and fire him.

Thirty-Four

So they'll go all the way. Nothing is sacred. Not a mother's death, not the sadness around her last resting place. Just go ahead, turn it into a ghoulish cartoon, into reality television. Charlotte could scream out to viewers, expel her outrage across the airwaves – she pictures her fury rucking up the land and sea, a tsunami of disgust. If people could only understand, could imagine their most delicate memories hollowed out and filled with filth, they would want to bleach this villa, this island, off the face of the earth.

The housemates are fearful. She watches them drum their feet nervously on sun-loungers, drink like fishes and talk about the pressure in this game, how it's driving them crazy. 'Oh, it's messed up,' Shelly is saying. 'He fell quite a way.' They don't know the half of it. The ropes moved of their own accord, and he was far more badly injured than they saw.

Heidi touches her scar, barely healed, a blemish on her perfect skin. Who is next? Charlotte can sense their revulsion, their reluctance to set foot in the escape room. At last they feel as terrified as she does. Yet, even now, some of the talk is about how to manage the situation and try to be safe, rather than a straight boycott. Aside from it being where the food appears, the sinking floor is central to the show. If they don't do the challenges, how will finalists emerge? It has been weeks since a new contestant arrived by speedboat, so this must be the home stretch.

Bugs, skeletons, cobra tattoos in Memphis – they run through her mind like a ghost train – Mak's yell as the line of light narrowed on the rising water, the dead-fish smell that lingered for days, the lurching USA states and blood running from Heidi's nose, then this sick riff on her mum's woodland burial. It was the version in her nightmares, drained of colour, denying the beech leaves were ever luminous green and rustling, snuffing out the mauve-breasted wood pigeons. And the webs... an attempt to make the drifting spider threads she must have mentioned – perhaps in a single message to the school counsellor or someone – ugly and malevolent, thinking they could scare her.

Then there was the hum. No mistake, this time. It was layered on top, an extra dash of horror. That they knew about it pulls her to pieces.

There are five lines of wispy cloud, like fingernail-scratches across the sky. The housemates get louder as they become inebriated. Charlotte nurses a beer, leaning on the railing and looking across the beach, still strewn with scratchy driftwood and storm-mess. When she thinks about Asher's face turning strawberry-red, his drowned gulps, fingers useless against the rope, she can't help wondering why they did it to him and not her. Why was she allowed to climb safely to the ground? What the others didn't see, and don't want to believe, is the way the web basically shook Asher through a gap and then half-strangled him. It was almost spiteful, the way it was done. Every room is skewed towards her personal nightmares, yet it was Asher lying there with a broken leg. She takes a swig of beer. If they want to hurt her, why don't they just do it?

The bottle slips through her fingers, stopped by the wooden rail. Of course, he was trying to help her at the time. Is this a pattern she has missed? Mak was giving her a hand, and so was Heidi, albeit briefly. She looks over her shoulder at the housemates who are left. Brash, faux-sweet Pacey, Spike – openly mean and thick as rawhide – the contortionist, the chef, and the Colombian model who is so disdainful of Charlotte that they have barely exchanged two words.

It is a warm evening but she finds herself shivering at the thoughts crystallising in her mind. They are picking off her allies, but she has never been scratched. Why?

Is it possible she is being saved for later, like a gladiator in ancient Rome, set aside for the biggest beasts, the bloodiest showdown? Her heart judders into action, and she slinks away to the furthest corner of the terrace, as far as possible from the escape room. The hibiscus flowers mist their honey towards a pair of circling butterflies. As usual, her thoughts seem far-fetched, impossibly sinister. But remembering how it sounded when Asher fell, the cry shaken from his throat, makes everything real again.

Across the pool, the housemates are talking about shows where contestants have had painful or gross-out experiences. *Naked Down a Mine. Fifty Days in the Jungle, Deathbed Life-Swap,* and a dozen more she has never heard of. She remembers watching similar shows herself on obscure, tacky channels, eating pizza with Tamsin and Luka, distracted by the tinkle of some tramp playing her piano three storeys down. In these tricksy shows, people's nearest and dearest were replaced with face-matched lookalikes, or they signed up to marry someone chosen by viewer voting, or to win mystery plastic surgery specified by their partner. Charlotte often ended up watching through her fingers as men and women on survival shows cut their feet on volcanic rock, ate eyeballs or swam through flooded underground chambers. *Oh right* – went the thought process – *they're actually going to let that snake bite her. Oh right, the guys are going without water, isn't that dangerous?* Then there would be helicopters airlifting people away, contestants tumbling out and weeping on the presenter's shoulder, 'Man, that was tough. Hardest thing I've ever had to do.' And everything was fine again.

She has been prepared, inoculated by all those little shots of horror. She can tell from their conversation that her housemates are the same. 'They're making it tougher,' Spike is saying, 'that's the way it goes.' Everyone assumes Asher is now receiving medical attention, and he might not even kick up a fuss, once he's bandaged and handed a microphone for his moment in the sun. People want to see bravery, and to whine would be to throw away all the gifts the show might bestow. Charlotte yearns to watch the aftermath, to sneak a viewing on the maintenance guy's television. Asher deserves to get something out of this – all the acting jobs his heart desires – and when he does, the natural balance will be restored. It's a deal with the devil that everyone understands: you take what they hurl at you, then your stock gets a boost. Only now does it become clear that she is as guilty as anyone; she had no sympathy for the people on these shows. The things she watched, never once leaping from her seat in alarm, getting on the phone to the studio, and complaining that their treatment of contestants was outrageous. If you are watching a screen, no empathy is required. Maybe that's the appeal.

'Sit the hell down, Charlotte, you're making me nervous.' She looks over to where Pacey and Spike are dangling their legs in the pool, and realises she has been pacing around, carrying her unspoken monologue up and downstage. The smell of moist decking awakens her to the present moment. Nervous? This whole thing is making her a wreck. If she really is their prize gladiator, penned up in anticipation of the big showdown, what can they possibly have in store?

The door creaks as she shifts it open a crack. *Ajar*. It is very late, no one around, but that is not to say she won't hear the sickening grind of shutters, the room sucking back its furniture, ready to morph into a new nightmare. She gathers the clothes she needs, plus her pillow and sheets, and drags them quickly through the living area. Her bedroom has become a rat trap, and this way she'll never again have to set foot on that treacherous metal floor.

These kitchen areas look different at night, cleaning bots gliding around like stingrays on the seabed, producing little venom-squirts of bleach. It won't be the most comfortable set-up, especially with the lack of curtains and potential to be disturbed by late-night revels, nevertheless she dumps her bedding around the armchair in the cosy corner.

At this point a thought occurs: even though the others have spread out, there should still be a spare room somewhere. In fact, it will be Asher's room, the one down the corridor by the ping-pong area. Silent in her Jimmy Choo slippers, she climbs a metal staircase onto the next level, turning the corner onto a windowless landing. She tries the handle to his bedroom. It doesn't give. There is no lock, no key. It must have been sealed automatically. They have thought of this, of course. No chance of switching rooms.

As she turns back, feeling her way along the wall, something catches under her throat. It is cold, rubbery, like a plastic-coated wire, and her forward motion means that it digs in. A pinch on her windpipe. A single, seismic throb. It tightens. Her scream is hot breath barely laced with sound, her neck seizing, snappable as the stem of a glass. Too dark to see the cable's origin, she flails upwards and finds more, a sort of wide loop that her fingers wrench down and away, and once it is off she crouches, as though in a tunnel, and blunders down the creaking steps, slipping, seeing sparks, the night crackling with terror. Sweat streams down her face and her lungs burn, and she does not stop until she is outside panting in the moonlight, pure disembodied heartbeat. The infinity pool burbles innocently to itself, smelling of chlorine, of disinfectant.

This is how they will do it.

Because the other thing about reality shows is that they can't shake off an association with suicide. Networks are forced to offer counselling to contestants, who struggle with the intense scrutiny that follows. She closes her eyes and sees herself in the yellow dress on screen, talking weirdly about fir trees, staying apart from the others. Then there was that mad dash that landed her in a stormy sea – on the dinghy that *just so happened* to be there. She has played her part perfectly, has fallen neatly into their trap.

They'll do it with some cord dangling in the night. A tragic accident – she must have been playing saboteur again and digging out the electrics, the narrator will say – or maybe they'll spin it more simply, lassoing her so she is lifted by the neck up to a simple light fitting, toes floating ballerina-style, just above the floor, even though nobody expected her to go this far... She hugs her legs on the decking, shuddering in time to her heartbeat. It's the last domino falling, the mental health end-of-the-road. There will be a scandal, apologies from the network, outcry, a princess-of-hearts moment on social media, and ultimately – so ultimately – case closed.

Thirty-Five

Anylocks have hit a million sales. They are delighted with their unusual, off-beat new influencer, so bold as to make a show of herself at the governor's party. A dozen celebrity feeds carry pictures of silvery hair above perfect folded wings, Tamsin's short stature ideal for showing it off.

Funny how being 'up to the task' implies the need for height. She lives in a world of the high and mighty, of aiming high and reaching for the stars. Language doesn't favour the short, just as fortune doesn't favour TunnelFairy, though everyone who takes a selfie with her seems to find their wishes coming true. The eco-jewellery maker who created her charm bracelet has now been appointed to make a thousand of them for the Emir of Qatar, and every collaborating influencer has seen their follower count go through the roof. Rollo's quip about rubbing her hair for good luck seems to keep causing ripples, doing her image no harm at all. Tamsin might be stuck, sleepless every night as she tries to work out her next move, but TunnelFairy is going places.

Anylocks now values her to the tune of a higher fee-per-post, a personal driver, a part-time security guy and a second image consultant, much to Dee's distress.

'I don't understand why they would bring someone else in… do you?' She has been following her client around all morning, demanding to know where she has fallen short.

Until she opened the door to him, Tamsin was happy to share in this disapproval of a superfluous extra stylist. But when she saw him standing there, grinning brilliantly, it wrung an unexpected joy from her heart.

'Joss,' he held out a hand.

'I remember.'

In daylight, the American's clean-shaven cheeks made her think of a chestnut fresh from its case.

'Small world, the Republic,' they both said, almost at the same time, and then he ambled inside and took charge, bringing up a calendar of appointments on her digital wall.

Currently he is brewing some sort of cleansing herbal tea, guaranteed to clear up her vodka headache, something his step-mum swears by, apparently, with nettle and fennel. He takes a Tupperware container out of his satchel, full of papery teabags. Emergency tea is not the sort of thing people tend to carry around in the Republic. She doesn't mean to stare, but questions raise themselves like the hairs on the back of her neck.

Joss gives off an efficient, slightly hippy vibe. He wears fabric trousers so loose they could be yoga pants, and a leather pendant nudges at his shirt collar. In different clothes he could be a businessman, an accountant, almost anything. On his bag there is a Stanford University pin, and she tries to picture him as a student. According to films, American colleges distribute people into tribes, so would he be nerdy, arty, smart, rebellious… a hard-ass? He seems too watchful and quiet to be a bully, though perhaps he was bullied himself because of this, or for being the wrong colour, or for doing things like bringing his own tea. As he pours the hot water, he catches her eye and she is yanked out of her trance, still uncertain what it is about him that is making her so curious.

'So TunnelFairy,' he says, stirring a cup of clear, greenish liquid. 'I've caught up with your story. Great segue from model-with-a-science-degree into full-fat mystical, if you'll excuse the f-word.'

'Mystical?'

'Rollo saying you're good luck? The unicorn?'

Foamy droplets fall from the cloth as he wrings it out, and an uneasiness spreads through her insides. How did she not see this until now? They've untwisted her ironic nickname and made her into a face-value fairy, and she has helped the whole thing along. For a moment she is unbalanced, grasping at the air for something to hold onto. He passes her a mug and, grateful, she lets the dusty steam of the sap-like drink ease the tension from her face.

'And rescuing the Baltimore kids…' he goes on. 'How did you pull that off? I mean – what a vote-winner! It was old-school heroism… with cameras on standby.'

'Vote-winner? It wasn't a ploy for popularity, Joss. The whole thing was a fluke.'

'Sorry,' he seems to wrestle with his expression of sharp glee, which spikes one last time – 'You sure?' – before subsiding. 'In the Republic you can't take anything for granted.'

Putting aside the brief hope that she might have found someone even marginally on her wavelength, she drifts towards the window, where marshmallow-pink clouds scud across a sea of light. Joss follows her, taking a vape device from his shirt pocket.

'So... you're an engineer, right?' He says it with faint bemusement, as though acknowledging a small but weighty elephant in the room.

'Tunnel engineer.'

He nods, taking a puff. 'And this is a side hustle? Not that I blame you. A few months here really helps with the mortgage, huh?'

She meets his look, as if affirming his suspicion. Let him think she is after the money, the thousands in Luvcoin that sponsors are raining down around her.

'What is that smell?' It is familiar and comforting, with a tinge of wrongness.

'This?' He holds up the vape. The scent is like something caramelised, with a hint of soap. 'It's supposed to be "bacon frying," though it can't really compare. I went veggie and it's the only thing I really miss.'

'Didn't you have a plate of meat at the party?' There were those pink bendy slices being carved from the slightly-too-geometric hog roast, dripping with honey glaze.

'Oh, that was lab-grown.' He offers a disarming smile. 'So long as nothing goes to an abattoir on my behalf, I'm good.'

As she recalls, he had quite a lot of faux-ham in his roll at the party, somehow maintaining an appetite despite those freaky Rollo-faced waiters. On the sofa, a couple of outfits are laid out in starch-wrap.

'These are for this evening?'

'No, tomorrow,' he says. 'A photoshoot down by the harbour. This thousand-berth cruise ship called the *Midas* is docking and it's quite a sight – painted gold from top to bottom.'

'Bit on the nose, isn't it?'

Joss laughs. 'In the Republic, all wealth is good wealth.' He proceeds to tell a tale about the owner of the ship, and by the time they are leaving for the evening's premiere she is starting to understand why the Republic is seen as a haven for tax evaders and money launderers, people who make use of a stable cryptocurrency to veil their deals in mystery. When they go outside, the evening is like a warm, wet flannel on her face, almost as though she is re-emerging into the Caribbean from a colder, more calculating world. She ducks her head into the limo, hungry to know more, but Joss has switched to the flimsier subject of hairstyles and accessories. The aftertaste of the tea is astringent in her mouth. He has a job to do, after all, and she is his client.

Her head lolls against the leather and, staring out at the scenery, she mentally flicks away the pink princess annexes, the helipads and the golden lions on gateposts; she shoots down the drones and unplugs the hologram hounds. Let one big wave come along and wash all this crap into the sea.

Even if she wasn't beholden to a sponsor, Tamsin would still need to keep posting. The Republic's security policy requires you to share what you are doing whenever your devices indicate you are awake. Otherwise there is a fine or, for habitual offenders, eventual deportation.

The harbour provides an opalescent, slightly oily backdrop, punctured by a diving cormorant. Tamsin's outfit is baby-blue, slipping off one shoulder. As she poses with the golden bulk of the vessel moored behind her, the photographer becomes frustrated, accusing her of being on autopilot, her eyes not focusing where they should. 'In profile,' he calls. 'Left foot forward, turn a fraction towards the ship.' But how is she supposed to concentrate? The situation with Charlotte could be going critical, and she's had no luck getting anywhere near her. Good fortune flits around in her wake, like a tantalising butterfly, settling on every head but hers. Though of course it is ridiculous, thinking of it this way. The cold, hard essence of the matter is that she – Tamsin Wilde – is not smart enough to come up with a fix.

A woman in coral-print leggings approaches with the confidence of someone who is supposed to be there, and a plastic-smelling, almost comedic microphone – like a foam orange on a stick – is thrust so close to Tamsin's mouth that she could bite it.

'TunnelFairy, how stoked am I to find *you* here? How

are you doing today?' It is a lifestyle blogger, bouncing hopefully on her rainbow trainers. The photographer groans and replaces his lens cap.

Beneath them, the sea sucks at the jetty and there is the smell of salt-crusted wood, serrated barnacles creeping upwards with each wave. Joss is waiting by the car, his hand flashing open as he gesticulates on a phone call. It is high time she got back to him.

'Excuse me—'

'I've gotta ask — what do you think of Rollo's vlog today?'

'Haven't seen it, sorry.'

Before she can slip away, the blogger grabs her wrist. A tablet is thrust out, and Rollo appears on screen, walking along and sipping whatever drink he is currently promoting, his speech diminished by the air-rush of cars. 'Apparently she can't act, either,' he is saying. 'What is she actually famous for? Getting mistaken for a model. That's it, isn't it? Who knew you could make a career out of that?'

Slap, slap, slap, the salt water seems to applaud this entertainment, but Tamsin hands back the screen coldly, and says:

'Who knew you could make a career out of your dad owning a gym?'

This elicits an explosive giggle, the interviewer curling inward as though to gather this precious material into her devices. Tamsin's veins are full of fizz. The small, sensible part of her knows there is no point riling Rollo, not while she is still on Republic soil. But another voice says, 'fuck it'. Her new security guard is reassuringly burly and she feels comfortable climbing into the car's cream leather interior beside him, her two stylists sitting opposite.

Joss joins her on the terrace, where she is watching the sea stick to the sky, delicately green before it ripens into sunset.

'It's just a reaction,' he soothes, taking the tablet from her hands. 'What do you expect if you go to someone's Me Day party and your followers grow more than theirs?' There has, of course, been a certain amount of cruel commentary online about whether or not she is pretty enough to be mistaken for a model. Rollo has fed the trolls, or rather, given them a taste for her.

'It's just so… petty.'

'I know. But don't take it personally. When Rowena made headlines with her self-defence channel earlier this year, he banned her from the Republic *and* published some embarrassing photos from when she was a kid.'

'And that was just sibling rivalry.' She weighs a pebble in her hand. 'Did she retaliate?'

'Rowena? Oh, definitely, though I can't say how. She's a bit more crafty than her brother.'

Tamsin thinks back to the angular, attractive woman who showed her Rollo's faux-library, kept her guessing at every turn, and ended up in most of the night's pictures.

'More strategic?'

'More creative, certainly. Whatever the truth is, she absolutely nails it as a bisexual icon, and did you hear about her gladiatorial-style games? All those poor suckers who'd do anything for the follows…' He blows a cloud of vape towards the sea. 'Though if I was styling Rowena, I'd be telling her she's on a knife edge.'

'Why?'

'It's her brand. Fashion tasers and pseudo martial arts, and finding people's 'crumple buttons'… When does self-defence go too far?'

'When is it just… offence?' Tamsin plays along.

'Yeah,' he agrees, laughing. 'Everything she does causes a sort of horrified stir, and Rollo doesn't help, letting her chuck people into the sea at parties when it suits him. She sells a lot of merch, though.'

Curious now, Tamsin gets her specs to project Rowena's profile, which shows the younger Boone in some fetish-inspired sportswear, lying on a judo mat with one knee pointing sharply to the ceiling. A message flashes up: 'You are now following Rowena Boone' and Tamsin swears under her breath. Scroll through enough pictures and the algorithm is triggered. She opts out, realising, much to her surprise, that her own follower count now exceeds Rowena's.

She hoists herself onto the railing, wanting to continue this analysis, to hear Joss's thoughtful, musical voice sizing up and ranking the Republic's big hitters. It was nice waiting with him before this morning's photoshoot, eating frozen yogurt by the harbour. Beyond the rental boats, the water looked dusty, opaque as paint, and they learned from a local that a dead coral reef had been ground up to extend the breakwater. Probably just jellyfish there now. They swapped ideas on what to do about them. Joss reckoned he would get celebrity chefs to fry them up, offer incentives to rave about the results, then there would be a fishing frenzy and everyone would be eating jellyfish soup or sushi or candy. A tad underhand, bribing the chefs, but at least it was a solution.

What troubles her is how someone like Joss can be satisfied trotting round after influencers, having to fuss about what shoes they wear or whether they post a product shot at the right time of day. The job doesn't match the personality, and she wants to know why. Unlike her other stylist, he has almost no stars in his eyes.

'All this. Don't you ever find it…' she hesitates. He looks at her, and already he has understood what she means. She bites her lips together. Luka's voice chimes contemptuously in her head. *Stay in character, you dolt.* Typical if she let her guard down in front of an attractive man and ruined things.

But is there any point keeping secrets if she can't think of a way to accomplish her mission? She gazes out to sea, picturing the unseen island, a passing heaviness in her feet as she puts herself into Brunel's shoes, frowning as he might have frowned across some unbridgeable river or gorge. Earlier, a chance conversation revealed that Joss has heard of her favourite engineer, but only – strangely – because of a book he had as a child: *The Little Book of British Ghost Stories*. It included that old yarn about the two skeletons, a riveter and his boy, being found within the double hull of the Great Eastern steamship when it was scuttled. Not actually true, though plenty of workmen died on other projects, drowning or being blown up in tunnels, Brunel occasionally risking his own life trying to save them.

'Imagine you're him,' Joss said, as her heels dug into the salt-eaten decking and she sidled reluctantly towards the photographer. 'Big golden ship, newly launched... you're looking pumped.' Silly, of course, since Brunel would have just tucked his thumbs into his waistcoat and cast his features into the ultimate neutral expression. Even as she rolled her eyes at Joss, she took quiet joy from having someone in her corner again, knowing at least a sliver of the real her.

Berries are growing beyond the balcony, a faint aroma of rotting fruit wafting from the beach. Just as she is stealing a glance at him, Joss's eyebrows shoot up.

'Good news,' he says. 'Rollo is trying to destroy you.'

'He's what?' She can barely grasp the tablet as he hands it over. The thought is like acid in her mind: *he knows*. Rollo's quip about her being mistaken for a model cut worryingly close to the bone, but it was not what she feared most. Why didn't she keep her mouth shut? Now he is probably questioning her entire story.

The clip is only seconds long. She recognises the lurid orange colour-scheme of the life-blogger's website. Damn that woman – she will have made everything sound as provocative as possible, and now Rollo has hit back with another vlog. It begins with a shot of his party, purple lights picking out the rattan chairs on the terrace, a burst of chatter. Tamsin's face appears at an unflattering angle – where was the camera? – and Rollo is heard talking about her mum. He asks: 'And who's your pa?' to which she replies: 'I don't know.' Her fingers whiten around the tablet.

'Wait a second,' she says. 'That's been edited.' One cocktail is not enough to wipe her memory: there was some other question in between, and he has snipped it out. Now Rollo is with the interviewer, speaking into the big foam microphone. She plays him Tamsin's jibe about his dad owning a gym, and he holds up his hands, offering a crocodile grin.

'Hey, she's got me there. I had a head start, actually knowing who my pa is.'

Only now is it dawning on Tamsin what he is trying to suggest. He is beefing this up into a story, and the comments are already building. It is almost familiar – this sense of someone taking a part of her and twisting it to suit their own ends. In this case it is so ridiculous that her fingers ache to flick it away. Rollo, who has benefited so much from his famous family, seems to think he can mock her lack of pedigree – in this day and age. Yet the internet, of course, is serving up enough loyal fans to chime in with his catty remarks.

Dee rushes through the French doors, sweating lightly in her ivory suit.

'Crisis stations,' she gasps. 'I'm sorry darling, he's had a clear run at the gossip sites…'

Joss leans on the railing beside Tamsin. 'I think it's fine,' he lifts his shades, regarding her. 'If anything, he's shot himself in the foot, trying to make this into a slur.'

Dee detonates. 'Fine? Are you out of your mind?'

She glares at them, but Tamsin is almost steaming with

relief. Part of her wants to laugh – a light, wild bark – at how nuts this all is. The maddest part is that Rollo knows nothing about her father; he has simply taken a punt on what he hopes is a sensitive issue.

While Maeve appears, sporadically, in Tamsin's online footprint, there is no sign of her dad. He was an Icelandic guy who met her mum at a party spread across the compartments of the London Eye. The day after, when Maeve tried to call him, the number didn't work. Maybe he was married, or it was a one-night thing. Her mum would hardly have given it a second thought if not for the discovery, a whole three months later, that she was pregnant. In Tamsin's opinion, only someone who revered fate to a ridiculous degree would decide to keep the baby. Yet Maeve did, and she decorated her second-hand pram with festival wristbands.

Iceland is a small country, and Tamsin did make a few attempts to find her dad, particularly during her teens. But a first name and Maeve's vague description (soft hair, owl-like, frowny) were not enough. Nowadays, having heard some of her mum's remarks with an adult ear, she is no longer troubled by her failed efforts. He has fluttered away into her past, just a disturbance of air.

'Are you gonna set Rollo straight and shut him up?' Joss says, twirling his vape-pen.

The strength seeps from her limbs. It was a clumsy shot in the dark, on the governor's part, but one which, to her annoyance, could potentially find its mark. The world has no right to open such a long-closed door.

'Can I borrow this?' She takes his tablet and switches to

her LOVE account. It is already flooding with supportive messages and stories of lost relations. *I have no daddy, either*, writes Martha, 13, from Wisconsin. It is sweet and heart-warming. But even if her followers approve, it is as though she has been given a makeover without her consent. If she tells the truth, she will be sharing something that does not belong to TunnelFairy.

As though to underline this thought, someone posts a picture they have found of Maeve wearing her tiny 'festival shorts' and being held horizontally by about six young men. Tamsin's jaw tightens. She swings her legs over the rail, leaping down to the scrubby sand beneath.

It has been some time since she last looked up her mum's Social account. Right now her status is: *My first cup of English tea in a month*. Maeve has been in India, and must have emerged from her yoga retreat. The first thing she will see, when she plugs back into the world, is her daughter gone viral, in crazy clothes and crazier hair, on the red carpet or hooking arms with DJs and fashion designers. Tamsin has no wish to witness the level of excitement this will generate.

In many of these photos, Maeve resembles a version of her daughter, only stretched into someone thinner and more energetic, with dry hair that holds a soft curl, and a big crescent-moon smile that could outlast the latest of late shifts. Her history is written in these images, photos blurring with lower-res cameras, with the raw, primal blush of youth. There is a feverish rhythm to the way Tamsin swipes, until she reaches her mum's famous collection of celebrity selfies.

Even narrowing it down to the right date-range leaves a lot of choice. She discards one after another. They are too old, too young, too married, too famous, not famous enough, not interested in women. But this last one has a ring to it. An old rocker. A household name, even for most of the LOVE generation, and his reputation certainly fits the bill. Sweat trickles into her eye, and she knuckles it furiously. Maeve looks so happy beside him. She looks ecstatic in all these photos, and beautiful, too. Bringing these people filtered water in the green room and leading them to the Pyramid Stage made her a somebody, and she was good at her job. Glastonbury begged her not to leave, even when she was treading its eight-mile circumference with a baby in a sling.

The rest is easy. Her smartface lines up the gossip sites and creates an anonymous sender address. It is enough to caption the image with names – the date is about right, a year or so before her birth – and the message streaks away, like a cord that releases all Tamsin's adrenaline at once. What has she done? With her blood boiling, it seemed like a good idea. Now she is not so sure. No more than two minutes pass before she hears gasps from within the condo, then the smash of a dropped glass.

Her feet take her onwards, down to the sea, and she tries to match her breathing to its waves. Driftwood is all around, bleached bone-white and cracking. The sun spills diamonds onto the water and she opens her eyes wide, losing herself in the salt-sting of too much dazzle. Rollo will discover how wrong he was to say she can't act. All his petty remarks clump together in her mind: so pathetic, like schoolyard bullying. She leans down to the surf, as the wave retreats, and her fingers close around a smooth, pale stone. What Rollo doesn't understand, geotechnics being outside his experience, is that a substrate under pressure does not always crumble. Sometimes it crystallises.

Thirty-Six

Charlotte can trace patterns through the dew. She finds an imprint of the hammock on her arm, the skin pressed into diamonds. It was almost dawn by the time she stopped shivering and fell asleep. The sun-loungers on the terrace would have been more comfortable, but the house cannot be trusted. So instead she is here, crunching stray grains of sand between her teeth.

Now there is this balmy Caribbean dawn, the smell of people toasting croissants in a luxury villa, all colluding in a show of normality. She needs to remember Asher's bloodless leg, and the feeling of a cord across her neck. She must be strong and stay away from the house. They can't reprogramme the palm trees to throttle her.

Shelly returns from her morning run, and Charlotte sits up, the hammock doing its best to fling her off.

'Shelly?'

The woman slows. The hesitant eye contact tells Charlotte everything she needs to know about her current status. A second ago it seemed so reasonable to ask someone to go and check the ceiling by Asher's room. Not that the wire could have been imaginary, but there is a chance that stormy weather caused the panels to shift and let it slip down. Or Asher himself might have dislodged it – he once punched through one of the flimsy plasterboard walls in the snug. Charlotte's lips part, but the request won't come out, and now the contortionist looks pained. She offers up a wan smile, then jogs up the steps.

There must be others outside, perhaps having breakfast, because greetings are called. Charlotte hears her name, then Shelly's nasal purr: 'She's doing her own thing,' more indifferent than unkind. Someone laughs, and then it sounds like Spike who says, 'Get with the programme.'

Charlotte slumps, hair snagging painfully as it escapes her bun. It should bother her how unbothered she is about all the viewers out there, seeing and judging her. But they are no longer cheery emoji faces, plush hearts and warm words; they have cooled into something hard and unforgiving, a bleak ice-scape of eyes. For so long she has invited people into her life, perfectly aware that every fan would own a piece of it, part-ownership of her self. Fame was always worth the price. But if she goes rogue and acts out-of-character, they feel ripped off. These people thought they knew her, but now they're getting a different Charlotte. Frankly, the deal has soured for her, too. She swats at any camera drones that come close enough.

The house looks peaceful from here, no hint of a darker motive behind the show. Could someone – for some unimaginable reason – actually want her dead? Think of the outcry, if they succeeded. There would be no second season. The name of the franchise – perhaps even the studio – would be scorched beyond repair. They'd generate short-term notoriety for the show, but surely that would be outweighed by the tidal wave of negativity that would crash down upon the entire industry.

From here, the neatly sawn edges of the decking are visible, the tang of pool-chlorine reaching her nose. So much effort has gone into developing *Outta My Room* as a profitable brand. As Tamsin would say, it doesn't add up.

What studio is it, anyway? She looked it up online, a film house based in the Republic. Republi-KA, or something? She recognised its logo from the gladiatorial games earlier this summer – an island-based production she was glad she avoided. Charlotte rubs the chill from her toes, so chalky and numb they no longer feel like her own. The shadows that have danced in her mind – of people who might hold a grudge – begin to sharpen. A producer would be a likely candidate, someone with control over the show's format. The only producer she might have pissed off is the one who signed Rollo and herself for a chat show following the *Six on the Beach* win, which had to be swiftly canned. The other possibility, which she is reluctant to contemplate, is that this is some scheme concocted by Rollo himself, some ridiculously disproportionate revenge.

She rises, her bare feet sinking into lukewarm sand. It messes with her worldview to think that Tamsin might be right about exes, that all bonds should be neatly severed. Rollo, with his natural charisma and star-quality, his neat physique and aversion to sweat, a delicate soul airbrushing life to remove anything ugly or troubling. It could be refreshing. If a waiter was rude to her, Rollo would be instantly and publicly in touch with the restaurant via LOVE, and five minutes later the server would be gone, replaced by someone with a sunnier disposition. There were no tedious bits in films, because Rollo would skip them. *Life is too short for bads*, he liked to post, assuming people would read it the way he meant it.

She has always tried to think fondly of Rollo, but was she too quick to excuse his behaviour as Governor, too relieved her rejection had not harmed his popularity? The more she considers it, the more it seems likely he would have the means to create something like *Outta My Room*. With a few words in the right ears, he could even have made her other work dry up. A spasm goes through her neck as she bites down on the idea.

From one of the palm trees, a bird dives towards the terrace, perhaps for breakfast crumbs. The aluminium windowsills are painted pink, the same hue as her lipstick. It is so long since she last saw herself in a mirror: the smiling woman who buffed suntan lotion into her skin and flashed that lacy purple bra, the bubbly reality show contestant. At last the truth deals her a stinging slap; how did she miss this gigantic house-sized clue? The first time Rollo clapped eyes on her was mid-show. It was the setting for their relationship – and it's the perfect backdrop for his revenge.

Would he really do this? It seems like an age since they sat on the ridge amid that sunset haze of pollen, Rollo telling her he didn't love himself quite enough, taking her finger and using it to trace the sun, the stick-figure, the spoon-sized bird on his bicep, like a bas-relief. Since that talk, that spillage of secrets, the hieroglyphs must have doubled. It strikes her that this is something more than simple vanity. Loving yourself is an art which, once perfected, makes the world fall at your feet. There is an inner child wandering lost within those warm skin-walls, that boyish self she would see in the few seconds after he awoke but before he remembered himself, a spirit desperately trying to please the bigger Rollo, the governor, made of gold and charcoal and shades of his father, who promises a heaven of health and happiness. All he has to do is believe in himself – in everything he says and does – and he will be invincible.

But how does that song go? Devotee and deity… can never become one. There will always be childhood echoes of his dad congratulating Adrian for making the soccer team, Rollo watching the two of them and feeling the glass of milk tremble in his skinny hand. Yes – she thinks – he must make himself forget certain things. He has continued to this day, removing anyone or anything that might remind him of those feelings. Shutting people up, throwing people out. What it truly means when he 'Bermudas' someone if – God forbid – the rumours are true. He is the governor, and he won't tolerate anyone who makes him feel like a lesser being.

Her wholeness eluded him, too; he only ever wanted certain parts of her. Strange that he managed to be so consciously cruel in the interior design of the villa, with the rainbow-hued Bolivian throws, sea-creature kitchen accessories and Venice Beach mural – bringing to mind her few rock-bottom nights of sleeping on graffiti-caked, urine-scented benches. Rollo's attention to detail doesn't normally extend much beyond his own personal space, even if this space itself is immaculate, his very aura constantly groomed and honed.

In truth, she doesn't know what to believe, but the idea has taken root. One way or another, he is behind this. The reality show format is the giveaway, and she is an idiot for not seeing it sooner. A tremor runs through her bones, and at once she is lightheaded, her brain taut as an overfilled balloon. She looks at her hands, the fingers even longer and thinner than usual, the nails a mess. They tingle with the desire for violence.

It is good Tamsin has other things going on – she is grateful for that now. The last thing Charlotte wants, knowing what she does, is her best friend blundering into the middle of all this.

Thirty-Seven

Tunnel Fairy, you rock. We love you. We love his music. That's the beauty of the rumour mill — no truth required. Hearsay goes in and headlines come out. Even on respectable news sites, people absorb what they want and discard the rest, conditioned to act as their own selective algorithm. When everything else is personalised, why not truth?

Nothing has been more of a hit than today's photo, shared from a magazine site for extra authenticity. A man with tan-furrowed skin, smeary sunglasses and the glint of a lone earring almost lost in the graininess of the image, his arm around the waist of Maeve Wilde, fresh-faced Events Coordinator at Glastonbury. They stand on trampled, almost fermented grass, luminous with light through tent-canvas. The photo is having quite an impact, and Tamsin did not expect all these aftershocks. She endures a gut-ripple of fear every time someone asks a question. It was meant to be just one post, nothing more. No follow-ups.

The estate of the rock star in question denies it, of course, though interestingly they do so in a muted, *not to our knowledge*, kind of statement. The safest thing is for her to deny the rumour, too, both to prevent any helpful relatives offering her a DNA test and to preserve what is left of her mum's dignity. This is the biggest worry. Maeve could be fine with it, or she might be furious – there's no way to tell. Tamsin is geared up to rant alongside her if necessary: these gossip magazines, can you believe them? What are they implying, that her mum slept with every musician who felt lonely in his trailer?

Or maybe it is a badge of honour to have caught the eye of someone so famous, and she will be in no rush to set the record straight. His reputation is doing all the work, making it seem likely he could have fathered a child and not known. But people are never kind to women, and it would kill Tamsin to see her mum subjected to the sort of vicious trolling that Luka suffered, or worse.

When she thinks about the possible outcomes of what she has done, and how little it has achieved, she can understand why Dee dropped a tray of cocktails when she saw it, leaving the kitchen still sticky despite the efforts of its cleaning bots. Tamsin freely admitted she was responsible for sending the picture, anonymously of course. 'You don't need to look at me like that,' she said, 'I know it was rash.'

Heat builds beneath her clothes; she would like to rip them off and dive into the sea. The company that stuck her in a music video last week is exultant, like a prospector unexpectedly striking gold. Some people are too young, they don't remember his music, while others snap back angrily – *timeless*, is what he is. *Old-school*, with all its messy connotations. Joss, who initially feared alienating her long-term followers, now thinks they can make it work. Everyone is talking about the rumour, and she is not even sure what drove her to spread it. Something had to be done. Rollo couldn't be allowed to get away with it, trying to unravel TunnelFairy. There is something distasteful about the way he rolled up his sleeves and reached deep into something she'd created, messing with her diagrams and calculations, interfering in her design. How dare he add insult to the injury he has already caused, the harm he continues to inflict upon her closest friend?

Joss steps through the French doors with a cursory *knock-knock* on the wooden railing. He is holding a pale yellow playsuit, and she shakes her head.

'All these pastel colours are too bloody cute. It's time for a new look, I reckon.'

'Uh, okay, let's circle back to that. Have you checked your feed? If I had a switchboard, it would be lighting up.'

Joss is right: her follower count is off the charts. Tiny avatars beam at her, hurl armfuls of hearts her way. Are these all real people? It's a medley of emojis and symbols, users saying she brought them luck with their driving test or their daughter's oboe recital. She has not checked for ages, but she knows her stylists have set up an algorithm creating personalised responses to anyone who types the word 'luck' in any language, making sure TunnelFairy radiates good vibes. It's silly, but she lets them get on with it.

Some of the messages are ones of reassurance: they say it doesn't matter to them whether the rumours about her dad are true or not, they think she's cool either way. These are the ones that bring an astonished tear to her eye. Before she knows it, she is dictating a reply: 'Relatives are great, but I love my extended family too. Thanks for keeping me going.' The words solidify and are suddenly cast iron across her profile. Did she really just say that?

'Nice,' says Joss.

'Oh,' she waves a hand, puffs out her cheeks to blow away the embarrassment.

'Did you know,' he says, 'that when you go into a guitar shop and pluck a string – say 'D' – every other D-string in the shop will eventually start vibrating?'

The stories come thick and fast, *my mum, my dad, my friend, my stepdad, my aunt*. Charlotte's veneration of her followers always seemed odd, yet it is hard not to feel a certain appreciation for these stories of lost relatives, of single-parent upbringings and lonely child-rearing. Joss is right – it is the longing to be tribal, even across the ether, to resonate with others. You have to pluck the right string.

Nobody else has a story about a famous father, but many remark on how neatly this puzzle-piece seems to fit, as she claims her rightful place in the celebrity landscape. The rumour is like extra-strong concrete poured into her foundations, making TunnelFairy stand firmer. It is getting easier to muffle the tiny, deep-down voice that keeps telling her she's a fraud.

'Dee told me I'd fanned a fire I could easily have extinguished,' she says, and is gratified to hear him laugh.

'Do you think Rollo got to be Governor by putting out fires?' He holds her gaze. His teeth are faintly translucent with internal imperfections, almost like quartz. 'I'll let you get on with breakfast.'

Finding herself strangely lifted, she continues to peel the stubby bananas on her plate. If only she could know what Joss really thinks of her. So often they hit upon the same idea, and the moment is like a struck flint, sparking beautifully between them. But how much of his attention is due to her follower count? If their paths first crossed in some drab London pub, would his soft, redwood eyes slide right past her? What would he make of how solitary she can be, the evenings spent doing her little geometric drawings as she waits for Pip to get back from a night out?

Part-way through breakfast, a message appears on her specs. She feels a shadow fall. It says:

What are you playing at, and why are you still playing?

The message is from an unknown number, yet she does not doubt that it's from Luka. A quick check of his account confirms he is no longer getting trolled, so why can't he leave her alone? Perhaps there is some nugget of annoyance at the way she took over, that she – not he – chose how their wonky love-story should end, her beach house sickly-sweet with roses and forgiveness. She rubs her forehead, picturing the ale-soaked bar of the Pike and Pitcher. This stopped being his project a long time ago. He must be scrutinising the latest rumours on LOVE, watching her step towards an open limousine door amid fawning fans, the champagne nicely chilled. From his perspective, all is lost. He has given up hope of hearing from his adored ex, so he is prodding at Tamsin from afar, grumbling in the dark, letting that old nerve jangle – the one set in motion when Charlotte fell into the arms of a rich boy.

Luka was, of course, looking forward to seeing the governor exposed, knocked down a few pegs once Charlotte told her tale. He is sitting on the lower end of the see-saw, waiting to rise in her affections, hoping to atone for his past mistakes. Or would he just make them all over again? Would he put her ambitions under the microscope, claiming superior knowledge of her true potential? Would he be able to control his natural instinct to be controlling? Tamsin shades her eyes against the sun. From here, it is Luka who looks small. What does he know about the Republic? It is wrong of him to accuse her of playing, no matter how things may look from afar.

She begins to reply, feeling an emptiness that has nothing to do with her uneaten food. Such is her hunger for a pep talk, a little support from home, that she would almost risk a candid conversation. *New plan...* she begins. Then she deletes it. *Right now...* That too is deleted. Her head sinks into her hands. What the hell can she tell him? There is no plan.

Companies are queuing up to give her products for free. She eats the finest meals and has a bulging new wardrobe. A million years ago, when they were planning this, Luka made her hold on to her accidental spike in followers, sensing they could be used as some sort of currency. The more she sees of the Republic, the more this rings true, yet she can't seem to make it pay. What use is all this influence when her friend remains trapped?

Sails and rigging clink against masts as she exits the music film set, where she was cajoled into singing a few lines they will need to autotune thoroughly. Her hair is flyaway thistledown, the sea an extension of her blue-teal iridescence. They dress her up in these outfits, and people snatch photos of her, but why? She hasn't *done* anything. They want a piece of her, and it feels like a physical pull as they take and adore it and claim it as their own.

The yacht club welcomes her with its beach-hut shabby-chic, laced with cigar smoke. All she does these days is change clothes. Who would believe she used to wear the same trackie bottoms for a week, nights included? In her dressing room, she slips off her heels and closes the door, aware of Dee mid-way through a phone call on the balcony.

'But if your client gets on the wrong side of the governor you… manage it, don't you?' her voice rises in pitch with each new retort. A certain tension is apparent in the figure behind the slatted wooden shutters. 'It's not about me. I only wanted to know what his background was… He's so…' In the pause, Tamsin realises her stylist is talking about Joss. The two have been at loggerheads since the dad rumour. 'Sure,' Dee goes on, 'but what client? Who was it? Well, that's frustrating. Yeah, we're on track to get the video done today, and I'll talk to her about the party idea.' Heels strike tiles, and Dee steps back over the door frame. 'Oh, hi, are they looking after you?'

'Yeah, we're done.' Tamsin hesitates, unzipping her dress. 'Were you talking about Joss, just then? I caught a few words.'

Dee smiles and flaps a hand. 'It was nothing, really.'

'I'm curious about him, too.'

She has asked Joss about his background, heard some details of his Seattle upbringing and teacher parents, his crazy Californian camping trips and political marches, plus a spell caring for his younger sister who has spina bifida. He is starting to add up as a person, but not as her stylist. How many knowing looks dare she exchange with him, when he points to some other influencer and picks their story apart? That affair, that breakdown, that juicy little morsel that just so happens to coincide with so-and-so's new product launch. He's a connoisseur of constructed lives… like hers.

The stylist's perfect fuchsia lips drop open as she considers.

'Well, you're right – we should have no secrets. I was just trying to reassure myself, I guess, about his… qualifications? They told me his last client was someone big, though there's a non-disclosure clause slapped on it, so I don't know who it was.'

'Well, what other celebrities use smart-hair?'

'Oh, it wasn't for Anylocks. Most image consultants are freelance.' She takes Tamsin's hands in hers, silky as talcum powder, nails like polished gemstones. 'It's you I'm worried about. You deserve the best.'

She observes her stylist, a pencil-neat person, happiest as a conduit between celebrities. Interesting that Dee should want to check up on Joss, though a lot of it is obviously to do with territory. Tamsin would feel the same if she were making headway with a project only to have some guy swoop in to share the credit.

What was she going to do, take Dee's golf cart to the restaurant, when the stroll is so short and pleasant? There are tiny white flowers creeping between buildings, a faint scent of coconut. She is passing the quiet end of the Strip when it happens, in broad daylight. The guy filming is noticeable because he is walking backwards, holding up a phone to capture the approach of his mate, who strides towards her on a collision course. He looms up: a large man wearing a pale grey t-shirt that says, in very bold type, *Gonna R*pe Ya T-Fairy*. The pavement is narrow, no one around besides a few seagulls. He is not moving fast; she could run, so why don't her legs work? They totter, stiff as wooden pegs. The guy has a fringe of dirty blonde hair peeping from the front of his balaclava, which features a cartoon grin. His shoes are yellowish suede, thick soles the colour of toffee. He stops, opposite, and a low moan is wrung from her as he leans forward, pungent with pit-stains, fat fingers outstretched.

On the edge of hearing, there are other footsteps, as though her terror has attracted onlookers, sharks drawn to blood. Just as her stuck lungs pulse, unable to make a sound, the man stops. Almost robotically he stiffens, swivels round, and marches back the way he came, followed by his companion, who now films the back of the t-shirt: *Euurrr No I'm Not!* He snaps his fingers in delight, both of them cackling, picking up the pace.

She stands in a bubble of shock, ears dulled to the din of shouts, other voices, feet skittering ahead. Her slow mind takes hours to pick apart the scene now taking place further along the pavement. A dozen figures leaping on the two men, one diving for knees so the filmmaker falls, the phone bouncing twice before it is crushed under a white stiletto, just that single *crick* of a screen breaking. Then the voices come nearer. 'Are you okay?' People telling her not to worry, that the footage will never see the light of day. 'We've got you,' they say, giving her hair a friendly pat, a little rub. 'We got you.'

By the time she reaches the restaurant, Dee is outside fidgeting.

'Everything all right, darling?'

'Yes,' she whispers, not quite ready to tell her tale.

Like a slow-acting medicine, the reassurance begins to kick in. People recognise and welcome her, and she distributes smiles like seed to hungry birds. They want to see her resilience, the legendary TunnelFairy positivity, and summoning its appearance seems to be enough to make it real.

All that kicking – the t-shirt man rolled over, obviously feeling it even through his blubber. Just as they drew her away, she heard a security man ask what was going on, the 'dickhead defence' swiftly cited and accepted. When she tells Joss about the incident, the violence, he will never let her out without a bodyguard again. *Mistaken for a model.* It would be the work of a moment for the governor to hire a couple of thugs in an attempt to humiliate her, to underline his insult. She should be freaked out, but instead it feels like something has changed, her aura growing stronger. Is she is simply too well known, now, for Rollo to get away with any of this shit? Her dad is a rock star, after all.

'Skinny champagne!' Dee calls to the waiter. Having received a sales report, she has perked up considerably. Over lunch, they will discuss a partnership between Anylocks and certain fashion designers, who are here along with their models, already picking croutons out of the salad.

A waiter is carving paper-thin slices from a blushing cube of non-animal meat. She glances at Joss, wondering if he will make the connection to where they first met, which must be — unbelievably — a mere fortnight ago. He catches her eye, and nods briefly, smiling. He was right from the start, of course. Popularity is what keeps you safe. She tries to analyse his look. There is complicity there, and respect, but what else? In the mirrored wall she examines the shimmer of powder along her cheekbones, her hair in an ice-blue Nordic plait, almost a crown. Does she have any magic to work upon him?

'Miss Wilde?'

The waiter reassures her that if the menu is too long to read they can use her data to conjure up the perfect meal, a few childhood flavours. Her ears pulse with unheard chatter, and perhaps she is still in shock. This restaurant, these smells and sounds, have just settled around her, making up a new reality. London, and her job, and her mum and Luka are two-dimensional, like a film she once saw. Right now, as she pinches her sunburned wrist, it feels like she has booked too many days of holiday in one place.

There is a lump between her flesh and the polished wood of the seat. Reaching down, she finds a ring, a fiddly little thing between her fingers. It has a chunky diamond set in a swirl of gold. An engagement ring. Dee catches sight of it and lights up.

'Oh, beautiful!'

Joss leans over and takes a quick photo. A couple of the fashion designers notice the ring and start to examine it. 'Is this a very shy proposal?' one jokes, provoking an exchange of awkward sidelong glances. Another takes it from Tamsin's hand. 'This is a Clive T. Auger, a small but excellent studio. I'm sure I've seen this piece before.'

'There!' Joss shows them a post from earlier that morning.

We have retraced our steps in the Republic to no avail... the Wimbledon champion explains, adding that the ring was due to be adjusted, a fraction too large when her boyfriend got down on one knee. No wonder she lost it. Without another word the item is handed back to Tamsin, packaged in a murmur of congratulation. She is vaguely aware of devices flickering, capturing another oddly fortunate moment.

Thirty-Eight

They are stuck behind an overturned pineapple truck on the cross-island road, in a queue of SUVs that absolutely cannot be held up. They have places to be. Every few minutes a car door opens and someone's PA stumbles out to go and harangue the tow-truck driver, or bang the dirty yellow side of the lorry. Closing the windows is not enough to dull the racket of horns, so Tamsin digs out headphones from her bag – big, noise-cancelling earmuffs that some company has provided – and starts ploughing through Gogglers podcasts. They are pretty much the most influential indie commentators on the Republic and, amid the inane chatter, TunnelFairy occasionally gets a mention. Her eyes droop, wanting to close, but she hears the words *Outta My Room* and sits up, stretching her stiff legs into the ample footwell, careful not to kick Joss, who is sitting opposite.

'We came across this blog before, didn't we?' Dick remarks.

'That's right,' says the other presenter. 'He's crew, this guy. Thinks he can sell shit from the show and stay anonymous – he is so busted!'

'Now this stuff about Charlotte on the roof… I think he's making it up. But you've gotta keep an eye on these things, so we've reported it to the producers, just in case…'

Tamsin's hands creep up to the headphones as if she could touch what she is hearing.

'He doesn't actually think she'll jump…'

Her lungs have stopped. The fragrance of the air conditioning is soapy on her palate. What is going on? In an instant, her smartface has performed a search on everything referenced in the podcast, and up pops the blog that Luka found when he searched for the filming location, run by a guy whose name clearly isn't Jerónimo. The headline chills her: *Suicide Girl*. It must be a hoax, an attempt to add some drama to his posts. There is no footage of Charlotte getting onto the roof. More to the point, it is not in her nature. She has never been prone to depression. Still, the words are icicle-sharp on the screen. When the podcast ends, Tamsin almost wishes she never heard it. There is no way to silence the tiny, irascible voice that keeps questioning everything, that whispers about what pressure does to people.

Her body is yanked back – just the car moving on, but it makes her tense spine click. The road is clear, and they pull up at a tower that seems to be made entirely of blue glass, a structure she has seen from across the island with a newly opened viewing platform for tourists. She remains in her trance until the lift doors are swishing open.

'Wait,' she gasps. 'What are we doing here?'

Dee hits the button to hold the lift.

'You're cutting the ribbon, darling, you know that.'

She is, of course, the perfect influencer to open such an innovative building. It smells of new carpet, with glinting screws and pin-thin calk around every fixture, but what are building regulations like in the Republic, and how easily can they be bypassed? Her heart pumps with enough power to send the lift shooting upward, the only direction she can go. The land falls away. There is a lot of air, a lot of sky. From here she can see distant, artificial islands, built to suit the personalities of their owners. Islands that cannibalised other sinking cays, sucking up their sand. Gilded Springs shrinks in the distance, the Turquoise Grand jagged as a tooth. Beyond is a green dot that might be the islet, hardly visible.

There are no other floors until you reach the restaurant and 360-degree bar. The lift ejects them onto the viewing platform, and a waiter comes over with a tray of green cocktails, scenting the air with mint and honey. People line up to meet her, but Joss steers her to one side, to where glass panels hold visitors back from the hundred-metre drop. Someone has left a greasy handprint just below her eyeline. 'Hey,' he whispers, 'something wrong?'

His face is so close she can see the slant-tipped hairs he has shaved, a faint spice lingering around his shirt collar. It would be such bliss to come clean about all her desperate plans, pour out her fears to the last drop – especially this new concern that she might have lost track of Charlotte's state of mind.

When she says nothing, Joss moves a fraction closer and powers down his smartspecs. The proximity alone feels comforting, the warm air between their bodies like a hug. He speaks in the lowest possible voice: 'You've gone way beyond having to take any shit, okay?' he regards her. 'Look, when Roland Boone first made Governor, he was the only game in town. How do you think he's doing this time?'

She shrugs, nonplussed by the digression. Rollo just does whatever the hell he wants, every minute of the day. A yacht in the marina will catch his eye and, before you know it, he is posting a video of himself on board, telling his smartface to locate the owner and purchase it. He boasts that, if he really wanted, he could buy dinner with the most powerful individuals in the world. He'll gatecrash any party, stumble onto any stage or into any DJ booth and take over, and they love him for it. People congratulate Rollo just for being Rollo. If Joss could only know how little this topic of conversation appeals right now.

'He's made too many dickhead moves – most of the residents think he's nuts.' Joss's voice is breathy and earnest. 'Remember I told you he swiped the sand from someone's private island to build a concrete stadium? He lets Rowena humiliate every visiting dignitary, and the sea is full of jellyfish… My point is, his whole thing is getting a bit stale. Whereas you…' He gestures to the rose-red ribbon, the bar manager waiting patiently with golden scissors.

The flutter in her stomach returns, that sense of being

swept along by some current she doesn't fully understand. As his meaning becomes clear, it reverberates along each of her limbs; Joss has twanged her whole being. This is the strength of his ambition. He is looking at her with flecks of light in his eyes, tracing her outline as though she were a human-shaped graph.

'I can't,' she hisses, moving away from him, back towards the throng. Squabbling with Rollo is one thing, but why would she compete with him? The very idea fills her with dread. Joss didn't watch the woman in the plum dress plummet. Then there is the harbourmaster who, according to her colleagues, has taken a suspicious and lengthy holiday following the incident with the dinghy. Tamsin understands what he is suggesting, but it's a whole new ballgame, and not one you would want to lose.

'Think of the money.'

'Not everything is about the money, Joss. He's dangerous, don't you get that?'

He puts out an arm as she tries to pass him. 'That's the whole point,' he says. 'When you're in a bear pit and the other guy's got your scent, it's too late to hide. You need to win.' This is what he believes. This is what scares her.

With steps that barely falter, she goes towards the bar and is introduced to the manager, who tells her, with great gusto and a hint of poetry, that up here he is closer to the stars… but never truly starstruck until now. It is enough to make her realise, as the conversation swirls, ice cubes tinkle and devices click, that by engaging with Rollo and sending out the rumour about her paternity, she has made her move. She is already playing the game.

Thirty-Nine

Sun salutation, forward fold, downward dog. The group bend and stretch on the hotel terrace, prayer flags strung up behind the teacher. The mechanics of yoga are appealing, though she would not want to spend a month in some remote part of India learning about it, as her mum has done. Will Maeve emerge from the Ashram, her innermost self refreshed, all her chakras aligned, only to find the media clamouring to know if she slept with some old rock star thirty years ago? Perhaps her knee-jerk reaction will be to deny it, and that might be enough to kill the rumour dead. It is better if the gossip keeps going, but by now Tamsin is so worried about trolling she almost hopes her mum will nip it in the bud.

In the foyer, her image consultants are making arrangements with the hotel events manager for tonight's party. They don't need her right now, so she slips away into the gardens, where skin-temperature leaves aspire to create their own little cloud forest. As though the yoga class conjured it up, a blinking icon appears on the edge of her vision, a call from Maeve. Every tendon tightens as she answers.

'Mum?'

'Hi. You're in the Caribbean now? I didn't even know you were going on holiday.' It has been long enough that the thrust of her mum's voice, so useful for controlling unruly crowds, catches her unawares.

'How was yoga camp?'

'Oh, fabulous, obviously. I met some great people. Ate a lot of dal,' she sounds so upbeat, it is puzzling. 'But why are we talking about my boring old trip when we could be discussing you, viral child? We've got a lot to catch up on.'

Tamsin rolls her eyes, up to where a yellow bird is pecking at a rubbery stem.

'There's no need—'

'I like the *Vogue* one,' Maeve goes on, 'we should save that for the Christmas card. Anyway, about what they've been saying…'

'Yes?' At once she is alert.

'Let me tell you what's happened in the past twenty-four hours.'

The garden smells of warm compost. In the distance, there is the incongruously peaceful sound of pan pipes.

Tamsin's eyes close. 'Okay.'

'Three style magazines are bidding for an interview, even though I told them I'd be disclosing absolutely zero intimate details. Some American rag wants to fly me over to meet a collector of festival paraphernalia in Palm Springs, *business* class,' the words hiss like pressure being released.

'Last night at The Packet, two guys asked me out. Actual hotties, mind, not the usual septuagenarian car-polishers who think they can have someone twelve years younger… and that's not the half of it.' She pauses, and in the breath she draws, there is barely-contained, brimming excitement.

She tells her daughter about eye-watering interview fees and offers of stays in luxury hotels, her inbox stuffed with invitations. It has been months, maybe years since Maeve sounded this happy. Perhaps this is how normal people react to unexpected fame. Is there something wrong with Tamsin for never being this thrilled, no matter how much she earns, or how many celebrities she meets? It might be different if she didn't have a mission to think about, like a stone in her shoe.

Every key-change of her mum's chatter raises the level of relief now flooding her system. But there is one thing she has to say, before Maeve gets carried away and lets something slip.

'Mum, you know about the Republic, don't you? How their security policy means they can potentially access all conversations…'

There is an infinitesimal pause.

'Say no more, darling, I understand.' This is the only time she has been grateful for Maeve's sly grasp of how such things work; this piece of juicy gossip they both know to be untrue is a delicate thing, easily spoiled. Her mum has evidently decided to milk the situation to its fullest extent, reacting to all enquiries with coy, well-judged evasiveness. 'But I want to be seen on the red carpet with you,' she declares. 'When are we going to a premiere together? When are you back?' Her mum's calendar unfolds on screen. On the day of the Republic's election, Tamsin notices several appointments, including *Second-level wax*. She shudders.

'I've got to go, Mum, there's a little party for me tonight…'

'Aren't you a busy bee? What happened to the day job, did you jack it in?' Only her mum could sound this jolly at the thought of Tamsin giving up a decent engineering career. A twist of discomfort goes through her stomach, a lightning-quick reassessment of whether she is deluding herself: will Ogilby really take her back after all this? Maybe she isn't as good as she thinks. But this is not the time to be worrying about her job; she needs to focus.

'No, and let's not–'

'And what does Lottie say about you muscling in on her game?'

In a panic, Tamsin severs the connection and fires off a quick message: *Sorry - signal is rubbish here!* There is no easy way to explain why they should not be mentioning Charlotte, and even her old nickname could trigger a bot. Tamsin is under no illusion about the level of scrutiny right now. If any recent link between herself and Charlotte came to the governor's attention, he might probe a bit further. So long as Rollo retains control over *Outta My Room*, he has the ultimate bargaining chip.

There is also Luka, stuck in the back of her mind like a thorn. He could still destroy her with a few well-chosen remarks on social media. As she catches a glimpse of the ocean, between banana leaves, she fantasises briefly about putting him somewhere without access to devices, a tiny island, perhaps, just to keep him out of the way until all this is over.

Still, at least her mum is enjoying an Indian summer of vicarious fame. Tamsin plucks a frilly hibiscus bloom and tucks it behind her ear. Growing up, she came to see her mum's approval as overrated, or at least highly suspect. Maeve would laugh when she caught her twelve-year-old daughter drinking cartons of French wine, or doing stupid stunts or experiments. It wasn't so cool to skive off lycée if your mum cheered you on with knowing remarks about the 'school of life'. But now, at last, Tamsin is grateful to have someone on her side, not judging her for pushing the envelope with Ted, nor asking too many questions. This rumour thing could have had terrible repercussions, but instead it has brought a little joy. She allows herself to smile inwardly, to bask in a glimmer of this luck that people keep talking about.

There is hardly a breath of air to disturb the insects humming around each sugary flower. It seems like a million years since she was dashing through this greenery under storm clouds, evading flying chairs and naively assuming she would be allowed to walk out to the island. How could she ever have thought it a viable plan? There is no point even going to check if the turquoise-capped guard is there. Most of the security is invisible or, in a country where everyone sticks out like a sore thumb, unnecessary.

She kicks a coconut husk down the path. Will Luka work it out for himself? Will he check her follower count and understand that she is hoping to get that crown symbol that the LOVE network hangs over the profile picture of its most popular citizen every fourth of October? *Governor* seems a stuffy title, though since being here she is already starting to hear the word differently, rather tongue-in-cheek, as though it is an in-joke for the in-crowd. Joss has tried to reassure her that the Republic – still little more than a bunch of private islands – is mostly run by AIs and a handful of civil servants, and that the governor is really just a figurehead to encourage recognition from the international community. It is an influencer title, he says, not really a job. None of this does much to calm her nerves. She is not prone to panic, but the current plan has her blood running cold almost hourly. How is she even close to being the top influencer? Is it possible for a lucid dream to last several weeks? It doesn't seem real, yet Joss talks as though this is a straightforward process, even planning ahead – anticipating the moment Rollo realises she is after his job and becomes a threat. Her stylist has placed opinion pieces in popular blogs, drawing attention to stunts such as 'walk the plank' and 'Bermuda Triangling' people, hoping to make the incumbent governor think twice about foul play. Given Rollo's sense of being above all judgement, it may not make much difference.

Someone calls her name, and she hurries up the steps back to the lobby. The yoga group are lying in Savasana, as though they have all dropped dead.

A breeze tries to mess with her hair and fails. She is on the ridge, her off-shoulder dress perfect for this sunset selfie. Down by the lagoon, the bridges criss and cross. People lounge on the decks of their yachts capturing fabulous images of their trip, setting sail back to Florida or some Caribbean destination in the morning.

Back home, Ted will have the early stages of their next project underway, and she doesn't even know what it is. Something beneath the river, perhaps, or a Crossrail side-tunnel, some juxtaposition of cutting-edge technology and early Eocene clay. She can almost feel the track ballast crunch beneath her feet as she pushes through cold, wet air, looking up towards rows of rivets, bundles of cables, and always an icy drip that defies probability to hit the nape of her neck. Ted's warbling voice comes to mind, agreeing an extension to her holiday, and delivers a pang of guilt. This has gone well beyond taking the piss, and they both know it. Currently she has sworn to be back at the office on Thursday, bright, bushy-tailed and with an armful of duty-free treats. That was before Joss convinced her she had a shot at the little crown icon. The 'election' is on Friday.

She sighs. This mango-hued sunset makes the world back home feel less real, as though she isn't really jeopardising her career. Surely a few more days won't make any difference, and her employer will want to protect their investment. She focuses on Joss as he strides up the hill, hair and pendant bouncing. He sits down serenely, leaving a metre or so between them, and takes a puff of his pipe. Tamsin wrinkles her nose. She has already told him that Steak and Kidney vape – and how did he even find that? – is not necessary to remind her of home.

'How's it looking?' she asks.
'Good. Forty K behind.'

'Forty K?' Her heart sinks. That does not sound like a gap that can be closed in just under two days.

'It's not over yet.' Joss stretches out, legs wide. He looks so confident, as though he has a dozen aces up his sleeve. On the terraces below, people jog or glide past on e-skateboards. In the distance, she can just make out the governor's mansion on its promontory.

When you think about it, why does any country need a government, so long as it has laws? This small, rich nation is basically a dictatorship, though most people seem to see it as the opposite, something refreshingly simple and people-powered. Rollo has not made any promises or mounted a campaign, except sometimes in jest, parodying the hyperbole of the US presidential election candidates, the Republican and Democrat titans battling it out only a short plane-hop west of here, stepping everything up for these last crucial weeks. Even if Rollo does things that might be called political, he would spit out the term, because the People's Republic of Love does things differently. The coolest, most popular citizen will always be in charge, and with LOVE being the only social network to employ 'one genome, one account' technology, there is no real possibility of voter fraud, no question of trickery.

'Funny how far away the US election feels when you're here, in the thick of it,' Joss muses, as though reading her mind. 'I mean, this is proper loco, huh?'

'There are plenty of US citizens here – don't they vote?'

He shrugs. 'I can only speak for myself. Rollo is quite public about not bothering, since he's been Governor anyway, though he comes from a strongly Republican background. This is his country now.'

'I love my country…' she parodies the voice of his meet-and-greet airport hologram.

Joss smiles. 'Done with the selfies? Want to chill out here for a bit or get some dinner?'

Does he see her as a person, or a project? They both have a job to do. If she pictures herself as an image consultant, it warps into an engineering role, only she would be calculating the forces exerted on people, rather than buildings. Joss's passion for the job was never so obvious as earlier that morning, as he planned the party. Twirling a stylus in his fingers, his eyes were wet with screen-concentration as he pulled up dynamic spreadsheets more elaborately colour-coded than her own. Yes, she found herself thinking, you really are an image consultant, and you're crazy-serious about it. The ambition she observed has become more obvious by the day. It is good to have someone so capable on her team. Luka was an artist, but Joss has managed to make a science of popularity, quantifying and testing. They can develop this project together. Whatever happens afterwards… will happen. She hopes.

Her mind turns to tactics. 'Rollo's famous for being famous, isn't he, when you get down to it? But he knows what he's doing.' She has tasted it herself, that pressure to perform, to create an ever-wilder persona. It makes her wonder what is left of Rollo's inner self; does he have any friend close enough to know the real him?

Joss nods. 'It was *Six on the Beach* that really shot him up there, way ahead of the other Boones.' He gathers his ankles into a half-lotus. 'Y'know, I looked up his latest tattoo. It's inspired by a bird symbol that appears on the tombs of ancient kings, a link between the human and the divine – like, if you're a step above humanity, then you should be in charge.'

'Pretty cocky.'

She meets the amusement in his eyes, and vapour curls from his lips, blowing the meaty scent up high and away, like something equally absurd.

'I guess normally you curate an identity when you're young, put it out there, spend the rest of your life living it, right? But Rollo...'

Tamsin nods. While she cannot get her head around the governor's exact game plan, it is certainly about identity. The tattoo might be more signalling, designed to scream 'intelligence' like the Einstein quotes and Mynah bird, and even – briefly – herself, co-opted into his overall image. She thinks of the yoga teacher taking down her bunting of prayer flags, folding them neatly beside her mat. There are prayer wheels, flags and stones, and then there are the symbols lovingly etched on Rollo's skin. With every rise and fall of his lungs, he is renewing his faith in himself. Her spine stiffens as she contemplates this. If he is his own cult, how far will he go in his devotion?

The retreating daylight picks out buildings on the coastal kerb, raised to guard against the tides. It gives the island a kind of inside-out look. She thinks about the digital citizens, scattered far and wide, people who have a nationality already, but who fill in a form to be part of the People's Republic of Love. Somewhere in their identity there is a gap — disillusionment with their own regime, or distrust — and they have turned to the Republic to fill it. This is what they are looking for, something more.

'And what can I offer?' she muses. Rollo compels people to watch his every move. He has convinced everyone that he is modelling pure, unfiltered success. How can she compete?

Joss turns to her, and again she sees that hunger, that almost feverish enthusiasm, as though this is the only thing that matters to him. He twirls his Ray-Bans, full of rainbows.

'Why not luck? That's a good one, nice and secular, and... uh, inclusive.' He removes the lens cap from the camera around his neck, his eyes dark as its aperture. The twilight pinkens behind them. 'Everyone wants luck, but they don't know how to pull its levers. Unlike you.'

'Me?'

'A few weeks ago, a brand paying you hundreds of Luvcoin for this photo would seem like fantasy, right?'

He takes the shot.

She lets out her breath. Joss is a sly one. He is hoping to harness their shared love of control, convince his client to start pulling the levers of this crazy image thrust upon her — a fairy, a talisman. It was, of course, pure chance she sat on that tennis player's ring, and other people's good fortune is nothing to do with her. Luck has no basis in maths or physics. You can't build it or take it apart. How did TunnelFairy stray so far into this madness?

Joss focuses on his projection. 'Minus 39K,' he says, beaming. 'Way to go. Now let's get back to the hotel. Dee has everything ready.' He mimes clicking an earring, and she makes herself do it, feeling the slight tug on her scalp as her hair grows long and silky, and pins itself back over her temples, a look she hasn't sported since she was backcombed by a stroppy hairdresser on the set of *Eternal Winter*.

Overhead, the first hesitant stars appear like a multibillion-year-old magic trick. Tamsin tastes the watery air. Here, everyone puts so much effort into making it big, but one look at the night sky is all it takes to realise how small you are. She lags behind, transfixed by pinpricks of light, like promises of knowledge still to be found. Experiencing awe is said to make you happier, healthier and more appreciative of other people. It's a tonic that shifts your perspective.

Joss waggles his phone to show her the candy-pink glow of the LOVE network, a visual sugar-rush. This place is mad enough that Rollo has probably legislated against stargazing anyway – unless he is the star.

Forty

With the palm leaves shading her, the air is roughly body-temperature. She can hardly feel the cotton sheet beneath her shoulder blades, the beach perfectly aligned to her spine. Further off, the hot sand shimmers. What is it that makes her different from the earth, anyway? Just the tremble telling her she is alive. One day it will pass from these muscles, these little cells, and she will be a structure of carbon, inanimate, ready to be crumbled into ash by sharp fingers of fire. In a hundred years' time, part of her will be daisies. Her left thumb will be a pinch of fur, perhaps, or a tiny percentage of several rabbits. The brain she is using to think these thoughts will be air molecules inhaled by children playing, and will go into their bloodstreams, and she will be a part of them.

Never before has she let these ideas run their course, but then death is a terrifying topic. Charlotte normally derails it with a hasty interjection: 'Isn't that a bit morbid?' But now she is finding – unexpectedly – that if you endure it for long enough, space and detachment come too. Her chest barely rises and falls. What is life except this hum of particles that have enough energy to keep the shape known as 'Charlotte' projected and upright in the world? We are all holograms, in the hollowest sense of the word. And when the delicate suspension drifts apart, and the particles disperse into air and daisies and baby rabbits, all that's left is the hum.

Every morning flowers scent the air, hidden until they bloom. Her bedroom consists of a sheet laid on the sand, a pillow case of apples and biscuits cunningly suspended from a line strung between two palms, away from any vermin. She has dug a hole in which she stores two glass bottles filled with water from the outdoor tap, tasting only faintly of chlorine.

All in all, she is pleased with the set-up. The others come by occasionally to get a kick out of observing her, as though she is her own little micro-show, like Madame Crusoe or something, though they often find her daydreaming, or writing sonatas in the sand with a stick, and she does not respond to their taunts. No one has offered to bring her more food, and she is so determined not to re-enter the villa that she has been supplementing her provisions with some berries growing near the perimeter.

Any fans she has left would say she is not herself. But,

actually, she is. Amazing how it is possible to completely forget the kind of person you used to be. The anger at this show – a startling mushroom-cloud of fury – comes from a long-buried place, one that vanished beneath years of careful identity curation. Her old – oldest – self has returned amid an irresistible buzz of emotions, and it feels messy but joyful, like a park bandstand free-for-all.

The pillow is too fat, damp under her cheek, but it reminds her of hiding under pink tablecloths with Tamsin in the hotel restaurant, long before her mum died, long before she ran crying to the world with her pain. It becomes a habit, being seen. On a certain visit to the woodland burial plot she stood stupidly beside the beech tree, thinking she might as well be back in London. If a tear falls in a forest, and there is no one to see or hear it... does it fall? With the constant hum of the data centre, she could not even hear her own breathing. The sound smothered everything. It was as though her mum's musical voice, her strong fingers on a keyboard, and her laugh, had been pulverised in a blender and poured out in an even layer, an aural whitewash over the things Charlotte wanted to remember, in her mind's ear.

It catches her by surprise, this faint, traitorous longing to go back there anyway, even with the murky winter looming, even with the hum. Here, screened from the house by thick shrubs, in the midst of an unshareable experience – bar the odd camera drone that makes it through the canopy – visions are coming to her, things she has not pictured since she was a child: her mum texting in a bug-filled twilight, swaying on a hammock that was dampened, just like this sheet, by the morning dew. Her heart beats uncertainly as she awakens to a different grove of palm trees, where medics meander between huts and her mum strings up her waterproof backpack away from the rats, arms aching from a day of vaccinations. The gaps of sunlight smear easily into white coats, as her eyes fill with tears, and she moves her fingers, and sees other fingers, and her mum could be just over there, and there is something coming closer, on the edge of hearing. She sits up, every inch of her flesh sensitised and resonating. She can actually feel the hum, right now, coming in pulses, very near. Her heart starts to throb and her throat dries. Something is approaching, or is it already here?

When she lifts herself, twists in the sand, it takes several seconds to focus, then longer to believe her eyes. The little white flowers that opened this morning are spiralling up the tree. The hum unlocks, bursts apart into individual notes, like an atom exploding into a universe of music. At last she sees them, daubed with dust, chasing the chai-sweet nectar, landing delicately as if to bestow kisses. A hundred golden honeybees.

GOGGLERS ON THE ROAD [LOVECAST 2540]

DICK: One guy posted on her feed, asking for luck, and within the next hour his cancer results came through – all clear. A kid had a missing hamster return to its cage.
DOC: You don't believe all that, though?
DICK: Hashtag shrugs.
DOC: What I believe in… is the power of suggestion, and that people find patterns in random shit.
DICK: Either way, when we get to the party I'm gonna be first in line to rub her hair…
DOC: Keep your sticky fingers to yourself! You're not getting us chucked out–
DICK: Again.
DOC: Again. Apparently half the guests are arriving by chopper… I'm so frigging excited to be back in the Republic.
DICK: Yeah, big thanks to everyone who made it possible. You know who you are.

Forty-One

From James Baltimore's monster truck she can see into the upper levels of bars and blow kisses to people on balconies. A pleasure steals over her, satisfaction at how well TunnelFairy is functioning. Many of the media covering the Republic's novelty election are still asking who this surprise frontrunner is, spellbound by the tale of her secret celebrity blood emerging only when fate thrust her into the spotlight, or onto the cover of *Vogue*. The dad rumour is a spinning top that never keels over and, this morning, as she listened to his music, she found herself putting on eyeliner with a heavier hand than usual. The 'secret daughter' gossip has seeped into the mainstream. A good number of his fans have started following her.

By now she needs only minimal guidance from Joss, and has the confidence to deal out subtle burns to Rollo; she praised the videos her followers posted, called them all reality TV stars – real ones. It provoked a tidal wave of adoration. TunnelFairy, after all, is just an ordinary person who grabbed hold of a lucky break and bent it to her will.

On the sides of buildings there are projections of her face, or Rollo's. The election is very flexible, since citizens can, of course, follow both candidates on LOVE if they like. She doesn't want to jinx it, but the alcohol circulating pleasantly in her bloodstream is stirring up fantasies of facing Rollo, telling him the truth at last. This is the price he must pay for underestimating her. Not to mention screwing with her mate.

As the light fades, her entourage glows, reflected in windows as it finally leaves the Strip. Cheering is replaced by the ocean's slow, rhythmic applause. The truck bounces through the open gates of the Baltimores' mansion, past the golf cart and several sports cars belonging to guests. Dee will be somewhere inside, more than happy to be throwing an election-night party for her famous client.

James's hand is firm as he helps her down from the truck, taking care with her dress. It seems like months since she first set foot in the Baltimores' mansion, dazed and sandy and being hailed as a hero for giving their kids a lift. This time the guests jostle with expectant energy, applauding when she appears.

There is no time to wonder exactly why they are clapping. Her cheek samples the texture of a dozen other faces as she squeezes in for photos, hair brushing hair. The smile never drops from her lips. *Yes*, say yes to everything. *Yes*, she can reveal that a well-known film franchise wants her to play the part of so-and-so's daughter… she has forgotten the details, but *yes*, someone in Malaysia has indeed produced a TunnelFairy doll, and *yes* everyone here looks amazing with their Anylocks hair, and not at all like a bunch of whippy ice creams having a get-together. *Yes*, she is a lucky person, but you know the secret? A pause for effect, but they know, because she posted it earlier and got another two thousand followers, following her to learn how to *build your own luck*.

There are no more levers she can pull. She and Rollo are neck and neck. Joss beckons, and she hurries over to the leather sofa on which he is perching. He has been up for at least thirty-six hours, and Dee has been zipping about like a crazed insect, schmoozing at light-speed. Maybe she has burnt out by now and slipped away for a lie-down.

'Look at this,' he hustles her through a door into a darkened room. The incongruous odour of his black pepper vape reaches her nose. 'Rollo's increased his lead.' His voice is level, but she can tell this is serious. Joss holds out a tablet and shows her a dozen headlines.

Rollo Boone admits he felt overshadowed by brother
Daddy didn't love me as much
It was 'hell' in that house

More and more of them, as the PR machine kicks in, website AIs reconstituting the articles and spewing them across different networks.

'He released a vlog on LOVE,' Joss goes on. 'Must have been earlier this evening.'

It comes up on screen, a surprisingly smooth close-up as Rollo walks through the surf, water sloshing in the background. A low sun picks out the dimples between his muscles, the neat brushstrokes of tattoos. He removes his shades. 'So why,' he says, 'why does it hurt to talk about my dad? That's the question I was asked.' Tamsin raises an eyebrow, sensing stagecraft. 'Well, I've never really felt comfortable enough with who I am to say this before. All those seasons of *The Bare Boones*... I guess it looked like I was doing great. But actually... being on a reality show is the worst.' He shakes his head, his lips biting together.

In Tamsin's lungs, a frost has spread; she can barely breathe. Is he missing the irony here?

In the vlog, he squints into the squashed-orange sunset. 'I've always been the second-class brother. It's no accident that Adrian's the one in charge of our family business. Anyone who's never lived up to parental expectations give me a hey y'all.' He begins to tell a tale of his father's disapproval – hardly a secret – and how it scarred him. Rollo was not the man his dad wanted him to be. 'I got the grades, but Ade was better at sports and which do you think mattered to Dad? There've been times when I've thought... I won't tell you what I thought. It's been a long road, a journey we all have to go on. You get to know who you really are, and learn to love yourself unconditionally, 'cause no other fucker will. It's the only way... the *only* way. You might think all this' – he gestures to his mansion, the state yacht moored in its private harbour – 'means I've finally got there. You'd be wrong, bruv. But tomorrow, I promise, if you give me that hi-five, if you make me the first person ever to make it to a second term...' he knocks a fist against his heart, too overcome to continue.

'Nice,' Joss breathes. 'He's just pulled a soap's worth of drama out of his ass.'

'Daddy didn't love me – is that the best he can do?'

His famous family are always there in the background, like batteries he can draw upon, and something about this dispirits her. From beyond the door there are high-pitched, animated voices, reacting to his vlog. Is it the emotion they crave, proffered like some new, irresistible canapé? Or is it just the excitement of a two-horse race, follower counts going up and down? She moves to the window, where the moon is spilling bleach over the sea. What is happening with Charlotte? These last couple of days, the mantra has been pulsing dryly in her brain. *Suicide girl.* It isn't something she would ever believe, except now she'll believe anything. The only information on Jerónimo's blog is that her friend, a person who hates camping, is living outdoors, being eaten alive by bugs. The others are daring each other to steal her food. It has become impossible to second-guess her next move, much less her mental state, but it can't be good.

'We need something dramatic,' Joss glances back towards the party, and she watches him with a stab of frustration. It might be exhaustion, or hunger, but she has never felt so spent. Anylocks has a big stake in getting their influencer to the top, and she is grateful for his help, but they have tried every trick in the book. The Boones, for all their squabbling, are a powerful family. Unstoppable, some might say. Joss drums his fingers on the ledge; he catches her eye via the treacly reflection in the window. They both want the same thing, but all she can do is shrug.

'I'm all out of drama.'

Plus she is out of time.

Rollo has taken the lead and it is an hour until midnight. She imagines his indulgent smirk, his put-downs: 'Back in your box, T-Fairy…' Like being in the Ogilby Dobbs office with salmon-hued Sam Ockles telling her she was just acting up, treating her like an overgrown schoolgirl who wandered into this career by mistake. Her whole life has been about ignoring the signs, entering restricted areas, believing she can stumble into anything – even being Governor. What was she thinking? She snaps a bone-thick branch off the log on which she is sitting and hurls it as far as she can, hearing a *gloop* as the sluggish ocean gulps it down.

'Thought I'd find you here.'

'My god,' she clutches her chest. 'Joss. Don't you have a home to go to?'

The party next door has been raging for hours and everyone is so drunk and high they barely noticed as Tamsin slipped away. There seemed no point in staying. Rollo was on everyone's lips, his story making so much sense, making sense of him. He is going to win another year as Governor, while she is a mere viral sensation, a virus that flares up and then quietly leaves the system.

'Absolutely not,' he smiles. 'I'm a nomad.'

He says this as though it's a fun thing to be, not a rootless, unsettled existence. She picks off another twig and tosses it towards the waves. The beach outside her condo has a subtle night-time luminance. It smells of drying seawater, of distant rain that will fall unobtrusively in the early hours.

'I used to have a studio apartment in New York before I moved here,' he adds, a touch wistful.

Her little room in London feels pretty distant too, and it represents cold, hard failure.

'I've never made it to New York,' she murmurs.

'There's good sightseeing.'

She nods. New York has the world's largest steam system, more than a hundred miles of pipes beneath the city, and mysterious vents that rise from the pavements. In her mind the place has a coppery, steampunky feel. To go there would be to follow in the footsteps of Marc Brunel when he fled the French Revolution and became the city's Chief Engineer. She clears her throat, and the maze of sizzling tubes reluctantly evaporates.

'So anyway... the Boones will be celebrating, won't they? Rollo will get a victory tattoo and Rowena will shoot her tasers in the air.'

He chuckles. 'Nice image. Rowena will sulk briefly before jumping back on board her brother's gravy train.'

It has not escaped her notice, this easy expertise regarding the Boones. Given the theory that has been percolating in her brain, she is disconcerted to hear him talk about Rowena so freely. She inhales but says nothing. A line of stars winks out one by one, until it becomes clear an aircraft is passing overhead.

'I should have done things differently,' he peers at a pebble as though it is a faulty crystal ball, his fingernails like tiny crescent-moons.

'We both did our best,' she says. 'I know it's a blow. You're an ambitious guy, aren't you? Only satisfied styling for the highest office in the land,' she nudges him playfully, and he actually falls off the log, grunting as he hits the sand. This is so unexpected, so comic, that she can't keep her astonished laughter down. It rings out across the water. 'Relax – I guessed early on. You're the only one who doesn't gaze at Rowena and react with… what was it you said? A horrified stir?'

The stiffness of his posture tells her she is right. He cannot be blamed for backing whoever seemed like the winning horse, and Rollo's sister must have been a pretty good prospect. Who knows if he counted her as a client for long – presumably it didn't work out. Perhaps she and Joss went on a similar journey: if you can't join 'em, beat 'em. Or try to. Beating the Boones is no mean feat. Tamsin offers Joss a hand. He looks so shaken, and only partly from his undignified fall, that she casts around for a change of subject. The waves creep forward, and she inhales a breath of dewy, salted air.

'The tide is coming in.'

There is a pause, then Joss recovers his seat. He tosses his pebble from one hand to the other.

'It's a real push-and-pull relationship, isn't it? We love being by the sea, even with all its dangers.'

He is right. The ocean at night is fresh and dark, full of promise. Just offshore she can see the pencil-line of a concrete barrier, protecting these delicate condos from storms.

'Joss, can I ask you something?' she hesitates, squeezing

the *off* button of her smartspecs, realising that what she really wants to know is whether he is interested in her, or if it's just that they've been on the same page for so long. 'Why do you think I'm so keen on getting the little crown icon?'

'I don't know,' he says, shifting a fraction closer along the log. 'Sometimes I've wondered.' Beneath his measured tone she detects curiosity, like the cracks in this otherwise smooth driftwood. Of course she wants to tell him. He has performed miracles over the last few days, and she yearns to let him know that she has been working just as strategically. Plus she is tired of all the hiding, the half-glimpsed secrets. They are like two octopi camouflaged against the coral, spotting each other but too afraid to emerge. Who is going to make the first move? Perhaps the loneliness of the Republic is finally getting to her, because she can't wait any longer.

The chirping insects are like tiny cheerleaders, the beach expectant in the moonlight. Apart from a few crabs, who is going to hear? In an hour, it will no longer matter.

'Charlotte Hardey.' Amazing how good it feels just to say her name, when for so long she has trained herself to forget her friend exists. After a few false starts, it comes easily, and she tells him everything: from the first cry for help through to the evolution of her plan, her attempts to reach the film set, and to stay in character and pacify Luka, 'Who still hasn't responded, by the way, not that it's important now.'

He is silent long enough to make her doubt everything she has just said. The plan just kept growing, like a building on which storey after storey was added. Listening to herself, she sounds like Brunel describing some monstrous, over-ambitious project, some chasm-spanning bridge or sky-scraping steamship, all the risks she took and the time and money spent, trying to make it work.

His eyes gleam white as the conches at their feet. Is this a huge error, admitting that she was never bothered about being an influencer? Until a moment ago, she was certain that Joss, with his instinct for under-the-bonnet secrets, for the trivial undercurrents of fame and popularity, would get it. But is she wrong? Will he judge her for being – and she can hardly bear to hear this word, this profanity, dropping from his lips – a *fake*.

'Told you it wasn't about the money,' she mutters, rising stiffly. But he grabs her arm, not letting her go.

'Don't,' he says. He breathes out a long herbal-scented sigh. 'Damn.' Joss uses different voices for different people, and this is one she has never heard before, low and grainy. 'You were so driven.' His eyebrows flutter incredulously above his blown-apart expression. He seems dense with words, with things he wants to say. He looks at her, slides a few centimetres closer, touches her cheek with the backs of his fingers, a slow stroke, as though she is some rare and beautiful shell washed up on the beach.

There are things she needs to hear, but she is already becoming lost in the caress, the sincerity of his touch.

'I'm sorry,' he murmurs.

'For–'

'I just am.'

There are creases of moisture in the crook of his arm.

She leans into the saltwater heat of the night, and consoles herself with at least one question having been answered.

GOGGLERS ON THE ROAD (LOVECAST 2550)

DOC: Why is Rollo making such a fuss? He has more followers than Adrian and Rowena put together. Not being daddy's favourite hasn't exactly held him back.
DICK: Yeah, Adrian's just for gym obsessives – he's never been ahead of Rollo. Nor has Rowena.
DOC: A few years ago she was.
DICK: Huh?
DOC: Why do you think he went on *Six on the Beach*? He wanted a boost, but then he actually won, thanks to Charlotte Hardey, and that was it. Since then Rowena's never come close.

Forty-Two

At midnight the Republic's central bank will detect which citizen has the most followers, and for another year they will have command of a nation. Midnight is when she turns back into a pumpkin, when the dresses disintegrate and the champagne goes flat.

Joss nips into the condo and returns with two very strong gin and tonics. His large, dry hand briefly covers hers. The precise imprint of his lips is still furnace-hot on her face and neck, and it is very distracting, her whole being faintly sensitised, anticipating more. *Don't lose yourself* – a pulse reminding her not to fall too hard, not when he's keeping something back.

'This is good,' Tamsin says, clinking her glass against his. She lets a calm descend, a temporary reprieve. There is so much to say. Just as she musters her thoughts, he exhales sharply at something his specs are projecting.

'Luka,' he says, 'Luka Loxley?'

She shifts on the log. 'What about him?'

'There's a link posted on your feed. Shall I allow it? It takes you to a video on a gossip site. Woah, it's in quite a few places.'

What is Luka up to? He could still put her in an awkward position with an exposé. It would be a shame, though, after everything they have been through. She leans towards Joss and puts a hand on the rough hem of his shorts.

'We don't have to watch it.'

The video begins to play, revealing a shady room, a face and skinny figure that are instantly familiar. Internally she grimaces, knowing at once that this will be the culmination of his threats, the uncloaking of them both. It comes too late, at least, to spoil her already tattered plans. All it means is that she will have to hasten her departure, before the trolling begins. She glances at Joss; would he clamp his hand over her mouth if she tried to delete her LOVE account, right now?

Luka's pause for effect is excruciating. His head looks somehow acorn-like with that pudding-bowl cut, greenish under the light.

'So, TunnelFairy,' begins his monologue. 'Being with you was just sublime. Then, as you know, I had my lowest moment. Told you I didn't believe in you, even though you were right… about everything.' He makes eye contact with the camera, and it is a look just for her. Now she knows what this is. Astonishingly, she is hearing remorse, and something more.

'I fucked up. Couldn't see what was right in front of me. That's why I'm saying it here and now, in front of everyone. TunnelFairy, I love you.' A tear tumbles decisively down his cheek. 'You make my life better. You make the world better just by being in it. Will you take me back?'

He holds up a single red rose. Her lungs are still. Every inch of his acting clout went into that speech, his message deftly pressed into the air. The comments are starting to build, perhaps a thousand in twelve minutes. Laughter, outrage, droll remarks... but lots of the emojis have tears in their eyes.

A message appears from the same unknown number as before. He has become a digital ghost. *You don't know how close I came to ruining this*, it says. *Anyway, I'm taking my cue at last.* No apology, so it must be him. He has finally understood the new, epic scale of their project – she can imagine the slow thrill suffusing him as he realised what she was doing, the slim but tantalising prospect of unseating the governor. No wonder he wants back in. *Get her to call me, all right?* he adds, and she can hear the note of hope. The cheeky bugger. Despite everything, the message drenches her with long-awaited relief.

'He's done it,' Joss says quietly.

'It's not real,' she begins, blood rushing to her cheeks. 'Luka helped stage all this—'

'No, I mean he's done it.'

He points to her follower count. Five minutes to midnight and it is rocketing. The video is hitting feeds, and everyone wants to see what she has to say about it. Her profile is a magnet. A strange emotion surges through her: a combination of warmth for Luka and the burn of strong gin. The last seconds pass. The clock shows all zeros, but no-one turns into a pumpkin. It looks like a mistake, to see that crown icon hang itself on the corner of her photo.

'Go to his profile,' she whispers, and when Joss does so, Rollo's image is graced only by a standard flag icon. He is no longer Governor, just a common-or-garden celebrity.

'I have to call a car,' Joss says, before lurching back to hug her. 'We did it!' His body is quivering with excitement. When he lets go, she is frozen for a moment, but then gathers herself up and hurries back through the house. Out front, with the stars overhead, a gigantic golden limo is pulling up.

'You had this arranged?' Inside, it is all velvet and cushions and a built-in bar.

'It belongs to Government House. I'll meet you there.' Everything is happening at light speed. He films her climbing in, waving, and circles his hand until she gets the idea and doles out a few words of tearful gratitude to her fans, then he shuts the door before she can ask why he is not coming with her. There must be a lot to sort out, with her other stylist still unhelpfully absent, yet she is loath to leave him as the car bears her away.

'Madam Governor,' the chauffeur tugs his cap, and they pull away smoothly, barely a tinkle from the bottles. There is lightning outside, very close by – the flash of cameras. People are spilling out of Dee's house; there is a yell from the neighbour as people tread on her precious lawns. Tamsin can smell the night jasmine as she rolls down the window, hearing rapturous shrieks.

'TunnelFairy!'

She waves, and then they are behind her, and the car's automated bar service is asking whether she would like a drink, or perhaps a snack. In ten minutes or so they will be at Gilded Springs, ready for her to take up residence. It strikes her, with momentary trepidation, that Rollo might not be gone. She checks his profile, and stumbles upon a brief video statement. He's leaning on a banister, looking agitated.

'Losers,' he says. 'Come back when you've found your dicks.'

That's it. She can just imagine his stylists wincing, and sure enough the video is deleted, seconds later. Others have already duplicated it though, and links are being posted faster than they can be removed.

Then it hits her. They are going the wrong way. How could she let herself be ferried half-way across the island in the wrong direction? Shame runs through her veins, and at first her voice is too hoarse to get the chauffeur's attention.

'I need to make a detour. Can we go to the Turquoise Hotel?'

'The Turquoise Grand?'

'Yes, but can we... go round the back to the service area, and up the causeway?'

His cap is golden to match the car.

'Of course,' he says, with a brief chuckle and a backwards nod, 'Governor.' As he eases the vehicle into a U-turn, the little shot of happiness these words deliver catches her by surprise.

The road rises up the coastal kerb before swooping down too close to the lagoon, where water nibbles at the tarmac. She allows herself a split-second of mental sketching on how she would fix it, maybe create some better drainage channels. Then the Turquoise Grand glimmers into view, as iridescent and pristine as the day she arrived. What will Charlotte think, when she sees her in this golden juggernaut, a tiny flag flying from its bonnet with the Republic's single star on a background green with envy? It will be no easy task to explain that she tried a multitude of smaller plans, all swept from the drawing board – the only way to get here was to go all-in. Go big or go home. The zing she is experiencing is what anyone would feel who has pulled out all the stops, scaled things up beyond imagination: a mixture of trepidation and pride.

She pushes aside thoughts of Ogilby Dobbs, of Ted expecting her yesterday morning, whatever time that was in London, and finding no rum cake and airport sweeties, no tanned face to remark upon. The day was too crazy for her to think of messaging him.

A luggage cage glints by the hotel foyer, and porters look over expectantly, but the limo continues on until they reach the service entrance. Red interfaces with the security system, and Tamsin is thrilled to see gate after gate open wide. There are the bins, and ahead the causeway, as tyres grind through gravel, slipping a bit. The guard is still at his post, sitting in the same chair even though it is the middle of the night. He stands and walks into the road, and the car automatically stops.

The chauffeur's nasal drawl emerges from a speaker somewhere around the bonnet: 'Stand aside please.'

The guard does not move. His cap is at a jaunty angle. She winds down the window to get a better look. Then she gets out of the vehicle, not wanting to believe her eyes, keeping the open door in front of her like a shield.

'Impressed how quickly I moved on, T-Fairy?'

Under the angular floodlights, she failed to notice the shape of him. When he flicks off the hat, a familiar skull emerges, smooth as a gold-dusted truffle.

She starts to speak, but falters. As a lone figure under the night sky, Rollo makes no sense. She has never seen him without an entourage. On his own he is both pathetic and slightly menacing, like a wolf separated from its pack.

'I get why you're here,' he says.

'You knew?' If he has known all this time, why hasn't he used it as leverage? The familiar knot of fear tightens in her stomach.

'Not till just now. As they say, an hour is a long time in the Republic.' His teeth are radioactive in the moonlight. 'You think he's hot, right? Your big-time square of a stylist?'

Her knees unlock, and she takes a step backwards. Somehow he is already leaning against the car, his fingers curling over the open door. Moisture shines on his lips, as they crack into a half-smile, and the scent of cocoa butter is intense. How did he manage to eavesdrop on her conversation? Her brain rifles through the possibilities, and alights on her smartspecs; they must not have been properly powered down. No matter. She is the governor now, and he can't stop her. The causeway stretches ahead, a straight line across silvery water.

Rollo says, 'One thing I don't get, T-Face. If she's such a good bud, why'd she never once mention your name?' the dark gleam in his eyes belies his sympathetic frown. 'I mean, Christ, why are you bothering? I was there the whole time she was famous and she obviously didn't give two fucks about you. Rate yourself just a little, T. Save your loyalty for someone who deserves it.' He slows on these last words, giving them a contemptuous punchiness, then he waits. Internally, a part of her is reeling, struggling for balance, but her expression remains neutral. She tucks both thumbs into her waistband.

'Would you even remember? Name one of her friends.'

A straightforward challenge which he shrugs off, lounging more fully against the car. The chauffeur winds his window down a fraction. She should get in, give Rollo a last warning to move aside. He takes up so much space.

'Anyway, this whole thing is dumb,' he shoots her a mournful squint. 'I've been busy lately, as you're well aware. Hardly watched the show. When my PR guy found the suicide girl stuff, just starting to leak out, I'm telling you, I shat myself good and proper.' His shirt undulates in the breeze. 'I said to Rowena, "what the hell are you playing at?" She's an unnamed exec producer, but it's my production company. I was like: "are you trying to fucking bankrupt me?" I swear.'

His fingers circle illustratively, and Tamsin's mind spins.

'Are you saying this was a surprise to you?'

'No,' his hands come up. 'I'm not innocent. Not by a long shot. You know I've got nothing to hide, right? I said to Rowena that I'd like to see Charlotte lose a reality show. That's what I wanted. Proper lose it. That's all. I left my sister to have fun with it, barely watched the show, and, next thing I know, there's a crippling lawsuit in the making.'

The sea breathes out its plasmic, primordial fragrance, and Tamsin tries to tease apart what he is saying. There was always some nagging mismatch with Rollo's blasé personality and the calculated nature of *Outta My Room*. He is, of course, far too fixated on himself to take any sort of meticulous care over Charlotte's suffering. But Rowena… all the headlines and hearsay about the younger Boone flash through Tamsin's mind, along with what Joss said about her fascination with finding people's weaknesses. Of course she would enjoy dabbling in the show, a goldfish bowl within a goldfish bowl.

'Should have just Bermuda'd her ass,' he goes on, 'but I was mad, you know? Anyway. I'm guessing you haven't caught much of it lately? The show.'

She shrugs. The election has eaten up every waking moment. Her mission is straightforward as a plumb line: *Get to Charlotte*.

'Thought not. I wanted to get her out right away, but Rowena convinced me to keep her there and provide some discreet on-site counselling – and obviously we ditched the escape room algorithm. The show will end and she'll come out with dignity intact. Better for her. Way better for me and the other shareholders.' He exhales into the wind. 'Anyway, you've won, Tamsin.' His grin is gritted. 'Look at it from my perspective. Adrian has the gym chain, and Rowena has her self-defence brands. Don't I deserve to keep the film corp?'

She almost laughs. 'After all this, you're saying I should just turn around and let her stay there?'

"Zactly what I'm saying. Unless you want to screw things up for me and her both. It's what Einstein said – you never fail till you stop trying. This show doesn't have to be the thing that kills her career. She's already getting back in the game, and that really kicks ass if you hit rock bottom first.' His words surround her, like a fog he is conjuring. She can see how it will look for him of course, if the very first act of the new governor is to haul his abused ex-girlfriend into the spotlight. But the argument is starting to gnaw at her. 'Dang it, T-Fairy,' his voice reverberates through the limousine's bodywork. 'Finishing the show is the only thing that's gonna save her. She was clean out of work this summer – didn't you know that?'

He is so close she can smell the triple-distilled spirits on his breath. Of course she knew. But did she really listen? Charlotte was running out of jobs, out of money. Tamsin pictures herself blundering in, messing things up, as she has done before on far less important occasions. This wouldn't be the first time she has catastrophically misread the signs. She stands paralysed, the car humming in its own heat-haze. Once she bursts onto the film set, there is no going back.

Somewhere in the thrash of her thoughts there is one idea she can grab. It is not about what he says, or whether it can be believed. At the heart of all this is Charlotte, someone so familiar that she has become the unsolicited voice in Tamsin's head. As she meets Rollo's eye he shifts, crunching on the gravel. He can't get into the past they share, can't hear the hangers clatter as they flail around amid musty old coats, fumbling for the catch, searching for the exit. *No fir trees. No firs.* It's a line of communication like a string with a cup at each end, something analogue and personal, reaching from one world into another. Something that can be trusted.

'She was right,' Tamsin declares, shaking the car door free of his grip. 'It's like you don't know her at all.'

His mouth parts, just slightly, as he is dislodged. The truth will come out immediately, as soon as Charlotte is free. Is he naive enough to think he can shut her up? These are governor-level fantasies, and he's just some guy in a pricey shirt. It is fear, that tension in his shoulders, fear that makes him hold his centre of gravity so high he almost teeters. She compares this hovering figure with the Rollo she observed on International Me Day, lounging around and rearranging his golden world into a configuration that pleased him. The ugly associations of *Outta My Room*, the mental anguish, abuse and power-play are like fistfuls of mud, dirtying up his philosophy. It is clear that her friend's suicide scare marked the moment he lost control of his revenge-plan, when he realised it had gone rogue.

The causeway stretches across water that has its own mysterious glow. She spots pulsing orbs, poisonous and beautiful. Rollo peers incredulously through the open window as the limousine glides past. In the mirror she sees him grow smaller.

Part Three

THE GOVERNOR

Forty-Three

When you eat the terracotta berries growing on these rubbery stalks, you can enjoy the following hallucinations: bread-crust crabs, juicy parrots dripping jam on your pillow, insects that aren't there but whine like crazy, and night that really falls, as though it has tripped.

Much better than the things she found in the rock pools. They just made her throw up. These make her sick too, but with free entertainment. Plus the texture isn't so squidgy. Food ran out the day before last, and the sandflies are favouring her neck and ankles, but nothing can get her down. She no longer thinks twice before going to pee in the scrub, not caring if zoom lenses can see her squatting in a sarong. The other contestants don't bother her. She does not ask them for food. It is funny how words come back, how they can linger unheard in your aural memory for years. What she remembers her mum telling her, at some point when they were together, is that the only person who will be with you for your whole life, start to finish, is you.

You, the unimportant witness, elbowed out of the way so other people can see. You, the life-long witness, the only one to hear a clunk beneath each key of the antique piano, or rub pollen between your fingers, or panic at the deflation of a punctured dinghy. For years she has been skimming off the top of life instead of drinking deeply, trapped in its surface tension, forgetting what the rest of it tastes like.

It is late and the sea breeze is on the chill side. She dons another set of clothes; it is easier to keep warm this way because sheets slip off her newly strung hammock. The fabric is rough against the sunburnt patches alongside her bikini shoulder straps. When she nestles down and her heart beats in time to the rhythmic chirp of cicadas, she wonders whether the outside world still exists. Has there been a natural disaster, sickness or war, civilisation in tatters? Her stomach isn't quite ready to let her sleep. She listens to it, keeping control of the hammock's swing as she eases her legs down. A sip of water might help, but the bottles are empty. She upends them to make sure it is not an effect of the berries, that they are not tricking her by making the liquid extra-transparent. Then she takes them, one in each hand, and lurches through the sand towards the house, pausing when it spins. The decking smells of crushed nachos, of appetising cheesy powder. People have spilled over and left splashes of themselves around – a cardigan, some leggings, some voices trickling from the kitchen, though out here it is quiet. The infinity pool is coaxing her to dip a hand into its cobalt-blue waters, to drink its dark reflections.

When she finally gets the stiff tap to turn, something makes her look up. Beyond the fence panels, the highest shoots of bamboo wave like a crowd appreciating the moon. There is a click, and then a scraping sound, wood on metal. A small section has receded by an inch and is sliding to one side. The air stills. She always knew there would be a door somewhere. A hidden door to another world. Her head is throbbing, her body weak from the effort of throwing up, down to its last dregs of blood sugar. She can see specks in front of her eyes, like glitter at a premiere. If her legs could do it, she'd start her dash, but they are like tubes of water, and the exit doesn't quite seem real.

Left to its own devices for too long, the brain can no longer tell imagination from hallucination. One leaks into the other. When someone appears in the fence-gap, it looks like Tamsin. But the figure steps onto the decking with feet clad in lacy bronze sandals, hair impossibly long and burnished. Is it possible that a tired mind could create its own version of her friend, buffing the dull rusts of her inner Victorian shipyard into a brassy, trophy-bright tunic? Taupe-pink powder adorns the apparition's cheekbones, catching the light beautifully as she steps forward. When their fingertips touch, the figure will pop like a soap bubble.

'Charl.'

Her name is a bite of raw coffee. In one corner of her brain the fog lifts, just a little. How much personality is contained in a voice? If her imagination has synthesised this set of reverberations, it has done a bang-up job. She can almost believe this is Tamsin speaking.

'Charl?' the woman says again, breathless, as though she has run here. 'I'm getting you out.'

The vision is not receding. What if it is not the berries? The coloured patio lights, reddish, make her think for a moment that they are underground. It even smells earthy, starchy – she pictures the maintenance guy microwaving his jacket potato. Everything so far has been a ruse, and they no longer have the escape room to torture her. Is the latest thing some mind game involving lookalikes? She narrows her eyes for a sharper focus. The face is so smooth, and Tamsin has never been one to maintain a proper skincare routine.

Suddenly it drains her, the fact that they have mocked up the one person smart and loyal enough to have potentially saved her. Who is this clone, some poor actor down on her luck and willing to have face-matching surgery, hidden speakers outputting a voice mixed into the correct sonic signature? Perhaps the same person she saw on *Fanessa*, being interviewed before she was added to the cast. This level of cruelty is enough to break her.

'You couldn't just let the show end, could you?'

The figure, so stunning in her glamorous attire, looks around wildly.

'Charl,' she says, as if on a loop. 'Don't scare me. Tell me you want to get out of here.'

Wow, they've got her down to a tee.

'Just go.'

The words send a ripple through the woman, knock her eyes half-closed for a second, almost like she has taken a punch. Something inside Charlotte reacts to the expression of pain, compelling her to add:

'No more tricks.'

Why can't they just leave her alone? It feels like there is a cactus rotating in her stomach.

'Don't you remember asking me to help you?' She comes over and it is too much, that familiar scent wafting from her clothes. Charlotte is desperate to believe in her. Sensations are flashing through her mind, ancient memories of greasy light, cloaks and chairs in a 1940s bedroom, a wardrobe with dust like an old, woody spice.

'Lucy,' she says, the words slippery in her brain. 'Why were there no firs?'

Even if she has an earpiece feeding her information, no algorithm will make this woman able to answer as her friend would. Charlotte folds her arms, waiting.

The frown deepens. 'Usually because we couldn't get the back off the bloody wardrobe.'

Like magic, it is her. Tamsin materialises out of the clothes, the costume, as though she has wandered off a film set. When they hug, it requires a familiar bend of the knees.

There are tears, and she is laughing right through them. 'I'm kind of ill,' Charlotte announces. 'Get me the hell out of here.' And just like that she is stepping through the fence, out from the show, parting the bamboo as easily as a bead curtain. There is the yard with the corrugated lean-to, complete with scrappy chairs and a table, empty cans rolling beneath, and a cleaning bot in pieces, smelling of burnt rubber. The maintenance guy is standing in the middle of it all like his feet have been nailed to the floor, transfixed by the enormous limousine waiting on the road. Ahead is the causeway, and the wind blowing from that direction is a thousand times more refreshing than any she has felt in weeks. She looks at the diminutive figure beside her. Her friend, here at last.

'Nice shoes,' she murmurs.

Tamsin looks amused.

'I move heaven and earth to rescue you, and you notice the shoes?'

They reach the car, and the chauffeur opens the door, nodding and smiling. Overhead, a flight rises with a muffled roar, dark against the stars. Charlotte can't help looking up longingly, though it makes her dizzy.

'Where are we going?' she asks.

'We'd better just go to Gilded Springs for now.'

'Gilded...' Her teeth start chattering inexplicably in the warm wind. 'Why would we...' Light drains from the sky, blood from her head, and her last sensation is the smooth paintwork of the car, brushed by her fingers, then a dull crunch against her temple.

Forty-Four

Charlotte's bedroom has a view of the ocean, its depths mottled blue. There are so many flowers, and so much fruit in the bowl; it gives off a ripe, cidery scent. Tamsin tips a sachet of rehydration salts into a glass, stirring it with a silver teaspoon.

'Thanks,' Charlotte takes a sip. 'Can't believe I got so dehydrated.'

'At least your fever's down.'

The governor's personal physician has come for two long visits, giving Charlotte all the best care, though what she mainly wants to do is sleep, and this is the first time Tamsin has got beyond ten minutes of conversation without her drifting off. When will Charlotte be herself again? Right now she seems drained of her essence, skin darkly translucent around her eyes. On that first night, when her temperature was high, mysterious thumps were heard along the corridor, and she was discovered curled up in an armchair by the front door, entangled in a sheet. Even her naps, with fever raging, are so restless they drive her to the threshold of her room, where she sits in the doorframe, one foot planted limply in the corridor.

Tamsin has joked about it with her. 'Is the bed not up to your standards?' The mansion's biggest guest room is elegant, lightly floral and luxurious, everything stuffed with duck-down and carved from very blonde pine. But Charlotte was too ill to do more than muster a watery smile.

It is a relief to see her sit up and drink, and squint at the glowing paradise to be glimpsed through the window. Having heard the full TunnelFairy story, she is picking at it, as though it is a complicated meal and she hasn't found her appetite. Certain things need to be repeated, too incredible to digest. The fact that Tamsin is the governor – actually the one in charge – is a nugget that Charlotte cannot swallow. But it is no chore to go over it a few times. Tamsin is rather enjoying this pleasant aftermath, so long-awaited, relaxing with her friend while they eat pastries and drink the finest loose-leaf tea. She lists them once more, all the things she invented, from boob job through to old rocker dad – an epic tale of nobody-to-somebody. But instead of the expected laughter, her friend reacts as though every word is sharp, paling a little as both hands leap to her mouth.

'Effing hell, Tam,' she breathes. 'I've seen people torn apart for this, for faking up a life story, pretending they had cancer when they didn't, or that some amazing thing happened to them… People hate that. They hate it more than anything.'

The passion in her tone is unnerving, enough to coax a line of sweat from Tamsin's spine.

'I never pretended to have cancer. Anyway, it's all over now. We're going home as soon as you're better.'

Charlotte's hands unclench from the sheet, and she takes another breath. 'Yeah,' she says. 'It's all sound. But, Jesus, if I'd known…'

'If you'd known?'

'I wouldn't have wanted you to take the risk.'

Tamsin's innards are still feeling the after-effects of adrenaline. 'Well, what was I supposed to do?' she says, hearing the involuntary snap beneath her words. 'I heard about this Jerónimo blog… you on the roof, and I was freaked out. I honestly didn't know what was going to happen.' She finds a teary warmth gathering on her face. It has been so hard – the plans kept failing and failing – but it was all worthwhile. She leans in and gives Charlotte a shoulder-hug.

'Glad you're alright,' they both whisper together, then pull apart. Tamsin plucks a plum-sized grape and wipes it clear with her thumb. She grins.

'I had to sell out big-time. At a party, I actually signed someone's old DVD of *Eternal Winter*. Can you believe that?'

For the first time Charlotte regards her with the full depth of her dark eyes.

'That must have been cringe,' she says.

It is happening at last, this subtle radiation of gratitude Tamsin has been craving. She can smile. They can laugh about it.

'Yeah, when we get back to London the drinks are on you,' Tamsin says, the words sounding somehow out of place. 'Actually, that would be nuts. I have about twenty thousand Luvcoin in my account...'

Charlotte sighs. 'I have to admit, it's impressive how you got so famous. You transformed yourself, all on your own.'

The cups rattle on the tray and Tamsin fills them with a beautifully aromatic tea. When Charlotte saw TunnelFairy's profile, her mouth dropped open, lips mouthing the number of followers. What an achievement, and what a feat of theatre, yet Tamsin's pleasure was laced with a slight disquiet. Maybe she needs to talk it through a bit more, explain the mechanics of everything. Charlotte keeps steering the conversation back to Rollo.

'And the fact that he admitted it,' she gathers her hair and pulls it over one shoulder. 'He probably just said "make it happen" and it was all arranged.'

Hard to shake that image of Rollo standing on the causeway, saying he wanted Charlotte to lose at something, the casual, almost natural way that he and Rowena dreamt up a reality show. Genius – they would have thought – she'll have to take everything that's thrown at her. Charlotte doesn't for a second believe the claim that they were about to offer her counselling. It would have been a last-ditch attempt at damage limitation, once Rollo realised how messed-up the whole thing had become. Or perhaps he knew all along. Tamsin couldn't help clasping her neck in horror when she heard about those dangling cables. She shudders.

'I still can't believe we don't have a case against him. He tried to murder you.'

The Republic is ridiculous. No police force to gather evidence of such a crime, nor punish it. For Rollo, the whole system is disgustingly convenient. All they can do is wait for the justice that Charlotte is certain will naturally come to pass, once her story is told. So long as people believe her.

'Or was it Rowena?' Charlotte muses. 'She hated that Rollo got famous on *Six on the Beach*, kicking her out of the running to be Governor herself.' Rowena has, of course, dropped her brother like a hot stone now he can no longer offer her the freedom of the Republic. Her last update shows her getting on a flight to LA, pouting at the camera while the tassels of a diaphanous black scarf splay out in the wind. 'It's actually worked out pretty well for her, hasn't it, now you've given Rollo a walloping?'

Tamsin hesitates. 'Hard to tell with that family.' They are squabbling one minute and closing ranks the next. Even if Rowena was pleased at seeing her brother ousted, it seems unlikely she will escape unscathed, once the details of *Outta My Room* become public. Tamsin hears Joss's voice in her mind. The scandal might be enough to tip Rowena over that 'knife edge', associating her less with self-defence and more with sadism.

Charlotte gazes fixedly out of the window. 'I don't like it,' she mutters. 'He doesn't take insults, Tam. You stole this job from under his—'

'Will you stop worrying about Rollo?' The mansion is enmeshed in the latest security tech, safe as a bank vault, and now she is Governor she can keep tabs on every citizen, check every tourist visa and work permit, see every device, read every message. For good measure, she brings up Rollo's full details on the wall, his recent purchases of expensive lotions and drinks, the scribble of his movements on a map, showing he is still on a yacht belonging to one of his cronies. His world has shrunk, and since he is constantly posting vlogs it is not difficult to keep track of him. The latest shows him yanking at his skinny vest, setting the world to rights with a couple of guys in baseball shirts, the deck jostling with bottles.

'See? He's just twittering away to himself. As for Rowena—'

'Please turn that off.'

Charlotte's head lolls into the pillow, face softened by slumber. With a swipe, Tamsin dismisses the giant faces and closes the door.

Since they can't immediately leave, she has to act as though they are staying. Unfortunately, Gilded Springs is far from a hideaway. A chance conversation with the house steward about the number of digital walls, sometimes two in a room, reveals that there are web cams everywhere, and a film is continuously being made for the governor's LOVE channel. An AI edits out anything that is boring or a security risk. 'People want to know what you're doing,' he reminds her. This spurs a momentary panic. A dozen conversations replay in her mind, hiking her pulse, and she breathlessly awaits the answer to her question: what about the webcams in the guest room? 'Charlotte Hardey shut 'em down,' says the steward. 'On her first night.'

At least now she knows to be careful. Awareness of being watched makes it almost impossible not to perform, just a little, even when you are doing nothing, sitting on a satin bedspread, smoothing out wrinkles with a tanned knee. Followers want to see the situation they helped create, and share in it. They want to be the ones getting dizzy checking out the chandeliers, the crazy artwork, the seawater pools. Being in his shoes, or rather, under his spotlight, kindles a faint admiration for the way Rollo made it look so effortless.

How is she going to tell them it is all a sham? Since arriving in the Republic, she has waited for this. It's a bit worrying that the big reveal has lost its shine. Now she would feel embarrassed, almost apologetic, to tell her lovely followers that she lied to them. Charlotte has suggested they hold a press conference. 'I'll tell my story, and you can be yourself again,' she said. 'Get rid of this…' A gesture briefly traced the outline of TunnelFairy, the stylish leather plaiting on a top which was, at least, something she chose herself. Charlotte should have seen her in the beginning, when every outfit was like something from a kid's dressing-up box.

It is about stitching Rollo up, or 'defusing him', as Charlotte puts it, by thoroughly exposing what the Boones did to her. Usefully, the state limo was fitted with enough dashcams to capture his confession, a verification of what Charlotte will tell reporters. She also has the doctor to confirm the trauma she has suffered.

Tamsin has always admired this unwillingness to be cowed, her friend's refusal to be timid when put in the role of victim. Of course they can do a press conference, but it would be better to wait until they are ready to leave the Republic. One reveal is intertwined with the other, since Charlotte will have to explain how she got out, and TunnelFairy will be revealed as a project, a piece of theatre.

In the most recent episode of *Outta My Room*, the presenters joke about missing persons. They think the new governor visited the set on a whim, extracting Charlotte only because she was unwell. It is an interpretation that Joss and her other PR staff will have encouraged. She should have been more subtle, not dashed straight up the causeway when all eyes were upon her. Until the two of them are off Republic soil, she must be more careful.

Dee did not reappear after the election, but has sent congratulations and explained that she is taking some time out, a few days away on a beach featuring a slightly different arrangement of white sand and palm trees to the one outside her house. The makers of Anylocks are naturally delighted that their pet influencer has made top dog. The CEO herself has sent messages of praise and ever more staggeringly generous sponsorship proposals.

Joss has been kept busy by the media, but is starting to resurface, much to her relief. When the bloggers and photographers leave he takes her up on an invitation to soak in one of the Jacuzzis dotted around the rockery, with stunning views down to the sea. An attendant brings the frosty beers they have ordered, and she feels the bubbles gently buffet her thighs, one leg tucked underneath so her head stays above the roiling waters. It is too loud for much conversation, but droplets catch on Joss's curls and hang there, sugary in the sun, and he smiles and reaches his beer across for a clink. Her head lolls back and she wonders if Charlotte can see them, whether she will come to the window and wave, or if envy will coax her out. This mansion is like the grand prize in a competition, only a hundred times more sumptuous; a five-star hotel all to themselves, all inclusive, for free. How often does that happen? Tamsin takes a draught of icy, hyper-bubbly beer. They should be making the most of it.

She and Joss towel themselves off and seek shade indoors. Most of Rollo's stuff has been removed, and it makes a big difference having the digital walls reset to magnolia. She takes Joss through French doors, propped open against the wind, and into the glass wing, where gym equipment is mostly sitting silent, obviously not being quite so crucial to the energy supply as Rollo claimed. One or two kitchen staff are still pedalling, headphones on and oblivious to her presence.

'Is that a cannon up there?' Joss peers through the window over to the other wing.

'Just pirate props – they're on palettes waiting to be removed.'

'Takes a while to fully dislodge the Boones.'

They go through a golden archway, back towards the main foyer.

'I've never seen the place in daylight,' he says, bounding ahead. 'It feels familiar because it's so often filmed.'

'Slow down,' she dips her hand into a water feature, letting its metal-scented liquid course over her palm. 'Didn't you hang out here when you worked for Rowena?'

This is something she has been meaning to address, an unspoken edge to every conversation. She has been putting it off, not wanting to take risks as their mutual attraction delicately unfurls, but she needs to know he wasn't supporting Rowena at that particular time, that he had nothing to do with the psychological torture of *Outta My Room*. No matter how devoted he seems – and the dents of tiredness under his eyes proclaim how hard he has worked – if there is no trust they can go no further.

He hesitates. 'I... never actually worked for her,' he says. 'I did offer my services, but she has her own people and wasn't interested.' He tests his knuckles on one of the golden pillars.

'Sore point?'

'Not at all.'

He smiles, but it is covering something. From the beginning, it has been obvious he is at the top of his game, his standards a world away from Dee's. Perhaps he isn't used to being snubbed. It perturbs her to think that, following this failure with Rowena, he might have turned to TunnelFairy only as a second choice. Is that the reason for his sheepish tone? The thought lingers sourly.

'So,' he says. 'What's next on the tour?'

She wavers, wondering whether to probe further, but there is a certain pleasure in showing off her mansion – her spoils – the cool curves of brass doorknobs leading to vast mahogany-scented rooms. Heavy double doors pop open once her face has been scanned, and they enter an official-looking room decorated with sea charts. A central table features a model of the archipelago, carved islands protruding like wrinkled fingertips from a bathtub.

'The steward showed me this earlier,' she remarks. 'He says there's always a point at which new governors look confused and wonder where the actual governing happens, since it's all so amorphous and AI-controlled. So they created this – the map room.'

Joss tests the sharpness of one of the little pewter ships with his index finger. 'So where's the button that makes the whole Republic vanish into the sea?'

She laughs. 'Careful – most of it is voice-activated. You say 'open PR centre' or 'open central bank' and… there you are.' The maps on the walls become a set of graphs and flickering numbers, denoting how Luvcoin is doing against other currencies.

'That doesn't seem very secure.'

'It scans eyes as well, to check I'm actually in the room. It's so techy – but then it was set up by someone from Smarti, some Silicon Valley boffin.'

He catches her eye, and his look is unreadable. They have both been chattering away, small-talking around the important stuff again. He takes her hands in his, dry and soft as memory foam. She knows she has made an impression.

'Before you say anything,' he murmurs, 'I just want it on the record that I admire what you've done. Why you did it, especially.'

This is quite a compliment from someone who creates popularity for a living, almost as though he is addressing a fellow image consultant, a puller of levers. Despite his strangely formal tone, it is enough to make happiness surge through her system, a blush gathering on her cheeks. How long has it been since she felt truly happy? Her hand reaches for the warmth of his chest and his mouth opens slightly, but he does not lean in, or say anything further. Something about his posture is brittle, she longs for him to yield, to sway towards her. After a few moments, she steps back.

'I'm supposed to be the cautious one,' she says, with a sad smile. 'I never trust anyone on a first date, or even a second. It's one of my flaws.' The word conjures up connotations of a structural weakness or crack. She instinctively checks her reflection in the screen – a dark statue with an elfin look about her, a graceful strength.

'Flaws?' he breathes and moves forward. 'I don't think so.'

Her heart lifts, but he doesn't touch her. Tamsin sees herself through his eyes, and hates what she sees. Profound satisfaction. A project that is now complete.

Forty-Five

There is a simple, wonderful joy in saying 'Yes'. The word is like a shaft of sunshine across the floor, or the honey-scent of daffodils, something that instantly lifts her spirits. At Ogilby Dobbs provisos and piss-taking got in the way, as though her colleagues were afraid to heave a big, brassy 'yes' into the air and just let it resonate.

On the red carpet, people ask for things like helipads, moorings for their yachts and endorsements of their products. Off it, they ask if they can ditch these stupid grass skirts, have free access to a virtual doctor, and stop the beach raves during turtle nesting season. Mostly she says 'yes', and when she gets back to the mansion she begins to discover how easily her desires can translate into action. The whimsical nature of Rollo's legislation makes more sense now she knows what a frictionless process it is. A word to the Civil Service AI is all it takes to get an instant risk assessment and costing. If staff are required, they are hired, if expertise is needed, the AI puts out a ticket for consultancy. Everyone is instantly informed. In one night, Tamsin commissions a new cycle route, fixes the bottleneck by the lagoon and establishes the Republic's first, albeit tiny, National Park.

When she gets back from dinner on the Strip, she is moving shoe boxes when she finds her Brunel biography, buried beneath all the gifts. It is late, the mansion silent, and on her giant cushion of a bed she pauses to read a few lines. The accompanying sepia photo, that face with serious eyes concealing private playfulness, stove-pipe hat and nascent jowls, is a perfect counterpoint to what he wrote in his diary about riding through the countryside, learning to wear his reputation like a smart new coat. *I catch myself trying to look big on my little pony,* he writes. She has always known her idol to be driven by a dedication to his craft, a desire to build things that would be genuinely useful. He rode the bumpy new railways fantasising about people being able to drink coffee and write as they travelled. Only now does she see what else kept him going – the auxiliary motor of pride. It is obvious, when you think about it. He was a small man designing the biggest ship in the world.

She slips off her heels, six-inchers which she wore this evening so her head would not dip below the level of the crowd. Until now she has never thought of Brunel as having a real desire for greatness, to be immortal, but perhaps he did. If the importance of self-esteem – and self-care – had been recognised back then, Brunel might not have worked himself to an early death on the SS Great

Eastern, leaving his family to gaze sadly at the foundations of his Italianate dream-house in Devon, planned but never built.

Among the messages that appear during the night, there is one from James Baltimore. *Is she with you?* He demands, *Tell me the truth. Is she mad at me?* He is perplexed by Dee taking this sudden holiday, telling no-one and expecting the childminder to manage 24/7. *Where is she?* His concerns come in little puffs, in the early hours of the morning. He is lucky Tamsin is too wired to sleep. 'Relax,' she dictates back. She will look into it, with all the means at her disposal, but he needs to chill out. In the run-up to the election, Dee visited every influencer in the Republic, coaxing out a few posts in Tamsin's favour, her part-time job becoming all-the-time. Give the woman a break.

The sun is burning away the dawn haze. Yesterday, in the map room with Joss, she noticed a metric for Gross National Happiness. They measure it using a sentiment gauge that analyses the words and emojis citizens are using, and even their tone of voice.

'And that law, did you make it happen?' she asks the never-weary AI, tucking into her chopped papaya and yogurt. Last night she tried her first decree, asking every citizen to post one piece of good luck they experienced during the day. 'How is the GNH looking?'

'Gross National Happiness at seventy-five,' says the Civil Service.

'Up by nearly a tenth?' Not bad, for one small

experiment. Tamsin smiles to herself. Hard to believe she was worried about having this title slapped upon her. They could have called it president, king, queen, anything… but they went for Governor, someone who only governs the Republic on behalf of its true rulers – the people. She just steers them a little, as though adjusting the rudder of a ship. The role of Governor sounds so big and scary, but she can easily make a better job of it than Rollo did.

She steps onto the terrace and takes a breath of the balmy, orange-scented air. No wonder Charlotte moved here as soon as she could. It's a much better quality of life than in London or Los Angeles. Aside from the sunshine and easy access to the ocean, there is something special about islands. They are ripe with possibilities. She remembers seeing a play in which Thomas More, the inventor of 'Utopia', insisted that it must be an island, self-contained and sea-scoured. A place where you can start again and make everything perfect.

The only hindrance is that Charlotte is still not herself, unable to enjoy this time they have together. Tamsin wanders down to the rocks, the sea primrose-pale in the early light, and strips down to her bikini. The outer layer of her hair interlocks into a watertight swimming cap, its strands becoming a membrane and, after a brief check for jellyfish, she dives. The water is cool, never chill, and she emerges with streams trickling down her skin. An image of grimy bricks flickers across her mind and vanishes; the hot sun is bleaching away all the time she spent out of sight in soggy, centuries-old tunnels.

In the map room, on the model of the archipelago, there is a green triangle that reminds her of the praline chocolate you find in boxes of Quality Street, a reference that drew only a blank stare from Joss. Since she now has a right to all Rollo's secrets, the Civil Service bot happily answers her questions, and she learns that the island is a small eighteenth-century fort, somewhat overgrown. Early in his tenure, the former governor took a trip there and found an illegal chalet built atop the ruins. He started referring to the triangular islet as 'Bermuda' and, since it was a long way out from the archipelago and could be secure, he used it as a place to send people whose existence he found temporarily inconvenient.

Tamsin had to ask the bot to repeat this. Could it be true? Perhaps she should not be surprised, having dealt with *Outta My Room*, that another of Rollo's vindictive daydreams could become reality. His ego is like a weed she thought she'd extracted, only to encounter vigorous little off-shoots. 'There are actual people there?' she asked the bot.

'Yes,' it replied.

Having spoken properly with James, she agrees that there is something wrong with these messages from Dee. They are too bubbly, and uncharacteristically vague when referring to the children. It scares Tamsin to imagine that something may have happened to her former image consultant. 'Bermuda' is where she might be, so they are taking some security staff on one of the state yachts and will cross a few nautical miles of ocean to investigate.

Tamsin bustles around the mansion, trailing nervous energy in her wake. She chats to the walls about her trip, knowing cameras will follow her. 'Remember Rollo's thing about "Bermuda Triangling" people? It's not just online ghosting... turns out they were actually sent somewhere IRL. Maybe the fort has been converted into a spa and everyone's having a great time, but I doubt it.'

She throws a towel into a beach bag. Where the hell is Charlotte? There is nobody on the black rattan loungers, nor on the lawns. Once the security system has located her, Tamsin is obliged to go through the kitchens and across a yard of flapping sheets. The low-rise utility building has dry air and a starchy smell. Her feet detect the throb of a washer churning away, a drier alongside, its tray fuzzed with lint. Someone sits on a bench staring at the machine, as though watching television.

'I used to do this at home,' Charlotte says. 'I thought it was a right laugh to see the clothes flying about, knickers flashing into view.'

The air is thick, full of static. Tamsin squints through the dim light, then props open the door.

'Have you gotten hold of Asher yet?'

'Yeah, we've spoken. He's fully patched up now, but he said it was bad.' Charlotte pinches her arm. 'Even more traumatic than it looked, apparently. I can't remember any snakes myself, but he certainly does.'

'So... what's he going to do about it?'

'Oh, he'll come in on whatever we do. For the moment he's being placated with a role in some new crime drama – it's going to be the next big binge-watch.'

Tamsin exhales, glad to hear he isn't rushing to draw media attention to the show. 'We're going to "Bermuda,"' she says. 'Want to come? Could be fun, and it'll make good live-streaming.'

Charlotte interlaces her fingers, not taking her eyes from the machine. She is wearing a loose flower-print kimono and is looking better, but the stillness is unnerving.

'No, thanks.'

There is a pause. The tightness in Tamsin's stomach crisps into frustration.

'I thought you needed followers?' The rumble of the washer is relentless, something with buttons grinding and pattering against the drum. Only metres away there is gem-blue water, glittering in the near-equatorial sun, and waiters itching to bring them margaritas.

'Tam,' her voice is sudden, percussive. 'When are we getting out of here? I told you I'm well again. I don't understand why you're not rushing home, to your job, your flat. Why go on this jolly?'

'Jolly?' Tamsin lets her beach bag slump to the floor. The washing machine churns and gurgles. 'What about Dee? I can't just leave people there when I'm the only person with the authority to get them out. I just want to do this one thing—'

'But you also just wanted to fix the lagoon road and just get new suitcases and some other justs...' She sits with elbows on knees, cupping her chin like a petulant child.

'You're not...'

'Jealous? You were going to say 'jealous'? You're well off the mark, Tam. This is about you, not me. Remember when we were ten and wanted desperately to be famous? Look me in the eye and tell me there's not even a trace of that left.'

Tamsin's mouth drops open. If there was anyone who really knew her... but perhaps she was mistaken.

'I thought so,' Charlotte sighs. 'Why else would you want to keep playing in this... fucked-up dolls house.'

Heat floods Tamsin's system.

'I'm not playing. I'm also not the one who rushed off to live in the Republic, who used to call it—'

'It's not my home,' her response is swift. 'The only reason I lived here was for work, and maybe 'cause I'd sort of... won the right. I feel as conflicted as anyone towards the Republic, as you well know. It's not a real place, is it? Why do you think I leapt at the chance to film *Spill It* in the States?'

Tamsin doesn't want to hear them, but Rollo's words resurface in the ghost of an echo. *Why'd she never once mention your name?*

But it is time they were going.

'Look, we're casting off soon. Sure you don't want to come along?' If she doesn't, there will be no one to talk to about Joss.

Charlotte's head snaps up. 'Do I want to travel to an island prison designed by the same prick who built the one I've just escaped? Let me think...' Their eyes meet. The machine gnashes its bras and trousers, its hum vibrating through the floor.

'It's not like that. We'd be perfectly safe...' She trails off. There is no point arguing.

Charlotte gathers her hair over one shoulder. 'I know what's in your head,' she goes on, 'and you're right. I've been too much on my own, and I'm not quite… in my usual spirits. And maybe in the past I was a bit more at ease with the Republic than I am now. But here's the thing, Tam, you've changed, too. You did it for me, and I'm grateful, but the friend I know would never have brought me to live in my abusive ex's house. I keep seeing bits of his stuff, smelling him, thinking I can hear his music. Did it occur to you that going to a hotel might have been less traumatic?' Her hands burrow into the mound of sheets at her feet, and she drags them up to her chin. 'I keep waking up expecting to see his face, those tattoos, and to hear that voice…'

Tamsin is frozen, stalled on the word 'changed', after which she was expecting a compliment. Her dress sense. Her confidence. Instead there is this, to which she can barely choke out, 'Our house, Charl. It's ours. It's a luxury mansion. Can't we just–'

'Do I look like I'm enjoying it?' This blast of fire seals the deal. As the sheets slip through her fingers, Charlotte coils back into the posture of someone still suffering from stress, shrinking from shadows. Comfortable surroundings are not enough; she needs more time, that's all, and then she'll be herself again. If only she could know how much Tamsin is looking forward to having her back, bouncing and bold, like a garment fresh from the drier.

Forty-Six

Her yacht crosses the ocean like a pleasant thought, leaving laughter-lines in the water. If that laundry-room conversation had not left her mildly unsettled, Tamsin would be as stoked as everyone else on this rescue mission, hungry for the little green triangle growing larger on the horizon.

The cast-off was a photographer's dream, brass buttons grabbing the sun, foil bottle-tops askew among melting diamonds. She is wearing a dungaree dress with copper-chain trim, her hair neat as a closed flower. Comments appear on her feed – *I love your crazy soul* – lifting her spirits and dissolving the harshness of that tone still lingering in her ears. This *jolly*. As though Tamsin is doing it for fun or to show off, and not purely because it's the right thing to do. Someone has to put the place in order. If Charlotte were herself, she'd know that.

The yacht passes a bot-driven hovercraft with a deck full of benches. At first glance, it looks like a tourist boat, but then Tamsin sees the drones sitting dormant between each person, the glum expressions. People get automatically deported if they stop complying with the security policy, shipped to the nearest non-Republic island with transport links. It is a law she has been meaning to change, though it is unclear how much of the system she can safely overhaul, given that visibility is the main mechanism for law-enforcement.

She turns to see Joss setting up old-school deckchairs, helping the young waiter who is struggling to work them out. There is a lock of hair overhanging his forehead that she really wants to adjust, and it is a sign of her new-found confidence that her weight shifts to her front foot, inching her closer. Since that moment in the map room, she has tried to keep things light between them. It occurs to her that he might be deliberately holding back, knowing she will leave soon.

'Ahoy,' she says.

He looks up. 'We're making good progress.'

'Are we now?' she smiles.

The islet is close, dominated by a squat, greenery-swathed fortress. There is a certain déjà vu in approaching, perhaps because the skipper yells a warning about electromagnetic barriers. On this occasion, Tamsin is able to instruct the AI to deactivate them, and the yacht soon finds a rocky cove where they can anchor.

She insists on joining Joss and three burly staff in the dingy, though when they scramble inland her selfie-rod gets caught in twigs. Mitten-shaped leaves flutter down, smelling of cinnamon. They pick their way through a tumbledown gatehouse, blocks of stone held in a frieze of moss. It is eerily quiet, this island where people have been physically ghosted.

Finally, they enter a courtyard and are astonished to find a double chalet of ham-pink wood, faded in the sun, washing strung from lines in between. Sunburnt faces begin appearing in windows, then people rush out. 'Eight, nine…' she counts. 'Wow, his bad books are a bloody library.'

A moment later she recognises Dee, wan without the makeup. She is missing her neat jacket and losing strands of hair from her ponytail. The stylist embraces her rescuer, both of them tearful, and Dee's voice dries up as she asks about her kids. She glances nervously at the camera.

'Rollo,' she gets out a few desiccated words. 'He did this. And to think I once served him canapés.'

There are voices raised in joy and confusion. People direct their thanks towards Joss, who exudes his usual calm authority. He explains that Tamsin is, in fact, the governor. She loves how quickly he does this.

Soon they are doing dingy runs to the yacht, three or four people at a time. The vessel develops a party atmosphere as it chugs out to deeper waters, its skipper turned DJ and taking requests from the freed inmates, who are well out of practice at handling their drink. Tamsin watches them from the deck above. These people were just put away, as though in a cupboard. The basic nature of

'Bermuda' – one level above a refugee camp – contrasts starkly with the ghastly finesse of *Outta My Room*. Here, Rollo just wanted flaws and irritations to vanish, without Rowena amusing herself in the process. The stamp of each sibling is more obvious now.

Tamsin shudders, glad to have left the island behind. She tries to mingle with those she has rescued, though many are busy making the most of the yacht's Wi-Fi. It seems that bots were set up on their social accounts, built from a lifetime of data. Dee, wandering fretfully up and down the deck as she makes phone-calls, has discovered that the usual messages have continued to be sent to her mum, and no one in Singapore even realised she was missing. Also among the prisoners is the harbourmaster, a gruff woman who is astonished to discover her online activities ticked along on their own. An amateur poet, she had the deadline for an international poetry contest jotted down in her diary, and the AI version of herself must have submitted something. 'You have won first prize,' she reads aloud. 'I don't know whether to laugh or cry.'

Dee joins Tamsin at last, almost out of breath from her frenzied calls.

'I was sedated, you know, after the party. I woke up covered in sandflies on that awful rock,' she rubs at a green stain on her skirt. 'Who does he think he is, treating people like that?'

'It means you were doing your job too well.' Tamsin speaks calmly, but in truth they are all a bit shaken by the transformation of 'Bermuda Triangle' from a joke, in

Rollo's silky smooth voice, to a place where vats of rainwater were allocated for washing or drinking.

Tamsin also saw crates of salt-fish, flatbreads, dried mango and other foods, deliveries which apparently arrived on a tiny robotic boat. Rollo didn't starve his inmates, at least, but the sheer lunacy of setting up this oubliette shows how deep his insecurities run. He must have felt so threatened by these people – mostly women, it has to be said – so scared they might scratch the paintwork of his ego.

'Spoilt little jerk-off,' Dee concludes, plucking the olive from her drink and throwing it into the sea.

The engine is barely audible as they cruise towards the lagoon. Perhaps they will drop off the castaways here, just as people are gathering for the evening light show. Tamsin relaxes, managing to catch the small black napkin beneath her cocktail before it blows away. The cosmopolitan was poured too long ago and is now lukewarm and syrupy. She smiles at Joss, who catches her eye and strolls over, joining her on a deck chair. When they tell people how they met, it will be an odd story. She was speaking TunnelFairy's lines, while he was doing the bidding of Anylocks. He looks as though he is going to acknowledge the surreal atmosphere pinned in place by the woody clack of deckchair feet, the fruity booze and indigo sky. Instead he says,

'Rescue operation mark two successfully complete. You have a knack for this. I bet at school you were the sort of person who'd save people from bullies. Small but weirdly strong and a bit scary, am I right?'

She stirs her cocktail with a cherry on a stick. 'Only about the scary part.'

He smiles. 'You care about people. Most new governors just want to throw the biggest party, fill their garages and wine cellars and be told how wonderful they are.'

Her drink is not refreshing, but the sweetness makes her keep sipping it. She has never been one for parties. Her most exciting evening so far has been spent hunched over the model archipelago, asking the AI all kinds of questions about how it could be ringed with new breakwaters, linked with land bridges, making it more like one solid, spider-shaped landmass. A thing of beauty.

'There's a lot I could do with the place,' she muses. When she posted, half-joking, about what might be done, retrospectively recycling the full-up landfill, planting new reefs and improving infrastructure, her followers were a bit bewildered, but then she found words of encouragement from other heads of state and island associations, which meant so much more. It is like moving up a gear. Eighteen islands and a blank cheque. The Republic is already well above sea level, more than other Caribbean nations, but it could be even safer. There's a lot of potential, with the right person in charge, someone who will do it resourcefully.

This morning she received a strange email from Ogilby Dobbs HR, encouraging her to return despite her unauthorised absence. They clearly want to hang on to a golden goose of publicity, but the tone was irritating, suggesting her fame was just some fortunate outcome of their recruitment drive. It makes her wonder why she gave so much of herself to a cut-throat, barely-ethical company, taken in by their talk of the Ogilby 'family'. Needless to say, she did not reply. Here, she can assemble her own team of engineers and get things done overnight, projects far bigger and more stimulating than any Ogilby can offer. Maybe she'll start her own business and compete with them for international contracts.

'What are you smiling about?' Joss asks.

'Oh, nothing.' She stretches. 'Joss... What if I stayed here, in the Republic?'

He pauses, replacing his drink carefully on the deck. 'Uh, why would you do that?'

She gazes upward at the seagulls following in their wake. Surely he knows the answer.

'Well,' she says, 'I could fix up the sea walls... and stuff.'

Instead of picking up on her playful tone, he is silent, one of a range of silences he has recently perfected. His profession requires him to keep quiet when he disapproves of something a client does or says. She matches his muteness, until he sighs.

'If you're interested in coastal defences, I know US projects that would snap you up. We lose acres of wetland every hour. In Louisiana–'

'But what about here? Islands are even more vulnerable. One big hurricane–'

'Tamsin, I've told you before,' his voice sharpens. 'This place is just... money. You can't fix it.'

'How do you know what I can and can't fix?' The words send her hurtling back to those downstairs offices where the graduates start out, a supervisor dousing every bright idea with sarcasm. 'I want to revolutionise—'

'Revolutionise it for whom, Tamsin? A few rich white guys in denial about climate change, who think they can 'rise above it', quite literally, by building higher and higher?' He stands, tapping his temple as though to chastise his slow brain. 'I knew this would happen. You've done what you came to do, but now you want to hang around, writing your name in coral reefs…'

Until now, his every word has been solid, like handrails making her world more reassuring. The deck bobs up and down with the swell, and she regrets the sickly cocktail.

'That's unfair.' Her plans are based in solid engineering.

'You're having too much fun as Governor, blithely living the dream – without a clue what's hanging over you.'

'What *is* hanging over me, Joss? You talk like there's some higher power, when I'm the one with the algorithms at my beck and call. I control the bank, the borders, the laws – everything. What exactly is threatening my security? Am I supposed to be worried about the Boones, like Charlotte seems to be, when I won the election fair and square and they have *nothing* right now?'

She is a lighthouse of rage, electricity crackling behind her eyes, lifting her from the deckchair. A fine spray lands upon them both, as though to salt and preserve this moment. Never has she felt so shaken, so quickly. Who is this man? After all they shared, he is just like the rest of them, unable to see her potential. Perhaps she should tip him over the starboard bow, make him swim back to the islet.

'If I'd known you were planning to stay...' The sentence just stops. He turns towards the back of the boat, locking his gaze onto the furrow they are leaving behind.

She has felt it before, that sense of some beam or supporting pillar missing. He is trying to make her feel small, or is lashing out for some private reason of his own – projecting, or whatever it is called. Charlotte would know. Where is she, anyway? The lounge, the kitchen, the breakfast room with its sunny window seat... all of them are lacking the outline of a woman with dark wavy hair. They may as well be an ocean apart again, they have so little time for each other.

Tamsin changes into a leather skirt for tonight's party – a small soirée for the Bermuda evacuees. Her shiny top has wheel-shaped buttons and her silver hair flows in a cool wave, twisting in impossible curls. How did this become normal? Back home, it was only when people recognised her as a grown-up child actor and posted pictures with *This is how Tammy May Wilde looks now*, that her attention was drawn to the grungy, boyish look which must have grown upon her organically, as she desperately tried to snuff out 'Lucy'. Ogilby Dobbs helped the process along, thickening her skin with its heavy PPE.

The bed is so springy, and she can't resist climbing up for one quick test-bounce. The thing is, it's hard to kill a part of yourself stone-dead. That still-young side of her reached joyfully for TunnelFairy, the glamorous, life-grabbing, good-luck persona that triggered streams of heart emojis bright as sweets from a piñata. Only now, when she looks back, or tries to, towards the Lucy who waded through chemical snow and pushed away the apple, does the muffling become apparent, a layering of fame upon fame, its edges smoothed. She catches handfuls of silky hair as it flies up around her face. *Eternal Winter* has been out-snow-globed by this new fantasy.

The weirdness of this realisation is accompanied by an urge to find Charlotte. Perhaps she is in the garden, or one of the many bathrooms. When Tamsin asks the house AI to locate her, the reply brings her to a standstill.

'She left?'

Sure enough, the palatial guest room is empty. It never occurred to her that Charlotte would fly alone. Couldn't she wait another couple of days, another twenty-four hours? Unless – and the thought has a raw, unfamiliar taste – she couldn't bear being on the edge of the spotlight any longer. Was it a touch of jealousy that hastened her departure?

Being left behind carves out a hollow inside Tamsin, a desolation in these empty, humid rooms. Maybe she could call home, call her mum. But Maeve might make some remark, like calling the Republic a luxury resort, or a bit fake, or expressing some trace of puzzlement… Tamsin goes to the window, scanning the sky for planes. It occurs to her that she could take a car to the airport, see if being Governor still means getting exactly what you want.

'House?'

'Yes?' says the house AI.

There is a certain echo to the voice. She hesitates. How long ago did Charlotte leave? The room has been made up as it was before, the bedcover free of wrinkles and stacked with cushions. In fact there are no signs of a guest except the open wardrobe doors. They gape almost obscenely, sighing out a dry musk of antiquity despite the furniture being new. She goes over and lays a hand on the wood, then closes them.

'Nothing.'

Forty-Seven

In the cool, conditioned air where invisible ears await her commands, Tamsin mouths the lyrics of rock music and finds comfort in a photo blooming across an immense digital wall. It is the one in *Vogue*, and it draws her closer, her shoes like fresh raspberries bouncing across the cream rug. There she is, bright-eyed and attractive, an engineer breaking the mould. How could she ever have found it embarrassing?

She bumps into a coffee table and causes something to roll across the floor. It is hollow like a pipe, and it turns out to be a vape, a neat gleaming thing that retains its aroma of allspice. Instinct makes her swivel, heart-rate spiking, as though Joss might be about to reach over her shoulder and reclaim it. His unsavoury words linger like flavoured vapour around the abandoned device. She sinks down on the rug. What she wouldn't give to have Charlotte's tremendous bear-like warmth wrapped around her. But of course her friend is not here because, even cleared out, the house still has Rollo's mark everywhere: the flattened outline of a rowing machine on the carpet, the faintest whiff of cocoa butter. Things Tamsin would scarcely notice, but which would leap out at Charlotte.

The faux-fur has a supple, leathery underside. For so long she has been chasing an imaginary equilibrium, feeling the weight of all those times Charlotte took risks for her sake, going back to that cloakroom scuffle at school. Only in these last few days have things seemed to right themselves. Tamsin fixed it, didn't she? She's a great fixer of things. So why does it feel like something is still broken?

A tiny sound from the digital screen. Another *like* on the photo. It leaves her cold, on this indoor tundra, an Arctic explorer who has forgotten how to explore. This palace has hardened around her, its flawless walls providing security and keeping people out.

She stumbles to her feet and tells the AI to have a car brought around.

Tamsin has a cloak made of people. The two security personnel hold back the press of passengers who have seen her striding through the departure lounge and have come to take their photos, to yell out questions. It is not ideal to have them billowing out behind her as she faces Charlotte. The latter sits on a square airport seat with legs crossed, looking remarkably well and ready to travel in a sunflower-print playsuit, her yellow-wheeled case like a big shiny seed. Tamsin clicks her earring – a nervous tic – barely aware of the tug on her scalp as she mumbles her question.

'Have I seen your profile?' Charlotte's response is pure frost. 'You did a full rom-com chase to the airport to ask me that?'

The crowd throbs. All she sees is her friend's expression of contempt, her jawline as she turns away. A bad beginning.

'Charl,' she says, but a hand comes up, flat and vertical. A stop-sign.

'Are you wanting me to tell you it's fine to stay? Will you stop doing my head in if I say that?' Her slim, tanned fingers, delicate with silver rings, comb through her hair as she talks, as if to gather energy. 'If I had that many followers, I wouldn't want to let them go either… So relax, enjoy it. I'll see you back in the big smoke, alright? No hard feelings.'

The thrust of her voice goes in deep and roots Tamsin to the spot. It is a speech that comes from beyond this glitzy archipelago, from the age-old sinewy roots of their friendship, which is still there, clinging on like a parched and wizened tree.

There are thin shouts from the crowd: 'Why, TunnelFairy?' She ignores them and sits beside Charlotte, forcing her to shift along an inch or two.

'It was a project… I got excited,' she admits. 'It became… a vanity project. Joss pointed that out.' At the word *vanity*, Charlotte meets her eye. Some of the onlookers have lost interest and wandered away, only to be replaced by others. On the pale grey seat, she at last manages to show Charlotte her LOVE profile. Her friend frowns in annoyance, then widens her eyes, a hand coming up to cover her mouth.

'No, Tam…' she murmurs, going a little pale. 'Your crown!'

Once again TunnelFairy is an ordinary citizen, her picture adorned by nothing more than a standard Republic flag. It was easy to resign. The Civil Service just asked, 'Are you sure?' and told her it could not be undone, and then it was instantaneous. Charlotte seems both impressed and horrified.

'But… what will your sponsors say?'

Tamsin shrugs, patting the Anylocks tote bag under her arm. Packing a suitcase would have taken too long. 'I'm ready to go home.'

How good it is to see that wild grin at last, too toothy for the cameras. Something has been very wrong over the last few days. Tamsin is so ready to get on the plane, put Joss and all the rest behind her – not to mention this hungry, restless crowd. Why are there so many of them? Only a handful of flights depart daily from this airport.

'Everything is delayed,' says Charlotte. 'There's some sort of computer glitch, and they're grounding planes in case it's affecting air traffic control.' Her eyes dart towards the exit. 'When you arrived I was just starting to look at hotels.'

Tamsin thinks for a moment, 'I have a rented beach house on the south coast. It's not very big…'

Charlotte nods and rises. The security staff clearing their way with difficulty. 'TF, why are you quitting?' people wail, and Tamsin hurries along even faster. She needs to put a statement on her account before the curiosity reaches fever pitch.

'We'll leave you now, ma'am.' She is caught off-guard by the largest of her security staff, who doffs her hat before both women slink away to their motorbikes. It will take some getting used to, being a mere influencer once more. The car that eventually pulls up is her Anylocks-branded SUV, as though this whole process has been knocked into reverse, and she will dwindle back to someone modelling a hair product in a hotel.

Their vehicle progresses slowly along the causeway, making her restless. Her mind was already stowing its tray table ready for takeoff, her ears ready to pop... It seems impossible to get off this bloody island. Is the Republic like a real-life version of the LOVE network, designed to keep you online – or on the archipelago – for as long as possible? Well, why not? Rollo's 'Bermuda Triangle' was a real place, not a blocking technique. The line between virtual and real life has never been so blurred.

Many of the comments on LOVE are supportive, others melancholy, and some followers are weirdly angry at TunnelFairy deserting them. Her stomach drops as the car rises up the coastal kerb, passing the gates of casinos, clinics, car-charging centres and a whole lot of banana trees she never noticed before. They pass an inlet where a group of women are dragging what looks like a net full of plastic bags towards land. When she approved this project, just days ago, she thought it was a terrific idea to harvest the jellyfish and turn their gelatinous bodies into toffee, using a Japanese recipe. At the time, it delighted her – what innovation! – yet now she sees it actually happening, she is struck by how small-scale it looks.

The sand spits are like dollops of cream, melting into the sea's clear, salty soup. It was just starting to seem real, as though she could wave a magic wand and transform a whole country. Brunel snapped his fingers – a slow, sometimes painful, snap over several decades – and Britain awoke to a thousand miles of railway. Inhabitants of the most pint-sized countryside town found their world expanding, and she still travels on trains using those tracks, nearly two hundred years later. But back then the earth wasn't shrugging off its concrete, shouting *Get off my back* in letters high as tidal waves, in a roar like a hurricane wind. Palm trees flash by, wagging their fibrous fingers. From the start, she has been perfectly aware of the short shelf-life of artificial islands, yet she almost sacrificed everything for the opportunity to fix up a mirage.

Charlotte has been helping her compose a statement for her profile. The phrasing is perfect, a reminder that her friend has been doing this for years, that she is good at being famous. It is a drug she consumes in moderation. Tamsin pictures her among the washing machines, sharing quiet, supportive phone calls with Asher. It shames her to recall what a miniscule part of her brain she allocated to working out exactly how Charlotte was feeling. She was just a bit quiet, wasn't she? A bit different. But how was she different? Now, when she looks at her friend, Tamsin sees a person who is trying something new. For the first time, she is dabbling in being alone. Solitude. Previously something that terrified her. She is testing its waters, finding out what they contain and whether she can allow those thoughts to float out and surround her. For once, she is not sharing the experience; it is all hers. But Tamsin detects something sad about it, as though she is grieving because she has discovered a new way to grieve. One day, they will talk it through. This reminds her of another thing she needs to rectify: Luka has waited long enough for his phone call.

When they pause at traffic lights, her sense of unease grows. A slam rings out as a seafood restaurant pulls down its shutters, and someone staggers from a bar with blood on his face. Ahead, there is a flash of bright t-shirts, people spilling into the road amid fury-fuelled shouts. It is unclear what is happening. A long string of paper bunting that must have been put up for election day comes scudding down, sliding over the bonnet like autumn leaves.

Forty-Eight

What she does not expect to find, on the driftwood-strewn beach behind her condo, is Dee crying. There is something very intense about it, the stylist's oil-dark ponytail trembling with every judder, makeup smeared under one eye. Tamsin assumes that some of the shock of being kidnapped is still seeping out.

'Hey. You're safe now.'

Dee looks at her in confusion. 'It's gone,' she says.

'What has?'

'Everything. All vanished. There's nothing in my account.' A cough rattles her throat, dried-out from crying, Tamsin starts to call for a glass of water, then realises she has to fetch it herself. There is a distant slam of drawers, Charlotte humming as she settles into the bedroom they will have to share. On the way over, her smartface mentioned a problem with the central bank, though it didn't sound like anything serious.

'My account froze once, when I was at university,' she says. 'It does freak you out.'

'My first paycheque had just gone in. My first one.' Dee looks up, her eyes backlit with hope. 'You could look into it. Ask the Civil Service?'

Tamsin frowns, feeling the sun's heat on her shoulders, the hair polymer keeping her head a fraction cooler. She thinks of the map room, numbers writhing on the wall, figures that will probably no longer appear without that tiny crown on her profile.

'I don't think it'll do any good, but I can try if you want.'

The AI might answer her questions. Either way, she can pick up her clothes and gifts.

Dee pulls out an Anylocks-brand tissue and wipes her face. All this is hitting her hard. It perhaps accounts for her strangely muted reaction to Tamsin's unexpected resignation.

'So, it wasn't your thing, being Governor?'

Tamsin digs a toe into the sand. 'I'm ready to go home.'

Dee nods. She gazes across the ocean.

'Go soon.'

Lights flare in the distance, as though something is on fire. Ever since hearing about the planes being grounded, she has tried to ignore a growing apprehension, a nugget of worry. It was a throwaway comment, when Charlotte remarked that no governor has ever resigned before. Does it mess up the system?

Crossing the island once more, Tamsin realises she has been lulled into thinking that everything in the Republic is easy and breezy and without repercussions. All it ever took was a word to the AI.

'How does it work, Red?' she asks her smartface. 'Have I caused this bank problem? Can I fix it?' There were all those warnings from the UK foreign office about the deregulated nature of the Republic; a maelstrom of money with minimal checks. What shimmers in the heat could be its veneer of nationhood, peeling off to reveal chaos beneath. She yearns momentarily for the monotony of her London office, for tinkering with a small corner of somebody else's project and looking forward to her sandwich at lunch.

'Only the governor has access to the central bank.'

If the other thought was a cold trickle, this one is red hot. Adrenaline makes her muscles fuse.

'I guess... I'm not the governor now.'

'You're not.'

'Then who is?'

The voice is tinny, relentless. 'The constitution is very simple. Unless they resign, it is the person with the most followers.'

All the blood drains from her face, leaving a trembling giddiness in its wake. The car passes beaches white as washing powder, each bump making her stomach drop. Her defeat of Rollo is solid and immovable in her mind, like something that could never be reversed. A part of her assumed an AI would take over, since they pretty much run the state anyway, but the truth is that she didn't really think about it. Even after all this time, she still hasn't got to grips with how things work.

She stares at the projected profile picture of Roland Boone, a brand-new crown dangling from its corner.

'Shit.'

All-out war between them, and she has casually handed back his gun. The leather seat sticks to her thighs. Ahead, gates open and the mansion rises up on its pillars.

'Is he here?' It would be unwise to waltz into the house of a man who loathes her more than anyone in the world and can do exactly as he likes. 'Where is he?'

It only takes a second for Red to check. 'He is on a yacht called the Johnnie Ray, belonging to a Brazilian venture capitalist. It is coming into the lagoon.' Images and a map pin appear, and there is a recent vlog. From the look of it, Rollo is on an almighty bender, thrilled to be back on top. He is playing some sort of hoopla game with a red and white lifebuoy, surrounded by stunning women. 'Smashing it, killing it, *crushing* it,' he gurns at the camera, looking wilder than ever.

In and out, she tells herself as she hurries into the hallway, finding drapes billowing from open windows, as though the building is already being aired out for a new occupant. This place is mad, utterly insane. The digital walls are no longer showing the images she chose and, sure enough, the AI tells her she has a limited time to collect her things. Even with Rollo a distance away, she feels a red-hot jab in her stomach every time she rounds a corner, half-expecting to encounter his cold, dark eyes staring her down.

Her memory is too good at conjuring up his voice, 'Not your scene, huh, T-Fairy?' he would say airily, as the doors slammed shut, 'Too bad.'

When she has squashed down her case and zipped it, Tamsin glances through the window and sees a man walking up the jetty, silhouetted against the sunset. Instinct makes her duck down. He is dressed differently, but she can always recognise a person's gait – it is like a fingerprint but in whole-body motion. A minute later, she has crossed the garden and is joining him on the weatherworn boards, out of breath. Every face she has seen since leaving the airport has been distressed or frenzied, but his is tranquil as ever, easing into a smile.

'That was a close one,' Joss says.

Her own pulse is loud in her ears. By now she should be used to things being orchestrated, should be unsurprised to see a small fishing boat moored nearby – ready for her to board.

'A close one? What do you mean?'

'Come on, it'll be chaos from here on in – let's get going before Rollo rocks up.'

'Why are people saying their money has vanished?'

'Are you wearing specs?' He reaches over, pinches the thin titanium headband from her brow and tosses it into the sea, where it sinks without a sound. She is too astonished to move. 'Okay, now we can talk. So… it hasn't vanished, the AI just froze all Luvcoin transactions, though unfortunately this *is* going to kill confidence and tank the value,' he hesitates, 'so I guess it's kind of vanished, down to pennies anyway.'

What he is saying hangs thickly in the air, refusing to make sense. Numbers flash into her brain, cryptocurrency earned from sponsorship, mostly Anylocks. Has that gone too? She has never considered herself a money-driven person, but still... She looks back at the dove-grey metal frame of the east wing, the mansion lit up like a circuit board. By resigning, did she set off a chain reaction, a colossal, rippling malfunction?

'Joss, is this what you were afraid of?' Something clutches at her windpipe. 'Did I... break the Republic?'

His laugh is jarring, echoing beneath the jetty. There is something different about him: a looseness in his joints, a sense of abandon. It is faintly alarming, not what she would expect from a man out of a job.

'Are you okay?'

'More than okay,' he says. 'I was afraid you'd never resign – you kept stalling and stalling. But the crown was snugly on Rollo's head when...'

'When...?'

'I'll explain on the boat.' He reaches out, but she stands unmoving. Waves slap against the barnacle-crusted wood, the last sour breath of the day rising around them. Joss sighs and lowers his hand. 'When we were in the system, in the map room, I hacked the Luvcoin servers in the island cloud,' he says, looking away. 'We'd made the "Luvguard" AI think users were losing their passkeys, so it helpfully made a back-up of the whole lot, with just the one encryption key.' He mimes unlocking a door. 'But not long after I'd finished, the AI spotted my hack and reacted by stopping all transactions, like a bank freeze – real helpful.'

A dry laugh dies somewhere in his throat. He glances back towards the mansion, their combined shadows stretching inland like a red carpet. 'I'll make sure the media know that it happened with Rollo in charge. It almost coincides with him getting the reins back, which might work well…'

'You hacked it?' Like a film reel guttering and stalling, those moments with Joss in the map room return: his aura of heat as he came closer, the zing of his aftershave, his smile. It should be cheering to discover none of this is her fault, but instead she is smothered by a slow-setting humiliation. That whole time, was he only interested in her biometrics? Her voice turns to rags; she clears her throat. 'Hacks are normally about stealing money.'

His feet are in surfer sandals, body twisted towards the getaway boat, a man she thought she knew. But she can't let the pulse of anger command her. Not yet.

'True but… Not this one. I'm sorry,' he bites his lips together. 'I wanted to say something but… you picked up on it anyway, didn't you? Once or twice.'

'What,' she says, 'that you're not really an image consultant?'

'Oh no, I am,' he glances upwards as seagulls shriek. 'Among other things. It's just the big client wasn't who you thought…' He says a name that at first sounds comic, then leaves her reeling, dislocated with astonishment as it rings in the air, as it becomes apparent he is serious. Currently, that individual is challenging a Republican for the White House.

'You're having me on.' It is unbelievable, but even now it is firming up in her mind, fitting together with the other pieces, making sense of him. 'My god,' she swallows. 'And of course all this time you've been... you're still–'

'Still working for them, yeah. On the weirdest assignment I've ever had.'

The words circle like aircraft in her foggy brain, refusing to land.

'But why here?'

'Money, of course.'

'Money.' The word is vinegary and harsh in her throat.

'You know the Agnatov corruption scandal? The real doozy?' His drawl intensifies as he warms to his theme: 'We found out that he – the other candidate – was about to make a huge hush-money payment, discreetly, in Luvcoin, to make it go away. Thanks to our little grass-roots mission, those bribes have just evaporated. I've pushed the Luvcoin back through the exchange, paid the dollars straight to Greenpeace as an anonymous donation. We've basically cleared away the dark money – cleared a way for the truth, Tamsin.'

He has drifted closer to make his point, but the physicality of him feels different now. Her skin prickles and she steps back. White domes come to mind, images of Washington DC and Joss in meetings with a spirited young team, hoping that ripples created in the Republic will become waves.

'So, this is about interfering in another country's free and fair election?'

A hand covers his heart, his face registering mild offence. 'My country, Tamsin. And it's hardly free and fair anymore. They play dirty–'

'So you have to?'

'If it's our only choice.'

As a larger vessel passes, the fishing boat seems to nod, the water slopping and slurping under the jetty. What strikes her, amid all the madness, is that this is a very 'Republic' thing to say. My country, my call. She closes her eyes, inhales some salty air, then asks,

'If I hadn't quit, would you still have let this happen, everyone's Luvcoin being frozen?' She can imagine ordering the AIs to activate the mansion's storm shutters as she hid from an angry mob.

'Well, once the hack was detected, it was out of my hands. But,' – his fingers leap forward – 'if that were the case, I'd have stayed. I wouldn't have just left you to deal with it.'

The sun is florid, feverish, weak in its illumination. After what he has just confessed, why should she trust anything he says? Every link and rivet of his story should be questioned. For all she knows, he could be nothing more than a swindler, placing bets on currency fluctuations like the unscrupulous politicians who make things wobble for their own gains. Yet there is structural integrity to his story, and the more she probes it, the more a furious, electric tension builds under her skin. He could have told her the truth earlier, that night when they were awaiting the election result, but instead he carried on faking, pretending to work for Anylocks. Now he stands here and explains things as casually as an actor outside the stage door, making no apology for the role he has played.

'There's another thing,' he says.

'What?' She sways a little, the ground no longer firm.

'Since I was leaving – and I was pretty sure you'd be leaving, too – I pushed some of your Luvcoin through the exchange, as well as my own,' he throws her a cautious look. 'I thought you'd need the dollars when you got back. Anyway, the details are on a bit of paper – you'll find them tucked into that Brunel book.'

She swallows. 'You made me believe…' She should have paid more attention to the way he looked at her sometimes, like a machine whose efficiency might be improved. There were other warning signs, too: his ill-concealed belief in the Republic's rotten core, his reverence for the grand scheme of things. 'You could have let me in on it. Why didn't you trust me?'

Exhaustion flickers across his features. He takes her hand. 'Have you any idea of the risk I'm taking, telling you all this? You mean so much to me… I'm sorry. I should have said something earlier. It's just that this was… bigger than the both of us.'

The irony of this being about politics, the one thing the Republic was supposed to have eradicated. She should have known that beneath its foam of celebrity cash-splashing and exhibitionism there would be people in the shadows, working the controls. It is agonising to have been duped – she, Tamsin Wilde, the original cynic. She snatches back her hand.

'But you used me – my popularity.'

The light is crimson now, sticky as grenadine on her skin. Incredibly, he suppresses a smile, shaking his head. 'It's a little more complicated. You got a long way, far enough that we picked you as the frontrunner. But did you ever notice that certain things, strokes of luck, just seemed to… happen?'

She goes cold.

'Do you think it's so easy to gain hundreds of thousands of followers?' he goes on, his voice softening. 'Apart from our army of volunteers, we had to fund a follower farm – somewhere in Puerto Rico, I think it was – and we even got around the genome thing by hacking dormant accounts.' He takes a step towards the boat. 'The way you just fell into talk shows and music videos, the way luck followed you – remember the tennis champion's ring? That was all helped along by our dedicated team and our encrypted tech. We built your luck, for the last stretch anyway and, believe me, it was a pretty epic task.'

She is getting no air. The words overwhelm her, making every cell draw inward. As she shrinks, the looming frontage of Gilded Springs peers down, windows winking – a peep show with dozens of gigantic, amused eyes – and her limbs go limp, like a dropped puppet.

Joss has turned his attention to unhitching the mooring rope. 'Please… we don't have much time.' The fishing boat groans, waves foaming at its keel. 'Oh wait,' he says, as his skipper fires up the motor. 'You need to get Charlotte. I'll meet you at the harbour in, say, an hour? Or would you rather come round on the boat with me?'

His launch nudges the jetty. He has minimised her, made her small and flimsy. She shakes her head, hearing the flatness in her voice as she says,

'I'll be getting back now, if you're done with me?'

Joss is in shadow but she perceives a dulling – the tiniest, homeopathic dose of what she herself is feeling. The boat bears him away, still looking back, until he is just a smudge, an impurity in the polished copper sea.

Forty-Nine

They are out of bread, but Dee found a kilogram of frozen blinis this morning. Tamsin's fingers are sore from making dozens of pixie-sized sandwiches, which now circle despondently on the sushi conveyor belt in the kitchen. Why do people get so excited about fish eggs, or want to eat the livers of tortured ducks? The hampers she has been gifted are heavy on the fine foods, the chutneys and specialty teas, but sorely lacking in carbs. When you have to live on this stuff, you hunger for a bit of cheese on toast or a nice chip butty… or, at least, an extra packet of crackers.

The Baltimores' chef was one of many Republic citizens who made a swift exit, probably taking a job with a passing cruise ship. On the horizon, yachts chug selfishly towards other shores, and plane tickets are like gold dust. A week ago, Tamsin could see a dress that cost more than her first car and buy it with two words to her smartface. Now, nobody wants her Luvcoin. It has been this way for days, and those who don't have dollars squirreled away are having to hawk their finery for basic supplies. Back-street deals are being conducted in the currencies of surrounding islands, traders on fishing boats trickling in from the Bahamas.

She eats a one-bite sandwich, without relish, and goes outside to see if Dee is back – it has been hours since their host trundled off in her tiny golf cart. It is risky to go near the gates, but Tamsin is drawn towards their wrought iron curves, the *ting* as they expand in the sun. There is a clever grid beneath which allows only authorised people and vehicles through. Burnt-looking crabs scuttle through the roadside dust. The wind is blowing from the east and seems to carry a hint of smoke, of chaos. It's scary to imagine what might be happening on the Strip. They say civilisation is always two meals away from barbarism. Here, it's probably more like one brunch.

Dee has been a good friend since the 'Bermuda' experience, insisting they move from the condo into her mansion, for what little protection her gates and dogs can provide. It turned out to be a wise decision, since the trolls started appearing almost at once: SUVs parked on the verges, people filming outside Dee's compound. They come in the daytime mostly, yelling abuse and trying their luck on these hot, slippery gates, and a few of them have camped, their orange and blue canvas flapping in the breeze. Even now she sees them emerging, recognising her despite having washed her hair with *Are You Sure?* Anylocks

Remover, despite being quiet as a mouse on LOVE ever since she resigned.

The reinstated Governor is not responsible for these trolls. If she were Rollo, she would have blamed the currency blip on the previous post-holder, but he has not done this. Gilded Springs has been heaving with round-the-clock parties, and the governor answers questions about TunnelFairy like a man struggling to remember a dream.

She backs away from the gates, onto spiky grass that is blue-tinged and wide-bladed. Some of James's Italianate statues have flaked in the sun, revealing chicken-wire innards, completely hollow. She too has a thin wind blowing through the heart of her. How did she manage to turn into her opposite? If she had to choose between good luck and good engineering, the latter would win every time.

Joss took something, when he sailed away. The sun touched the horizon, and her achievements became his. He has left her with nothing but the galling awareness that she was never going to hit the big time on her own. If not for Joss and his shadowy army, Rollo would still be leagues ahead, luxuriating in his whims and wealth and whatever cult he could cultivate. Even at the height of her success she was always a fake. She just didn't know it.

As she circles round to the seaward side, Charlotte comes into view, looking like a film-star in her broad-brimmed hat, her ochre dress. She is seated by the pool, shelling pistachios and stealing glances towards the horizon. They are together at least. They escaped the escape room. Yet Joss has staked a claim on this, too. Without his interference, her best friend would still be on *Outta My*

Room, left to the chill, star-spattered nights and a surging fever. Tamsin shivers, rubs her wrists. She feels weakened, the lack of sleep leaving dark dents beneath her eyes. They are stuck in a paradise-gone-sour, with no way out.

'What's up?' Charlotte lifts her shades. There is a pile of shells in front of her, the tiny green nuts gathered in a bowl. Until Dee returns, these and the blinis are pretty much all the food they have.

'Nothing.' Tamsin twists a twig from the bougainvillea. Had she known it would come to this, the flights booked up for days, the cruise ships unaffordable and Dee's yacht being patched up in a dry dock, she would not have been so quick to turn down Joss's fishing boat. 'I was an idiot,' she says, flicking her leaf into the pool. 'Why didn't I just say yes? There'd have been plenty of time to have a go at him later – after we'd been dropped off at Nassau or Miami or some airport.' Accepting his help may have required some serious teeth-gritting, but it would have saved a lot of hassle. On top of everything else, she seems to have botched their only way out.

'Sit.' The chair screeches as Charlotte drags it, the ironwork scabby with white enamel. She waits until they are both seated, then leans forward. 'Now look, I don't know Joss and I sure as hell don't trust him. He could have dumped our bodies in the ocean–'

'Oh, don't be–'

'He nicked people's Luvcoin, didn't he? Lied to people on LOVE, and lied to you.' Charlotte shakes back her hair, her features settling into a familiar indignation. She was particularly horrified by Joss's manipulation of the network; messing with LOVE is sacrilege.

'But Charl,' she rubs her tired, tender forehead. 'Without him I'd never have been–'

'Ey,' the bark coaxes a faint echo from the patios. 'If you hadn't got your arse on a plane, where would I be right now? You did this, okay? All on your own.'

'Not all on my own.'

It was with several nips of guilt that she finally rang Luka yesterday morning, so the call would come at a decent hour, and stepped into the next room while he spoke to Charlotte. It was so strange to hear his voice, the same as ever. As she smeared chutney on a cracker, muffled exclamations could be heard through the walls. You deserve this, Luka, she thought, but don't overdo it; don't be *too* delighted with yourself. Nevertheless, the pitch was jumping with every other sentence and there were cries of, 'Yeah,' and, 'I know, right?' The sound of them agreeing with each other was unexpected, almost unsettling. It was probably Charlotte being polite, rather than some fundamental shift in perspective, or was it Luka who had softened? Either way, he must have been pinching himself.

Charlotte throws a pistachio, and Tamsin catches it, taking pleasure from her friend's faith, this staunch – if misplaced – belief that she will be able to get them out of their current fix. Because of this, it hardly matters that her followers are flaking away at an alarming rate. She closes her eyes and the taste of Irn-Bru registers magically on her tongue, as though they are drinking on a bench somewhere, like old times, the fiery rum-shot an injection of molten metal. There's a lot to be said for the people in her life who know what she is like, and like her anyway. They remind her how to feel strong.

Tamsin hears a *ping* from her phone, another warning for not having posted anything. TunnelFairy has been silent, a hard-hearted sprite. There will be penalties if she does not share something soon, though the bots are welcome to extract a fine from the worthless cryptocurrency in her account. Staying quiet on LOVE may have been enough to keep Rollo off her back, but Rowena is a different beast. At first, she mockingly defended her brother, asking archly how he could derail the economy when he doesn't have a clue what it is. But then, like a last sting in the tail, Rowena declared that it must have been TunnelFairy who screwed things up before jumping ship. It is the younger Boone – of course – who sent the trolls to her door.

Ever since learning of her involvement, they have discussed Rowena a great deal, trying to understand what cogs were turning beneath that razor-sharp make-up and lacquered bob. Did she feel anything at all, as she watched Charlotte suffer? Had she done this sort of thing so many times before, with her weird combat games and product testing, that for her it was normal – normalised? Rowena is busy in LA, but her retail empire and impenetrable celebrity enamel are not enough to mask the bleakness Tamsin can detect in every action. People are playthings and, when her toys don't provide any genuine human connection, Rowena just plays harder. She wants the most fascinating individuals in the world to be right up close to her, so she can be bored of them. Tamsin has seen it firsthand. Maybe this, too, will eventually exhaust her, and she'll stop.

From the gate, a distant shout. People want their money back. It's understandable. Charlotte stands on tiptoes to get a glimpse of the road. The situation is not promising, with food running low, trolls outside as well as online, and their host worryingly late. But Tamsin is a problem-solver, and her mind is already sifting through schemes by which they might hitch a lift away from the archipelago. Dee wants to wait for James to return from his VIP cruise, but that could be weeks.

With her mind occupied, it takes a moment to realise that a sky-blue Maserati convertible is progressing up the drive. Their host emerges, and waves goodbye to someone who looks suspiciously like Ada, the short-tempered interior design guru who lives opposite. Dee's heels clip-clop on the tarmac as she powers towards the house, two brown bags of groceries in her arms.

'Hello, darlings,' she greets them. 'You won't believe what a crook he was, the man I had to barter with at the fruit stall. Those shoes I brought? I told him they were Chanel, worth a thousand dollars. 'Slippers for my aunt now,' he says, and gives me five pineapples. Then the golf cart battery went flat…'

The pineapples jostle in their bag, juicy and golden, making Tamsin's mouth water.

'Ada was such a sweetheart, though, when she saw me on the road,' she adds, a smile kindling. 'How are you both doing?'

'Going a bit stir crazy, but apart from that we're sound.' Charlotte scoops the pistachio shells into the open hamper to stop them from blowing into the pool. She heads to the kitchen with Dee, and Tamsin is about to follow when she notices her slim tablet on the table. Some part of her still expects Rollo to turn malevolent, and she can't help checking his feed. The length of this current vlog is staggering – another thirty hours straight. He is broadcasting like crazy, his reaction to the anarchy and food shortages to 'Be right here for y'all.'

With Dee's poolside flowers nodding fragrantly over her shoulder and birdsong on the breeze, it is unsettling to see a ghostly image of the governor clutching a bottle of premium vodka, talking so fast as to be barely comprehensible. She can almost see the damage, the effect of being knocked off the top spot for a week until, sweaty and wide-eyed, he re-took his virtual crown only hours after announcing that he was ditching LOVE, starting a whole new network, maybe a whole new digital country. 'Do you still rate me?' his eyes ask. A drop of sweat trickles down his temple, and he runs a hand over his eagle tattoo. He is so close to the camera that his breath is audible, bouncing off the lens. Tamsin's skin flushes as she remembers that radiation of warmth and healing, the love of a million strangers making everything okay, like the best drug in the world. Even when it burns, you still want it. Even when it bubbles up into an acid bath, stripping away your insecurities, until you become this flawless thing, until flaws are almost unimaginable.

'Don't switch off…' Rollo happens to say just as she shuts it down, swallowing hard, and turning her gaze to the bay's lazy sparkle. There is a hum just here by the pool, a whole lot of bees, as though nature has found a single flowerbed in which to exist. She feels the reverberation going through her like a small motor, or a powerful fan, and then she is buzzing herself.

This is Rollo's land, even if it is slipping through his fingers. It still astonishes her that he could get away with so much. No one thought he would have the arrogance to tidy away real individuals, to blow up petty online squabbles to life-size. It has taken her a while to get her head around the Republic, but at last she understands how it works, and how they will make their escape.

Fifty

Only now, sitting on her suitcase, has she rediscovered her neglected book. This arty little biography is really the story of the SS Great Eastern, Brunel's monstrous steamship, six times the size of any other vessel afloat. His remark, 'Call her Tom Thumb if you like,' when the directors pressed him for a name, was delivered with characteristic dry humour, but the ship was what finished him. Fragile and exhausted, he suffered a stroke when he heard of a setback on its maiden voyage.

Too big and too expensive. Like the Titanic. Except that the SS Great Eastern, built half a century earlier, sustained a far worse tear in its keel on one voyage to New York and carried its passengers safely onwards. Its double hull and impeccable workmanship made the Titanic look like a tin bath by comparison. That's why, despite Ted's aspersions, she will always believe in fairytale engineering.

Brunel worked on an epic scale, but what she truly admires is the way his projects reached beyond their time. Big stuff is meaningless if it does not last, if it sinks to the bottom of the ocean or falls prey to tides – like the man-made islands of the Republic. This is still the land of giants, but their existence is fleeting.

Built on money, Joss had said, before going on to make it vanish. Was it worth it? He might not have been so proud of himself if he'd heard Dee crying on the beach. Charlotte is still aghast at the way he emptied so many digital wallets, and has called him a criminal so many times that Tamsin felt compelled to argue. 'I did look up the Agnatov affair,' she said, 'and it is the sort of thing a candidate would try to bury with dollars.' Everyone seems so resigned to the ebb and flow of dark money these days – it has doused many a scandal at Ogilby Dobbs – but Joss did actually make it evaporate, or some of it at least. Whether having the right person in the White House will justify his actions, she cannot say, but he obviously believes in what he is doing.

It was strange to hear herself defending Joss. How would it be, if they met again? The prospect, organic and unanalysed, is pleasant, like the mysterious floral sweetness in one of his teas. Whenever she sees his name in her messages, she gets an unbidden, traitorous hit of dopamine. Her neurochemistry doesn't care that he betrayed her. She wants to separate him from what happened, her shiny dolls' house of a world being torn apart, awash with political currents beyond her control. But even the bewilderment, that awful sense of being used, has matured into something mellower now a little time has passed. She hates that

TunnelFairy was a component of someone else's plan, but somewhere within the deep-filled humble pie there is a taste of relief. It never quite made sense that she could get so famous for doing absolutely nothing. There are advantages to seeing the bigger picture. At least reality has settled back into a pattern she can recognise.

In the longwinded messages Joss has sent since leaving, there is clear regret at not taking her into his confidence. They combine awkward apologies with attempts to underline his point about the Republic being small fry, sending her links to gigantic projects, telling her that in the two hours since his last message, another football field of coastal wetlands has vanished. It is both touching – as he must still be working hard for his paymasters – and a bit annoying. Only when she comes back to them, very late at night, does she start to see the barrage of facts as yet another language, the one he thinks – hopes – they both share. Joss was slow off the mark, realising too late that she could have been convinced by his plan, that for her the grand scheme of things is not just something she can appreciate but a full-on guilty pleasure. Grand schemes make her feel alive. For better or worse, TunnelFairy is out from underground.

A piece of paper flutters from her book, and she reaches to the decking to retrieve it, seeing some scrawled numbers and notes from Joss on how to access her dollars. Luvcoin is currently about as valuable as Monopoly money, and the game is over. She lays down her biography, smoothing a hand over the front cover – Brunel's neutral expression, those sideburns – only for it to curl, affected by the humidity. The afternoon is thick as a blanket and seems to have melted the angry throng beyond the gates, who are probably off to queue for fruit. Charlotte strolls barefoot along the edge of the sundeck, flip-flops in one hand, long brown hair spiralling in the breeze, taking in the unusually clear view of boats crossing the bay.

Soon the two of them will hear the whirr of drones, and will be escorted to the daily hovercraft which goes to Grand Bahama or New Providence, the cheapest and most humiliating way to eject people who refuse to post their activities and whereabouts online, who don't comply with the security policy. Tamsin has had her penultimate warning. *You will be deported…* it begins, sounding petulant, making her want to laugh. The trick is to see the Republic like a person, like a vain friend. No need to leave – you just stop pandering to them and they push you away.

Charlotte is both excited and nervous to be departing in this manner. 'Orla has been in touch,' she says. 'Some nice offers to buy the story, and that'll set me up for a trip back to the States. A docu-drama on young musicians…'

Tamsin's spirits dip momentarily to hear her friend will be leaving so soon. She directs a sigh up at the pink cladding of Dee's princess annexe and pictures herself back under King's Cross, the air like a cold sponge on her face, her neon trousers rolled up at the ankles, eyes adjusting to the combination of darkness and a piercing beam from her torch. She imagines emerging at Paddington, among the echoing Victorian ironwork, and wanting to feel small in a good way all over again, and the thrill crossing her heart like the play of light on water: *Why not go further? Why not add a steamship, go all the way to New York?* The city that never sleeps, where steam rises from the streets. From the tip of the Empire State Building she will gaze upon it, from the Hudson River to Governors Island. Her first job will be to grasp its sheer magnitude. The big apple.

Acknowledgements

With thanks to Tim Kindberg for his expertise on cryptocurrencies and AI, and to Jen Velu for her help with economics. Rachael Penny gave me superb advice on London settings, and I appreciated Ivy Moland's insights on geology and tunnel engineering. As ever, I'm grateful to my lovely agent Julie Crisp, and to Stuart Debar at SRL Publishing who has been brilliant to work with. The support of friends, family and fellow writers is instrumental in getting any book off the ground, and I'd especially like to thank all the wonderful beta readers who helped this novel evolve.

SRL Publishing don't just publish books, we also do our best in keeping this world sustainable. In the UK alone, over 77 million books are destroyed each year, unsold and unread, due to overproduction and bigger profit margins.

Our business model is inherently sustainable by only printing what we sell. While this means our cost price is much higher, it means we have minimum waste and zero returns. We made a public promise in 2020 to never overprint our books for the sake of profit.

We give back to our planet by calculating the number of trees used for our products so we can then replace them. We also calculate our carbon emissions and support projects which reduce CO_2. These same projects also support the United Nations Sustainable Development Goals.

The way we operate means we knowingly waive our profit margins for the sake of the environment. Every book sold via the SRL website plants at least one tree.

To find out more, please visit
www.srlpublishing.co.uk/responsibility